Bible Faith
Study Course

Kenneth E. Hagin

29 28 27 26 25 24 23   36 35 34 33 32 31 30

Bible Faith Study Course
ISBN-13: 978-0-89276-083-1
ISBN-10: 0-89276-083-4

Copyright © 1974, 1991 Rhema Bible Church
AKA Kenneth Hagin Ministries, Inc.
First edition 1974. Second edition 1991.
Printed in the USA

In the U.S. write:
Kenneth Hagin Ministries
P.O. Box 50126
Tulsa, OK 74150-0126
1-888-28-FAITH
rhema.org

In Canada write:
Kenneth Hagin Ministries of Canada
P.O. Box 335, Station D
Etobicoke (Toronto), Ontario
Canada M9A 4X3
1-866-70-RHEMA
rhemacanada.org

Contents

Chapter 1

How Faith Comes—Part 1

So then faith cometh by hearing, and hearing by the word of God.

—Romans 10:17

But without faith it is impossible to please him: for he that cometh to God must believe that he is, and that he is a rewarder of them that diligently seek him.

—Hebrews 11:6

Notice particularly the first part of Hebrews 11:6: *"But without faith it is impossible to please him."* If God demands that I have faith when it is impossible for me to have faith, then I have a right to challenge His justice. But if He places within my hands the means whereby faith can be produced, then the responsibility rests with me whether or not I have faith.

Faith Comes by Hearing the Word

God has told us that without faith it is impossible to please Him, but He has also told us how to get faith. If we don't have faith, God is not to blame. To blame God for our lack of faith is nothing in the world but ignorance. If we lack faith, we are to blame.

This is also true concerning faith for salvation. Faith for salvation also comes by hearing, and hearing by the Word of God (Rom. 10:17). Paul said in Ephesians 2:8: *"For by grace are ye saved through faith; and that not of yourselves: it is the gift of God."* We know that faith comes by hearing, and hearing by the Word of God, but how are we to get faith to get saved? Romans chapter 10 tells us.

ROMANS 10:8–10, 13–14

8 But what saith it? The word is nigh thee, even in thy mouth, and in thy heart: that is, THE WORD OF FAITH, WHICH WE PREACH;

9 That if thou shalt confess with thy mouth the Lord Jesus, and shalt believe in thine heart that God hath raised him from the dead, thou shalt be saved.

10 For with the heart man believeth unto righteousness; and with the mouth confession is made unto salvation. . . .

13 For whosoever shall call upon the name of the Lord shall be saved.

14 How then shall they call on him in whom they have not believed? and HOW SHALL THEY BELIEVE IN HIM OF WHOM THEY HAVE NOT HEARD? and how shall they hear without a preacher?

Men are saved by hearing God's Word, because the scripture says, *"faith cometh by hearing, and hearing by the word of God"* (Rom. 10:17). You cannot believe and have faith without hearing the Word.

In Acts 10 and 11 we read about Cornelius, who, although devout, had not yet been saved. He had not heard the gospel yet, so how could he have been saved? No, Cornelius was not saved until he heard Peter preach.

An angel of the Lord appeared to Cornelius (Acts 10:3). The angel who spoke to Cornelius couldn't preach the gospel to Cornelius because angels can't preach the gospel; God sent men to preach. Remember Jesus said, *"Go YE into all the world, and preach the gospel to every creature"* (Mark 16:15). But the angel *could* tell Cornelius where to go to get someone who could preach the gospel to him (Acts 11:13).

The angel instructed Cornelius to call for Peter: *"And now send men to Joppa, and call for one Simon, whose surname is Peter: He lodgeth with one Simon a tanner, whose house is by the sea side: he shall tell thee what thou oughtest to do"* (Acts 10:5–6).

Acts 11:14 reports that the angel said that Peter would preach the gospel to Cornelius: *"Who shall tell thee WORDS, whereby thou and all thy house shall be saved."* This verse also shows us that men are saved by hearing words—God's Word: *"So then faith cometh by hearing, and hearing by the word of God"* (Rom. 10:17). You can't believe without hearing. So many are trying to believe without hearing.

How does faith for healing come? The same way— by hearing the Word of God concerning healing. In Acts 14 we are told the story of the impotent man who received his healing because of what he heard.

ACTS 14:7–10

7 And there they [Paul and Barnabas] PREACHED the GOSPEL.

8 And there sat a certain man at Lystra, impotent in his feet, being a cripple from his mother's womb, who never had walked:

9 The same HEARD Paul SPEAK: who stedfastly beholding him, and perceiving that he had faith to be healed,

10 Said with a loud voice, Stand upright on thy feet. And he leaped and walked.

The casual reader of the Word of God might say, "Isn't it wonderful how Paul healed that man?" You've heard that said, and so have I. But Paul did not heal the man. The man was not healed because Paul was an apostle. The man was not healed by Paul's faith. The man himself had the faith to be healed. But notice what had to take place before this man was healed: *"And there they* [Paul and Barnabas] *PREACHED the GOSPEL"* (Acts 14:7).

So Paul did three things:

1. He preached the gospel to the man.

2. He perceived that the man had faith to be healed.

3. He told the man to rise up and walk.

The man also did three things:

1. He heard Paul preach the gospel.

2. He had faith to be healed.

3. He leaped up and walked.

The man was not healed by some *special* power that Paul had. The man himself had faith to be healed. Where and how did he get faith to be healed? He got it from what he *heard!*

Remember Acts 14:9 says, *"The same* [man] *heard Paul SPEAK."* What did Paul speak? Verse 7 says, *"And there they PREACHED the GOSPEL."* If Paul preached what we call the gospel of salvation, how did the man get faith to be healed? The man got faith to be healed because Paul preached what *the Bible* calls *the gospel,* which also includes healing.

How I Got Faith to Be Healed

More than sixty years ago on the bed of sickness as a young denominational boy reading Grandma's Bible, the more I read the Word, the more I learned. I realized that I had never heard the *full* gospel, just part of it. The fullness of the gospel hadn't been taught in my church. But the more I read the Bible, the more I realized that I didn't have to die. The more I read God's Word, the more I realized that I could be healed.

Of course, the devil was right there trying to tell me that healing had been done away with. I had been taught that God would heal if He *wanted* to. But saying that God *could* heal, but that He might not want to is an even bigger insult than saying He *couldn't* heal. Both of them are lies.

I read the Word concerning healing. But the devil was right there to try to oppose me. The devil

brought to my remembrance all the doubt and unbelief I'd ever heard. He brought to my remembrance all that I'd been taught on the subject of healing. Something that helped me immeasurably was that even though people had told me that healing had been done away with, I couldn't ever remember hearing that faith had been done away with. I'd never heard that.

As I studied the Word of God, I saw that faith had not been done away with. For example, the text in Acts chapter 14 says that the man at Lystra had *faith* to be healed. And in Mark 5:34, concerning the woman with the issue of blood, Jesus said, *"Daughter, THY FAITH hath made thee whole; go in peace, and be whole of thy plague."*

Therefore, the Bible clearly shows that faith has not been done away with. The man at Lystra had faith to be healed, and concerning the woman with the issue of blood, it was her faith that made her whole. Faith comes by hearing, and hearing by the Word of God.

Notice in Mark 5:34 that Jesus didn't say that *His power* or His faith had made the woman whole. Jesus said to the woman, *"THY FAITH hath made thee whole"* (Mark 5:34).

When I saw this, I knew that if her faith made her whole, then my faith could make me whole too! And, thank God, it did. My faith tapped into the power of God and I was made whole! My paralysis disappeared and my heart condition was healed. Since then I've been going at a hop, skip, and a jump, and I have been preaching the truth of the gospel, including healing, ever since.

Let's look more closely at the man at Lystra who had faith to be healed. How did he get that faith? From what he heard. What did he hear? He heard the Word of God. Is there something about hearing the gospel that would cause a life-long cripple to be healed? Decidedly, yes. Emphatically, yes!

Healing Is a Part of the Gospel

Paul preached the gospel of salvation which includes healing. The Bible simply calls it *the gospel.* How do we know he did? Look at Romans 1:16.

ROMANS 1:16

16 For I am not ashamed of THE GOSPEL OF CHRIST: for it is the power of God unto SALVATION to every one that believeth; to the Jew first, and also to the Greek.

The footnote in the *Scofield* Bible says, "The Hebrew and Greek words for salvation imply the ideas of *deliverance, safety, preservation, healing, and soundness."* I am not ashamed of the gospel of Christ! It is the power of God unto deliverance, safety, preservation, healing, and soundness. Paul preached the full gospel, not just part of it.

We also know that healing was a part of the gospel that was preached because other scriptures indicate it as well.

ACTS 8:5–8

5 Then Philip went down to the city of Samaria, and PREACHED CHRIST [the gospel] unto them.

6 And the people with one accord gave heed unto those things which Philip spake, hearing and seeing THE MIRACLES which he did.

7 For unclean spirits, crying with loud voice, came out of many that were possessed with them: and many taken with palsies, and that were lame, were HEALED.

8 And there was great joy in that city.

Notice in verse 7 the miracles that followed the preaching of the Word—the gospel. Those healing miracles and deliverances all came about as the result of preaching Christ. *The New Testament knows no Christ without Christ the Healer.*

Physical healing—divine healing—is a part of the gospel. If there is no gospel of healing today, then none of us has a gospel of salvation to preach either because healing is included in the atonement (Isa. 53:4–5).

P.C. Nelson was a great Baptist minister. He said, "Healing is part and parcel of the gospel." During the time Rev. Nelson was pastoring a church in Detroit, Michigan, in 1921, he was run over by an automobile. The doctors said that one of his legs would have to be taken off at the knee. They said that if by some miracle it didn't have to be amputated, at the very least it would be stiff for the rest of his life.

But P.C. Nelson related that as he lay there in the hospital, the Lord began to talk with him. The Lord brought to his mind James 5:14 and 15.

JAMES 5:14–15

14 Is any sick among you? let him call for the elders of the church; and let them pray over him, anointing him with oil in the name of the Lord:

15 And the prayer of faith shall save the sick, and the Lord shall raise him up; and if he have committed sins, they shall be forgiven him.

Rev. Nelson said that he tried to excuse himself by telling the Lord they didn't practice that in his church. He said that the Lord reminded him of a man and his wife Rev. Nelson knew who believed in the anointing with oil according to this scripture.

The Lord told Rev. Nelson that he should call them and have them pray for him. So Rev. Nelson contacted them, and they came to pray for him. They anointed him with oil and prayed, and he was healed. His leg didn't have to be taken off, and his knee wasn't stiff. God's Word is good. The Bible says, *"faith cometh by hearing, and hearing by the word of God"* (Rom. 10:17).

Down in Texas several years ago, a fine denominational minister had a very outstanding ministry. Many of the denominational churches would sponsor him in citywide meetings. In his evangelistic endeavors he became sick.

And by his own testimony, within a couple of years, all of his own money was gone. He had had $10,000 in the bank, and that was a lot of money back then. But in two years' time his money was gone. He had to sell his automobile, his home, and most of his books in order to pay his doctor bills. He had been everywhere, including the Mayo Clinic to try to receive help, but was none the better; rather, he grew worse.

Finally he was hospitalized in California. The doctor said that he was going to die. The minister contacted his brother who lived in California to borrow some money so he could go home to Texas where he could die. Their eighty-two-year-old mother lived in Texas and he wanted to see his mother before he died. So his brother sent him the money and he went home.

The minister went to live with his mother at the old home place in Texas where he grew up. His mother was so glad to see him. He told his mother that he had come home to die. His dear old mother had a nineteen-year-old boy who lived there with her who did the chores around the place.

This nineteen-year-old boy became the sick minister's nurse; the boy had to turn the sick man on his bed and dress him. One day the boy said to him, "Why don't you let the Lord heal you? The Bible says that if there is any sick among you, let them call for the elders of the church, and let them pray for you" (James 5:14–15).

Here was a minister who supposedly knew the Bible and yet didn't even know that these scriptures were in the Bible. He had gone to school and studied everything but the Bible!

The minister told the boy to get his Bible and find that passage of scripture, but the boy had never learned how to read. The man asked him how he knew that passage of scripture was in the Bible. The boy said that his preacher had told him it was in the Bible. So the denominational minister looked up the scriptures and read them.

The boy told the minister that his preacher was having a healing meeting under a brush arbor and invited the minister to come. Arrangements were made for the minister to come to the meeting; someone brought an old Model-T Ford and made a bed in the back of it for the minister. They drove up as close to the brush arbor as they could, and after the service the preacher came out and anointed the sick minister with oil and prayed over him.

It was about midnight before the minister and the boy returned home. When the minister got home, he asked his mother to let the boy fire up the wood stove so she could fry him some ham and eggs. He had been eating baby food and soft foods because he couldn't eat any solid food. In fact, he hadn't had anything to eat except baby food in two years.

The man told his mother that he was healed. He told her the preacher had anointed him and prayed for him. The mother said later that as her son related this, she thought he had lost his mind. He also wanted his mother to make some old-fashioned country biscuits for him to eat too. She thought that since he was going to die anyway, he might as well die happy, so she did what he wanted and made the biscuits and fried ham and eggs. He ate that meal and didn't suffer any ill effects whatsoever; he was completely healed!

This minister then began to write about his healing and send articles in for publication in various magazines. Calls began to come in for him to hold revival meetings. He arranged a citywide meeting for Kansas City. The boy told him that before he went to that meeting, he needed to get filled with the Holy Ghost.

The minister said that by that time he was ready to believe anything that nineteen-year-old boy told him, so he asked the boy what he should do. The boy explained to him how to receive the baptism of the Holy Spirit and invited him to another brush-arbor meeting. When the invitation was given, the minister went to the altar, and he received the Holy Ghost and spoke with other tongues.

That minister has long since gone on to glory, but his writings have been a blessing to many of us, including the denomination he was a member of.

How did that man get faith for healing? He got it by *hearing the Word of God*.

Mark 5:25 tells us that there was a certain woman who had an issue of blood for twelve years. The Word tells us that she had spent all of her living and had gone to many physicians, but was no better. But then she heard about Jesus.

MARK 5:27–28, 34

27 WHEN SHE HAD HEARD OF JESUS, came in the press behind, and touched his garment.

28 For she said, If I may touch but his clothes, I shall be whole.

34 And he [Jesus] **said unto her, Daughter, thy faith hath made thee whole; go in peace, and be whole of thy plague.**

Where did this woman get faith to receive healing? She got faith when she *"had heard of Jesus"* (Mark 5:27).

I was preaching in Dallas in 1953 for several weeks in a Full Gospel church. Then I stayed on an additional three months while the pastor took a leave of absence. Besides preaching at different times during the week, I had a daily radio program, and I also conducted some special missionary services on the weekend.

One Friday night after the services had been dismissed, one of the ushers came and told me that a man and a woman from Forth Worth had come to see me. The woman was sick and wanted to be healed. I met with them, and the man related that he had been going to work one morning and had heard my radio program. He said that I had taught on the radio that healing was for everyone. He told his wife about that statement I had made, and they began to tune in to the radio program every day.

The man told me that his wife had had two serious major operations, and she was facing the third one. They had been praying that if it was the will of God for her to be healed, God would give them faith to believe that she would be healed.

They had come to me so I could pray for her. I told them that it was unscriptural to pray to God for healing using the words, *"If it be Thy will."* When you put an "if" in your prayer in praying for anything God has promised you in His Word, you are praying in doubt. Some people think they are being humble when they pray that way, but they are really being ignorant. In other words, when you pray in faith, you don't use an "if." You will get no answer to the prayer of faith if you put "ifs" in your prayers.

But when you are praying a prayer of consecration, committing your life to the plan of God, then you can use the phrase, "If it be Thy will," because you don't know for sure what the Lord's will is. When you are praying the prayer of consecration, you are not praying to change something. But the prayer of faith is the prayer to change things. "If" is the badge of doubt, and the word "if" shouldn't be used in your prayers if you are trying to change a situation.

I had given some scriptures on the radio concerning faith, but they hadn't registered on this man whose wife was sick because he still wasn't sure it was God's will to heal his wife. I asked him, "If the New Testament said that Jesus took your wife's infirmities and bare her sicknesses, then wouldn't it be God's will for her to have her healing?"

He agreed that it would. So we turned to Matthew 8:17.

MATTHEW 8:17

17 That it might be fulfilled which was spoken by Esaias the prophet, saying, HIMSELF TOOK OUR INFIRMITIES, and BARE OUR SICKNESSES.

This man jumped up and exclaimed that it was the will of God for his wife to be healed. His wife saw it too.

Then we turned to First Peter 2:24.

1 PETER 2:24

24 Who his own self bare our sins in his own body on the tree, that we, being dead to sins, should live unto righteousness: BY WHOSE STRIPES YE WERE HEALED.

Then we turned to the Book of Isaiah.

ISAIAH 53:4–5

4 Surely he hath borne our griefs, and carried our sorrows: yet we did esteem him stricken, smitten of God, and afflicted.

5 But he was wounded for our transgressions, he was bruised for our iniquities: the chastisement of our peace was upon him; and with his stripes we are healed.

The margin reads, "Surely he hath borne our *sicknesses* and carried our *diseases*" (Isa. 53:4). This couple said that all they needed now was faith. They knew that it was God's will to heal. They said that they knew they were saved; they had gone forward in a church when an invitation was given and had prayed the sinner's prayer. So I knew that they were saved.

I asked them if they had asked the Lord to give them faith to be saved when they had gone down to the altar to be saved. They said no. The man related that the pastor preached that they could be saved. The pastor had read the Word to the people.

In other words, they heard the Word concerning salvation. They had faith for salvation because the Bible says, *"Faith cometh by hearing, and hearing by the word of God"* (Rom. 10:17). So I told them that they had faith for her healing, too, for the same reason they had had faith for salvation. They had heard the Word.

This man said they were going to have to throw their first prayer away because it wasn't any good. I agreed with him. You see, as soon as the light comes, faith is there.

This couple already had faith because they had heard and understood the Word. The woman agreed with us. She said that all she had to do now was to accept Jesus as her Healer. So I laid my hand on her head and prayed. Then I asked her if she was healed. And she said that she surely was and that she knew it because the Word says so.

Sunday night during the service at that same church, the vestibule doors swung open and there was that same fellow again. He asked the pastor if he could say a word to the congregation. The pastor gave him permission and the man told the congregation what had happened.

He said that when he and his wife got home Friday night, she pulled her brace off and threw it into the closet, and said, "Thank God, I'm healed."

The next day when he came home, he found her stooped over the sink washing her hair, something she had been unable to do. The woman had been completely healed!

I also laid hands on the husband and wife, and they were filled with the Holy Ghost and began to speak in tongues. Years later, the wife was still healed. How did she get faith? *From hearing the Word!*

This man had also brought his mother to be prayed for, who was in a wheelchair with paralysis. After we prayed for her, she got up out of the chair and walked out of the building that night completely well.

In the gospel of Jesus Christ, there is provision for every need—salvation, deliverance, safety, preservation, healing, and soundness. Whatever need you have, the faith to receive your answer comes from hearing the Word of God. As you determine to feed upon the Word continually, you will see your faith grow to be able to receive the wonderful promises God has provided for His children.

Questions for Study

1. Who should we blame if we lack faith?

   _____

   _____

2. Why is hearing the Word of God so important?

   _____

   _____

3. In Acts 10, why did the angel tell Cornelius to send for Peter?

   _____

   _____

4. In Acts 14:7–9, the man was healed because he and Paul each did three things. What three things did each of them do?

   _____

   _____

5. In Mark 5:34, how was the woman with the issue of blood made whole?

   _____

   _____

6. How did the man at Lystra get the faith to be healed?

   _____

   _____

7. What do the Greek and Hebrew words for "salvation" imply?

   _____

   _____

8. According to James 5:15, what kind of prayer will save the sick?

   _____

   _____

9. When you put an "if" in your prayer in praying for anything God has promised you in His Word, you are praying in _____.

10. What will happen as you determine to feed upon the Word continually?

    _____

    _____

Chapter 2

How Faith Comes—Part 2

Now FAITH IS THE SUBSTANCE of things hoped for, the evidence of things not seen.

—Hebrews 11:1

God is telling us exactly what Bible faith is.

Hebrews 11:1 says that faith is the *evidence* of things not seen and faith is the *substance* of things hoped for. In other words, faith is *substance*.

Moffatt's translation of Hebrews 11:1 reads: "Now faith means that we are confident of what we hope for, convinced of what we do not see." Another translation reads: "Faith is giving substance to things hoped for."

Human Faith vs. Bible Faith

However, we must understand that there are a number of kinds of faith. For example, everyone has a natural human faith, whether they are saved or unsaved. But in Hebrews 11:1, God is talking about a scriptural faith—a Bible faith. Bible faith is believing with your heart.

There is a vast difference between believing with your heart, and just believing what your physical senses may tell you. Bible faith is laying hold of the unseen realm of hope and bringing it into the realm of reality. And Bible faith grows out of the Word of God.

Another translation of Hebrews 11:1 says, "Faith is the warranty deed, the thing for which you have fondly hoped for is at last yours." For example, you *hope* for finances to meet the obligations you have to pay. *Faith* gives you the assurance that you'll have the money when you need it because, faith is *"the evidence of things not seen"* (Heb. 11:1).

You *hope* for physical strength to do the work you know you must do. But faith says, *"the Lord is the strength of my life; of whom shall I be afraid?"* (Ps. 27:1). Faith will say about itself everything that the Word says, *for faith in God is faith in His Word.*

It would be a wonderful thing if folks would learn that and act upon that. Then, you see, the very strength of God and every blessing He has made available to them would become theirs.

Appropriating God's Strength by Faith

I learned what faith is when I was raised up from the bed of sickness. After I was healed, I needed work, but this was during the Depression Days and it was hard to find work. I had been bedfast for sixteen months and I needed clothes and other things for school.

I got a job at a nursery pulling up peach trees. We pulled up these trees by hand, one boy on each side of the tree. We had to pull them up for orders that had come in. I want you to know, that was work! It was especially hard for someone who had been bedfast for so long and who had only been up out of bed a few months!

We would meet each morning before sunup and begin work. Every day some of the boys would say to me, "Well, I didn't think you would make it today. You know, So-and-so fell out yesterday and had to quit."

I didn't believe in trying to push something off on someone, but I did believe in witnessing for God, so when they would say these things to me, it would give me an opportunity to witness to them about the Lord.

I would say, "Well, boys, if it wasn't for the Lord, I wouldn't be here. You see, His strength is my strength. The Bible says, *'the Lord is the strength of my life'* (Ps. 27:1). My life consists of the physical as well as the spiritual, *'and the Lord is the strength of my life; of whom shall I be afraid?'"*

When I would say that, it would make some of those boys so mad that they would cuss about it. I would just smile and say, "Praise the Lord, I'll be here tomorrow and every other day because the Lord is my strength."

Of course, if I had gone by my feelings, I would never have gotten out of bed because I felt like staying in bed. I never felt so weak in my life; I felt like I couldn't do anything—let alone a strenuous job like that! But I just stayed with it. I acted upon the Word because I knew what faith is.

So I would say to the Father, to Jesus, to the Holy Ghost, to the devil, to myself, and to those boys if they asked me, "The Lord is my strength!" Then after I prayed and asked God for His strength and confessed that I had it, I would never get any help or strength until I actually started to work. You see, it wasn't enough to have faith; I had to *act* on my faith.

This is where many people miss *what faith is.* They want to get what they are believing God for and *then* believe they have received it. But actually it is the other way around. You have to believe you have your petition, and *then* you get it.

So we would come to work and I still wouldn't have any strength. But every morning when we started on the first tree or sometimes the second tree, I would feel something hit me on the top of my head and it would go through my body, out the ends of my fingers and out the ends of my toes. It was the supernatural strength of the Lord, and I would work all day long under the power of that strength.

Finally, one fellow who weighed two hundred and fifty pounds said, "I'll tell you, when this old two hundred and fifty pounds is gone, there won't be one man left in the field."

I replied, "Why, Alton, God weighs more than two hundred and fifty pounds! When you fall out and quit, I'll still be here."

He cussed at me, but at 3 o'clock that afternoon he fell out! And it was the truth—I was the only man left. I was the weakest and the skinniest, but I was the only man left of the original bunch that started. And to show you how sufficient the Lord's strength was, the boss wanted to hire me permanently. So I proved God's Word.

Proving God's Word by Acting on It

You may *say* that you know God's Word is good, but you will never really *know* God's Word is good until you have acted on it and have reaped the results of it. That is what faith is: Faith is proving God's Word by acting on it. Faith is giving substance to the things hoped for.

I went to work in spite of my physical weakness. I acted on God's Word, and I reaped the results of my faith in God's Word. You see, I hoped for physical strength to do the work that I knew must be done. But faith gave substance to that which I hoped for.

God's Word says that *God* is the strength of my life. As I acted on God's Word, my faith gave substance to that which I hoped for—strength to get my work done. You see, a lot of folks just hope, and they stop there. But that is not faith, that's hope, and hope won't bring substance—only faith will. Faith *is* the *substance* of things hoped for. Hope doesn't have any substance, but faith gives substance to hope.

Someone might say, "Well, I *hope* God heard my prayer." But if that is all you are doing is hoping, you won't receive an answer to your petition because it is faith that moves God, not hope. Hope isn't what causes God to hear your prayer; faith is. If you are only hoping, there will not be an answer to your prayers.

However, your faith can give substance to your hope. In fact, faith *will* give answers to your prayers. Remember, hope says, "I will have the answer to my petition *sometime.*" But faith says, "I have the answer to my petition *now!*"

John Wesley said that the devil has given the Church a substitute for faith that looks and sounds so much like faith, many people can't tell the difference. He called it, "mental assent."

Mental Assent vs. Heart Faith

For example, many people see what God's Word says and they agree mentally that God's Word is true. But they are just agreeing with their minds. But mental agreement with the Word is not what gets the job done. It is *heart* faith that receives from God. That is why the Bible says, *"For with the HEART man BELIEVETH"* (Rom. 10:10).

Jesus talked about believing with the heart in Mark 11:23.

MARK 11:23
23 Whosoever shall say unto this mountain, Be thou removed, and be thou cast into the sea; and shall not doubt in his HEART, but shall believe [in his heart] that those things which he saith shall come to pass; he shall have whatsoever he saith.

Notice that the Bible never said one word about doubting in one's head. You can have doubt in your head and still have faith in your heart. But it is believing in your heart that will cause you to receive from God.

People ask, "How can I tell whether I have faith in my heart or whether I'm just believing mentally in my head?" You can tell because mental agreement or mental assent says, "I know God's Word is true. I know God promises me healing and the answer to my prayer [or whatever it is you need], but for some reason I can't get it. I can't *understand* it! Why then don't I have the answer to my petition!"

Folks who say that are just in mental assent, not in real Bible faith or heart faith. *Faith*—real faith in God's Word says, "If God's Word says it's so, then it's so. The promise is mine; I have it now!" Faith always says, "I have it even though I can't see it."

Now notice what the text said: *"Faith . . . is the evidence of things not seen"* (Heb. 11:1). Someone said, "Well, yes, but the thing that I've been praying about, I don't see. It hasn't come to pass yet."

But if you already had it, you wouldn't have to believe it; you would *know* it then. In order to come to that place of *knowing*, you have to take that step of believing without seeing, based only on your faith in the integrity of God's Word.

Many people want to *know* it first, and then *believe* it. That is, they want to know it from the natural standpoint of having it come to pass first. However, we know we have received what the Word tells us is ours because God's Word says it is ours. When we believe God's Word without seeing anything manifested in the natural realm, *then* what we are believing God for materializes.

Jesus said in Mark 11:24: *"What things soever ye desire, when ye pray, believe that ye receive them, and ye shall have them."* Notice that the having comes after the believing. Most folks want to turn that around and have first and then believe. But in common everyday language, Jesus was saying that you have to *believe* you have your petition before you *get* it.

I don't know about you, but I have never been able to receive healing for my body without first believing that I had received my healing—even when every symptom in my body was crying out, "You don't have your healing. You aren't healed!" I would just simply say to my flesh, "The Bible says, *'let God be true, but every man a liar'* (Rom. 3:4). So if you say I'm not healed, you are a liar because God's Word says I am!"

Then when I act in faith on God's Word instead of acting on what I feel, results are always forthcoming! It works one hundred times out of one hundred. But if you are going to sit around and groan and sigh and gripe and complain and wait for something to come to you, you will never get very far in faith—that is, real Bible faith.

Believe What the Bible Says— Not What Your Senses Tell You

If you are going to wait until you detect that every symptom has gone and your flesh corresponds with your faith and everything is fine before you are going to start believing God, then you're all out of order and out of line with the Word, and you'll never get very far in faith.

You see, the trouble is that so many people are like doubting Thomas, one of Jesus' twelve disciples. Thomas said, "I'll not believe until I can see Him and put my finger in the print in His hands and thrust my hand into the wound in His side" (John 20:25).

Then when Jesus appeared to the disciples, and Thomas saw Jesus, Thomas said, *"My Lord and my God"* (John 20:28). Did Jesus praise Thomas for his lack of faith? No, Jesus said, *"Thomas, because thou hast seen me, thou hast believed: blessed are they that have not seen, and yet have believed"* (John 20:29).

In other words, Thomas didn't believe in Jesus' resurrection by faith as you and I believe in it. Thomas believed because he saw Jesus with his physical eyes; he relied totally on his senses. But we believe in Jesus' resurrection because the Word of God says Jesus was raised from the dead.

This is where many people miss it in the area of faith without really realizing it. They say, "I believe in divine healing because So-and-so got healed." But that is not Bible faith! I don't believe in healing because I saw someone get healed. I believe in healing because the Word of God says healing belongs to me (Isa. 53:4–5; Matt. 8:17; 1 Peter 2:24).

I don't believe in speaking in tongues just because some people speak in tongues. No, I believe in the baptism of the Holy Spirit with the evidence of speaking in tongues because the Word of God teaches it. I would still believe in it even if I had never heard anyone else speak in tongues.

I believe what the Bible says, not what I see and hear. My faith is not in what I can see and hear. My faith is based on what *God* says. You see, when we develop our faith to the place where we believe what the Word says regardless of circumstances and physical symptoms, then we are believing the right thing, and that's what brings results.

Thomas said, "I will not believe until I see." And Jesus said, *". . . Thomas, because thou hast seen me, thou hast believed: blessed are they that have not seen, and yet have believed"* (John 20:29). Those who believe what the Word of God says, apart from what they see or feel with their physical senses, are the ones who are blessed.

ROMANS 4:17–21

17 (As it is written, I have made thee a father of many nations,) before him whom he believed, even God, who quickeneth the dead, and calleth those things which be not as though they were.

18 Who against hope believed in hope, that he might become the father of many nations, according to that which was spoken, So shall thy seed be.

19 And being not weak in faith, he considered not his own body now dead, when he was about an hundred years old, neither yet the deadness of Sarah's womb:

20 He staggered not at the promise of God through unbelief; but was strong in faith, giving glory to God;

21 And being fully persuaded that, what he had promised, he was able also to perform.

Notice the difference between Abraham's faith and Thomas' faith. Thomas' faith was just simply a natural, human faith. He said, "I'm not going to believe unless I can see and feel."

But the Word of God says that Abraham believed God's Word and he considered not his own body. Well, if Abraham didn't consider his own body, that means he didn't consider physical sight or physical feelings. What did he consider then? *The Word of God. He considered the promise of God, ". . . being fully persuaded that, what he had promised, he was able also to perform"* (Rom. 4:21).

I remember quite a few years ago, I was struggling along some of the same lines that many people do today in the area of healing. Even after I was healed, I had some of the most alarming heart symptoms that seemed to return to me. In the nighttime I would have some terrible struggles. So I did just what Abraham did. I had been praying and standing on the promises of God, but I could not get off to sleep.

Finally, I said to the Lord, "Lord, I must have some relief."

God spoke to me, "Consider not thine own body."

So I just relaxed and said, "Thank You," and took my mind off of my body and drifted back to sleep. Later that same night I woke up again and had some of the same symptoms.

I said, "Lord, I'm not considering my own body. What am I going to consider then?"

The Lord said, "Consider Him, who is the Author and Finisher of your faith and your High Priest" (Heb. 3:1; Heb. 12:2).

God tells us in His Word exactly what *not* to consider, and then He tell us what to consider. Or we could say it this way: God tells us in His Word exactly what not to consider and then He tells us *whom* to consider—the Lord Jesus Christ—the Author and Finisher of our faith.

Immediately I got my mind on Jesus, and I began to consider Him and what He had done for us. The Bible says, *"Himself took our infirmities, and bare our sicknesses"* (Matt. 8:17). I began to consider that scripture and to focus my mind and attention on Jesus and the Word, and I stopped considering my body with its symptoms. Then I was able to drift off to sleep. When I woke up every symptom had gone.

Too many times, we get our attention focused on the wrong thing. When it comes to healing, we consider our own bodies and the symptoms that try to attack our bodies. That is what we are thinking about and looking at, and the more we look at the symptoms, the worse we get.

You hear people say, "God hasn't heard my prayer yet and I'm getting worse. I guess I'll wind up being operated on." You will as long as you travel that road of doubt and unbelief! I preached at one church where there was a woman who testified every time she could, and at the end of every testimony she would say, "You all pray for me. I just believe I've got cancer."

Finally, the pastor got tired of it, and he stood up when she got through and said, "That's right, Sister! Keep believing it and you'll get it! Jesus said, *'According to your faith be it unto you'*" (Matt. 9:29)!

Sometimes folks say, "Brother Hagin, pray for me. I believe I'm getting a cold." It won't do any good for me to pray for them, because if they believe they are getting a cold, then they will get it because the Bible says, according to *your faith* be it unto you.

You keep on believing for it and you'll get it! You see, I'm trying to get you to see what it means to walk by faith and not by sight. So many people consider the wrong thing instead of considering God's promises in His Word.

Some people just get part of what I'm saying and go off thinking in an altogether different light than what I'm teaching. They think I am teaching that we are to deny all symptoms and just go on as if symptoms weren't even there.

We do not deny symptoms because they are real. Of course pain is real; sin is real; and the devil is real. But notice what the Bible said: "Abraham considered *not* his own body" (Rom. 4:19). So don't consider your body, but do consider Jesus, who is your High Priest and the Author and the Finisher of your faith (Heb. 12:2).

Center your attention and your mind on what Jesus has done for you and what He is doing for you as your High Priest. Jesus is doing something for you right now. He is seated at the right hand of God right now making intercession for you (Heb. 7:25).

HEBREWS 4:14

14 Seeing then that we have a great high priest, that is passed into the heavens, Jesus the Son of God, let us HOLD FAST OUR PROFESSION [our confession of faith].

We would do Hebrews 4:14 no injustice by reading it this way: "This is the reason we must HOLD FAST TO OUR CONFESSION, because we have such a great High Priest who has passed into the heavens, Jesus the Son of God."

The Greek word which is translated "profession" or "confession" implies that this verse can also be read, "Let us hold fast to saying the same thing." What does that mean? Jesus, our Great High Priest, is representing us at the throne of God. And Jesus is saying, "I took their place. I died for them as their Substitute."

Jesus didn't die for Himself. He didn't need to redeem Himself because He wasn't lost. But He needed to die for us because we were lost. He became our Substitute. He took our sins. He bare our sicknesses. He carried our diseases. He died for us. He arose from the dead for us and ascended on High for us. Jesus is at the right hand of the throne of God, saying, "I did all that for them."

Now we are to hold fast to our profession—saying the same thing here on the earth that the Word says. That's what puts the devil on the run. So get your attention focused on the right things—on Jesus, our great High Priest, and on His Word—instead of on yourself.

Keep Looking at the Word

I like another passage of scripture along this same line. In fact, these scriptures helped me when I was on the bed of affliction. I believe these scriptures helped me as much as anything in my lifetime.

PROVERBS 4:20–22

20 My son, attend to my words; incline thine ears unto my sayings.
21 LET THEM NOT DEPART FROM BEFORE THINE EYES; keep them in the midst of thine heart.
22 For they [my words] **are life unto those that find them, and health to all their flesh.**

I want to call your attention particularly to one verse. Verse 21 says, *"Let them* [my words] *not*

depart from before thine eyes." Many people fail because they see themselves fail. They keep the wrong thing before their eyes.

Understanding this was a turning point in my life because up until the time I read this scripture, I had always seen myself dead. I could picture every detail about my death. But after I read this passage of Scripture, I could see myself well, and I began to see myself alive. I began to see myself doing things I had never done in my life because of my heart condition.

I knew God had called me to preach and I could see myself preaching. So I began to get ready for it. Even while I was bedfast, I asked for a tablet and a pencil, and I got my Bible and began to prepare sermons. They weren't preachable and I never did preach any of them except one, but I was getting ready nevertheless.

The reason many folks fail is that they get ready to fail; they see themselves failing.

Now again notice what the Word says: *"Let them* [my words] *not depart from before thine eyes"* (Prov. 4:21). If you know that God's Word says, *"Himself,* [Jesus] *took our infirmities, and bare our sicknesses"* (Matt. 8:17), then if that Word does not depart from before your eyes, you are bound to see yourself without sickness and without disease.

If the Word doesn't depart from before your eyes, you are bound to see yourself well. And if you do not see yourself without sickness and disease and if you do not see yourself well, then that Word has departed from before your eyes. And although God wants to make His Word good in your life, He can't because you're not acting on His Word.

It's hard for me to follow the thinking of some people. To think that God is just going to do something for them without their doing what the Word says is just plain unintelligent thinking. God isn't going to move on your behalf if you don't cooperate with His Word.

You see, God can't move on your behalf, even if He wanted to, if you're not acting on the Word. If He did, He would make Himself out to be a liar, and the Bible says God cannot lie.

God gives us directions right here in Proverbs chapter 4 for taking His medicine. Proverbs 4:22 says, *"For they* [God's words] *are life unto those that find them, and health* [or medicine] *to all their flesh."* The margin of my Bible tells me that this Hebrew word translated "health" is also the word for *medicine.* So take God's Word according to His directions. God's

Words are medicine to all our flesh. But verses 20 and 21 tell us the directions for taking the medicine.

What is God's medicine? Does God have any medicine? Yes, thank God, He does. God's Word is God's medicine. *"For they* [My words] *are life unto those that find them, and health* [medicine] *to all their flesh."* But in order for the medicine to work, it has to be taken according to directions.

PROVERBS 4:21

21 Let them [my words] **not depart from thine eyes. Keep them in the midst of thine heart.**

Keep looking at what the Word says. You see so many folks are looking at themselves, at the conditions, at the symptoms. If God's Word assures you that He heard and answers your prayer, then if that Word doesn't depart from before your eyes, you are going to see yourself with what you prayed for.

That's faith in God's Word. When you see yourself with the answer based on God's Word, that's when you know your faith is solidly based on the Word of God. You see, failing to take God's medicine—His Word—according to instructions is what defeats so many folks in their prayer life.

Notice all of that agrees with what Jesus says in Mark 11:24: *"what things soever ye desire, when ye pray, believe that you receive them, and ye shall have them."*

You've got to believe you've got your answer before you get it! Someone might say, "I'm not going to believe anything I can't see." But even in the natural realm, we believe a lot of things we can't see.

For example, during World War II, when radioactive materials were loosed into the atmosphere due to exploding bombs, the whole world became concerned about something they couldn't see. You can't see or feel radioactivity, but you can definitely see and feel the result of radioactivity. It's a destructive power.

Also, scientists believe in many things they can't necessarily see but just as people became alarmed about the unseen radioactivity in this world and believed it even though they couldn't see or feel it, I believe in the power of God even though I can't see or feel it. I believe what the Word of God says about the Holy Ghost, the great Unseen Power of God, whether or not I feel or see Him.

Besides, I have had some of the greatest healings take place in my meetings when I never felt a thing. I have had some of the most marvelous things happen when the service seemed dead.

So, you see, feelings don't have a thing in the world to do with faith. God is with me, and His power is always available whether I feel like it or not. I'm not basing my faith on what I feel; I'm basing my faith on what God said. And He said, *"I will never leave thee, nor forsake thee"* (Heb. 13:5).

HEBREWS 13:6

6 So that we may boldly say, THE LORD IS MY HELPER, and I will not fear what man shall do unto me.

Is that what you are saying? Are you boldly declaring, "The Lord is my helper"? That's what you need to be saying!

"Well," someone said, "the Lord's forsaken me. You all pray for me. I don't feel like I once did."

Your feelings don't have anything whatsoever to do with what the Bible says. I've heard people say, "I don't know whether I can make it or not; I hope I can. You all pray for me that I'll hold out faithful to the end."

That is not what the Word says we are to boldly declare. So many people are boldly declaring their defeat and failure: "I'm whipped." "I'm defeated." "The devil's got me bound." But nowhere in the Bible do you find where He said to boldly say that.

The writer of Hebrews said, *"for he* [Jesus] *hath said, I will never leave thee, nor forsake thee. So that we may boldly say, The Lord is my helper . . ."* (Heb. 13:5–6).

So quit saying the wrong thing and start saying the right thing. Say, "The Lord is my Helper" (Heb. 13:6). Is He? Then say *that He is.* Say, "The Lord is my Healer." Say, "Jesus took my infirmities, and bore my sicknesses" (Matt. 8:17). Didn't He? Then keep talking about God's delivering power. Say the right things and believe the right things.

Friends, it is just simply wrong thinking, wrong believing, and wrong talking that whips folks. You see, the devil can't defeat you because Jesus has already defeated the devil for you. Satan doesn't defeat you; you defeat yourself. Or if he does, you permit him to do so. It's a consent of ignorance.

God has given us His Word to get our thinking straightened out, so that we won't be ignorant and so our believing will be right. And if our thinking is right and our believing is right, then our talking will be right.

So say, "The Lord is my Helper. The Lord is my strength." Real faith in the Word says, "If God says it's so, then it's so." If God says by His stripes I was healed, then I'm healed (Isa. 53:4–5; 1 Peter 2:24).

If God says He shall supply every need of mine, then He does it (Phil. 4:19). If God says He's the Strength of my life, then He is (Ps. 27:1).

In other words, real faith in God simply says about one's self what the Word says.

Thank God, I have what the Word says I have. I am what the Word says I am. If God says I'm strong, I am. If He says I'm healed, I am. If He says He cares for me, then He does. So I just simply quietly rest on the Word, for the Word says, *"For we which have believed do enter into rest"* (Heb. 4:3).

Quietly rest on the Word regardless of natural evidence that would satisfy the physical senses. *Real faith is built on the Word!* We should meditate in the Word and dig deeply into it and feed upon it. Then the Word will become a part of us just as natural food becomes a part of us.

In other words, what natural food is to the physical man, the Word of God is to the spiritual man. So this Word builds into me—the real me, the inward man—confidence and assurance. Remember, *"faith cometh by hearing and hearing by the word of God"* (Rom. 10:17).

Questions for Study

1. What does Hebrews 11:1 say that faith is?

   _____

   _____

2. What kind of faith is God talking about in Hebrews 11:1?

   _____

   _____

3. Bible faith is laying hold of the _____ realm of _____ and bringing it into the realm of _____.

4. Faith is _____ God's Word by _____ on it.

5. What did John Wesley call a substitute for faith that looks and sounds so much like faith, many people can't tell the difference?

   _____

   _____

6. How can you tell whether you have faith in your heart or whether you're just believing mentally in your head?

   _____

   _____

7. When does what we are believing God for materialize?

   _____

   _____

8. What is the difference between Thomas' faith and Abraham's faith?

   _____

   _____

9. What should you center your attention and your mind on?

   _____

   _____

10. What is God's medicine?

    _____

    _____

Chapter 3

What Faith Is—Part 1

Now faith is the substance of things hoped for, the evidence of things not seen.

—Hebrews 11:1

Moffatt's translation of this verse reads: *"Now faith means that we are confident of what we hope for, convinced of what we do not see."* One modern translation of Hebrews 11:1 reads: "Faith is giving substance . . . to things hoped for."

The Difference Between Faith and Hope

What God is simply telling us is that faith is laying hold of the unseen realm of hope and bringing it into the realm of reality. Too many times when it comes to receiving the Holy Spirit or healing or an answer to prayer, many people are just simply *hoping* they will receive.

Faith Is Present Tense

But it's not hoping that gets the job done; it's believing. The Bible says, *"Now faith is . . ."* (Heb. 11:1). If it's not now, it's not faith. Someone said, "Well, I believe I'll get the Holy Ghost *sometime.*" That's not faith, that's hope, because hope is always future tense or pointing to the future. But faith is *now.* Faith says, "I'll receive right *now*; I believe I have my petition now when I pray" (Mark 11:24). We need to realize this when it comes to receiving from God.

I speak along this line because the same principles are true concerning receiving the Holy Spirit, healing, or an answer to prayer. The principles of faith are the same in any area, whether it be finances, the baptism of the Holy Ghost, divine healing, or whatever the petition is.

And if you can learn the principles of faith, then it is easy to receive whatever it is you are seeking or whatever you desire from God that is in line with His Word.

I know from experience through the years in dealing with so many people that when it comes to receiving the Holy Spirit and healing, as well as to receiving an answer to prayer, many are just simply *hoping* that God hears them when they pray, or they are *hoping* that they will receive an answer.

I remember I was conducting a tent meeting in Waco, Texas, years ago. We started the revival on Sunday night. I preached an evangelistic-type message, and the next night I preached on faith. The next night we had our first healing service.

I always put folks in the same line to receive healing or to receive the Holy Ghost. I preached on the laying on of hands, and then after giving the invitation for the lost, I laid hands on the sick to be healed and laid hands on believers to receive the Holy Ghost.

The very first man in the line came to receive the Holy Ghost. I said to him, "Will you be filled with the Holy Ghost now as I lay my hands on you and pray?"

"Brother Hagin," he said, "I sure hope I will."

I said, "Well, then, you won't be."

That sort of made him angry. I meant that to help him, not to anger him, so I immediately said to him, "You don't receive anything from God through hope. It's by *faith* that you receive."

He said, "But I don't know whether I'm going to receive or not, so I'm not going to say I am."

I said, "If I offered you a dollar bill, would you say, 'I don't know whether I can receive that or not'?"

"No, certainly not," he said.

"Well," I said, "God offers you a gift that is just as easy to receive as it is to receive a dollar bill offered to you."

He said, "Yes, but I've been seeking a mighty long time. In fact, I've been seeking about thirteen years, and I haven't received yet. So I don't know whether I'm going to receive now or not."

He became quite upset about it, so I just reached out and put my arms around him and hugged his neck. I said, "Now, Brother, I'm here to help you. But under the circumstances, I could lay my hands on your head until I wore every hair off the top of your head, and you wouldn't get anything. So I just suggest that you go sit down on the front row and listen and watch, and see what's going on. Then you'll see the difference between believing and doubting, and between faith and hope."

So we prayed for several people for healing, and then we came to a young woman who wanted to receive the Holy Ghost. I said, "Are you a Christian?"

"Well," she said, "I'm a member of a church."

I said, "You understand that you could be a member of any church and not be a Christian. Salvation is not a matter of being a member of a church, it's a matter of being born again."

"Yes," she said, "I know that, and I've been born again."

"I accept your testimony," I said. "Don't let the devil talk you out of it."

Then I asked her, "Now then, do you believe in the Holy Ghost?" (Having come out of the same denomination myself, I knew everyone in that denomination didn't believe in the baptism of the Holy Spirit.)

"Do you believe in the baptism of the Holy Ghost with the evidence of speaking with tongues?"

"I certainly do," she answered. "It is in the Bible. It's in the Word."

Then I asked, "Will you receive the Holy Ghost now when I lay my hands on your head and pray?"

She said, "I certainly will."

She had her Bible in her hand, and she said, "You know, I sat there tonight and followed every scripture you gave as you preached, and it's all in the Word. And I certainly will receive."

I saw she was ready because I saw her faith in operation. So I just reached my hand out to lay on her forehead, and before I even touched her—I just barely brushed my fingers on her forehead—she threw up both hands and started speaking in tongues instantly.

I said to this older gentleman who was sitting on the front row, "Do you see the difference between just *hoping* you'll receive the Holy Ghost and really *believing* you'll receive?"

"Yes," he said, "I do."

On Friday night he came back, and he was the very first person in the line. "Well," I said to him, "I see you're back."

"Yes," he said, "I'm back, and I'll tell you something else. I've changed my hope to faith. Just put your hands on me, and I'll be filled with the Holy Ghost right now."

I reached out to lay hands on him, and I had barely touched him, when he lifted both hands and began speaking with other tongues!

Oh, it makes such a difference when you really believe God instead of just hoping you'll receive your petition from Him—whether it's receiving the Holy Ghost, healing, or any answer to prayer.

That man said he'd been seeking the baptism of the Holy Spirit for thirteen years, but really he had just simply been hoping that he would get the Holy Ghost. And you just don't receive anything from God by hope. You receive from God by *faith*.

Hope vs. Faith in The Prayer of Agreement

I remember on another occasion at the close of one service, a woman said to me, "Brother Hagin, I wish you would agree with me. In your message, you used the scripture in Matthew 18:19 where Jesus said, '. . . *if two of you shall agree on earth as touching any thing that they shall ask, it shall be done for them of my Father which is in heaven.*'"

I said, "All right, Sister. What do you want to me agree with you about?"

She said, "Do I have to tell you?"

"Certainly," I said, "I can't agree about something when I don't know what we are agreeing about."

She said, "This is a financial need."

I said, "All right, how much do you need?"

She said, "Well, my husband has a job and makes so much money, but an emergency has arisen. We need an extra $100. I just don't know where it's coming from. But I know God can help us and show us."

"He certainly can!" I said to her. "Then you want me to agree with you that God will provide an extra $100 this month."

"Yes," she answered, "that's right."

I said, "All right, let's agree. I'm going to pray, and you listen while I pray. You agree with what I pray because if we both pray at once, you may go one direction and I may go another. Let's agree. You just agree in your spirit right now."

So I prayed and I reminded the Father that we were agreeing according to His Word. I said, "We're on the earth, and You said if two of you on earth shall agree as touching anything that they shall ask, You would do it for us." I said, "We agree as touching this extra $100 that this woman needs this month. We thank You, Father, because we agree it is done. Thank You for it. Amen."

I said, "Is it done, Sister?"

Immediately (I'm not making fun of her. I'm merely stating facts.), she tuned up and began to cry, and said, "Brother Hagin, I sure hope it is. I hope so."

I replied, "Well, then, it's not. It isn't! Because we didn't agree. You are hoping and I am believing. There is no agreement there!"

This is exactly why some of our prayers don't work for us. Certainly, it isn't God's fault that prayer doesn't work. If our prayers don't work, it isn't God's fault because God never fails. If our prayers don't work, it is not Jesus' fault, because Jesus never fails.

God doesn't change, and prayer doesn't change God. He is just the same before you pray, when you pray, and after you pray. Prayer doesn't change God. Prayer changes circumstances, but prayer doesn't change God. He is always the same and that means He is always faithful to His Word (Heb. 10:23; 13:8; Rom. 4:20–21).

Dr. Lilian B. Yeomans said something that I read years ago and have never forgotten. It has been a great blessing to me through the years.

She said, "If I pray for any one thing or pray just one time for anything, and I don't get it, I start changing. I start changing because if I pray and that prayer isn't answered, there will have to be a change on my part before the answer comes. I know there can't be any changing on God's part, because He never changes. So if there has to be any change, it has to be on my end of the line. So if I pray and do not receive, then I start changing."

I've followed that policy through the years and found out that it always works one hundred percent of the time. We need to realize that we cannot substitute hope for faith and get answers from God.

Now don't misunderstand me. If you keep hope in the right place, it is a most blessed and wonderful reality to you. Paul said in First Corinthians 13:13, *"And now abideth faith, hope, charity* [love]*, these three; but the greatest of these is charity."*

Paul didn't say faith and hope aren't important; he said just the greatest of the three is *love*. But each one of them has its place.

For example, you can't substitute love for hope, and you can't substitute hope for faith. And yet, in dealing with many thousands of people throughout the years, I know that most people are trying to receive healing, the baptism of the Holy Ghost, or answer to prayer based on hope instead of on faith.

I know they are substituting hope for faith because of what they say to me. Many of them say to me, "If you take my hope away from me, I don't have anything left."

I respond, "No, I'm not taking your hope away from you. I'm just showing you that you have your hope misplaced; you are trying to make hope do what only faith can do—and that's receive from God."

Hope Is Future Tense

Thank God we do have a blessed hope. The blessed hope of the Church is the soon return of the Lord Jesus Christ, the resurrection of the saved dead, the rapture of the living saints, the hope of Heaven, and the hope of seeing our loved ones and friends. Thank God for that hope.

We rejoice in that hope, but that's all future tense. Jesus *is* coming again, whether we believe it or not. He is coming because the Word says so. The resurrection is going to take place whether we have faith in it or not. Whether we believe in it or not, it is still going to take place. The rapture is going to take place whether we believe it or not. And loved ones and friends who are Christians, who have died and left this world and have gone to Heaven, are there regardless of what we believe about it. And they will return with Jesus when He comes back.

My faith is not going to bring Jesus back. In other words, I can't believe that He will come at a particular time and have my faith bring Him back. If that were true, then the Church could believe and could bring Jesus back by their believing.

Jesus *is* coming, however. But, you see, that's all future tense because we don't know when that will happen, but we do know it will happen. And we do know it is a blessed hope. And we know it is a purifying hope, for First John 3:3 says, *"And every man that has this hope in him purifieth himself, even as he is pure."* This blessed hope is future tense. I do believe Jesus is coming, but He's coming back regardless of whether or not I believe it.

Looking for Jesus' return and waiting for that blessed hope is a combination of simply believing what the Word says and having *hope* in what the Word says. It is *future tense*.

But if I say, "I believe I'm going to get my healing *sometime*," that's not believing at all. It's hope, not faith, and hope won't bring healing to you. I've seen good people who were sick, yet died saying that. They were wonderful people who are now in Heaven, and I would not speak disparagingly of them at all because they were wonderful Christians. They just didn't know what faith is.

Someone said, "I believe God is *going to* heal me." But that isn't faith. That's hope. *Anything that points to the future or looks to the future is hope.* It is not faith because faith is now: *"NOW faith is . . ."* (Heb. 11:1).

Faith says, *"It is mine. I have it now."* Hope says, "I'll get it sometime." But as long as you are in hope and not in faith, whatever it is you are desiring will never materialize—it will never come into being. But the moment you start believing and acting like God's Word is so, your faith will work for you.

Changing My Hope to Faith

That's the lesson I learned on the bed of sickness many years ago. I had lain upon that bed for sixteen long months before I was healed. In fact, I'd been sick all my life and I never had a normal childhood. I never ran and played like other children and at fifteen years of age I became totally bedfast.

Five doctors, one of whom had practiced at the great Mayo Clinic, said that as far as medical science knew or had any record of, no one in my condition had ever lived past the age of sixteen. I became totally bedfast just a few months before I was sixteen years of age, and I remained bedfast until I was almost seventeen years of age.

I went through everything everyone does when they desperately want to be healed. Thank God for all the good books today on the subject of faith and healing, but there weren't many in those days. If there were, I didn't know about them, and didn't get ahold of them. I was just a denominational boy reading Grandma's Bible, but thank God, it reads just like my Full Gospel Bible does because it's the same Bible.

When I was trying to get healed, I cried and prayed, and said, "Dear Lord, please heal me." I begged Him to heal me, and prayed all night several nights, and nearly all night several other nights. When you are bedfast twenty-four hours a day, you can do a lot of praying!

I prayed many hours a day, day after day, week after week, and month after month. I was born again—but I wasn't getting any results as far as obtaining my healing. I'd pray and was sure God had heard me and had healed me because I sort of had the feeling that He had.

I don't mean I felt it physically, because I didn't feel any different. But I just felt like He had heard me.

I can't say that physically I felt that God heard me; but I'm talking about a spiritual sense of some kind.

When I would pray for healing, I would sense, *This is it; my prayer has been answered.*

But then I'd feel my heart. It was still not beating right. Then I would look at my lower limbs and they were still paralyzed. My legs were just bones with a little skin stretched over them—there was no meat or muscle in the thighs or calves.

Then I'd start crying and say, "Lord, I thought You were going to heal me. I just felt like You did. I just knew it, but You didn't."

I couldn't understand it, and for about a month or so I just wouldn't even look at the Bible. I decided I might just as well give up on my prayer as a bad job. Then I'd start slipping away. I'd go right down to death's door, right down in the throes of death. I held onto the head of the bed to try to keep from going. You could see where I held on to the bed, till all the varnish was worn off that headboard. I'd fight death with every fiber of my being. Then I'd come back to the Word of God again and begin to read it again.

As a young person I wanted to live so badly, so from the natural standpoint I fought death. But I couldn't see where I was missing it spiritually. I would try to act upon God's Word. And I'd get some results and recover from the attacks, but I still didn't receive my healing.

Finally, on the second Tuesday of August 1934, after lying on the bed of sickness for sixteen months, I said to the Lord, "Dear Lord Jesus, when You were here on earth You said in Mark 11:24, *'What things soever ye desire, when ye pray, believe that ye receive them, and ye shall have them.'* I desire to be healed. You said, 'When you pray.' I have prayed. You said, 'Believe.' I have believed."

I continued, "Dear Lord Jesus, if You stood here by my bedside in the flesh and I could see You with my physical eyes, and I could reach my physical hand out and lay my hands on Yours, if You were to say to me, 'Son, the trouble with you is you're not believing,' I would have to say to you, 'Dear Lord Jesus, You're lying about it! I do believe.'" (I said this in kindness and sincerity, not in tones of arrogance.)

You Cannot Believe Beyond Actual Knowledge

Now Jesus does not speak to a person physically, like someone else might speak to you. He's not here in the flesh, but the Holy Spirit is here. And Jesus said about the Holy Spirit, *"he [the Holy Spirit] shall not speak of himself; but whatsoever he shall hear, that shall he speak"* (John 16:13). The Holy Spirit spoke to my spirit on the inside of me: "Yes, you believe, all right, as far as you know." (A person can't believe beyond actual knowledge. It just can't be done. That's where many fail. They don't really know what the Word says.)

The Lord said, "You believe, all right, as far as you know. But that last clause goes with that verse of scripture, *'. . . and ye shall have them.' It says, '. . . believe that ye RECEIVE them, and ye shall HAVE them'"* (Mark 11:24).

Believe You Receive Your Petition Before You Have It

Then I saw it! It was just like someone had turned a light on inside of me. I saw it. I said instantly, "Dear Lord Jesus, I see it, I see it! I have to believe I receive my healing before I get it. I have to believe that I receive healing for my heart while my heart is still not beating right. I have to believe I receive healing for my paralysis even though from the natural standpoint I am still paralyzed. And if I believe I receive it, then I will have it."

You see, I'd not done that yet. I wanted to get my healing first, and then believe it. But you don't have to *believe* it once you get it. Then you *know* it. Faith is not sight. In other words, once you see whatever it is you were believing for, you don't need faith to believe for your petition anymore.

Instantly I saw what I had been doing. I had been hoping all of those months to receive my healing, and hope didn't work. I could never receive an answer to my prayers through hope—only by faith. That meant I had to believe I had my petition *before* I actually saw it manifested.

One good thing about it is, you don't have to have a Full Gospel church, a denominational church, or anyone else tell you how to receive from God. If you'll just follow the Word and the Holy Spirit, you'll find yourself walking in line with the Word because the Holy Spirit will always lead you in line with the Word.

You see, when I was lying there on my bed I could move; it was only the lower part of my body that was paralyzed. I could move my hands.

No one told me to lift my hands, and I can't tell you why I did, but I just did. I lifted my hands as I lay there flat on my back on that bed. I lifted my hands up toward Heaven and said, "Heavenly Father, dear Lord Jesus, thank God I'm healed! I believe I am healed!"

I finally had it in the right tense! I finally got it working for me.

"Now faith IS the substance of things hoped for, the evidence of things not seen" (Heb. 11:1). NOW faith is. If it's not *now*, it's not faith. The Bible says, *"Now faith is,"* present tense. *If it's not present tense, it's not faith.*

When I said to the Lord, "Lord, I believe I receive my healing *now*," that's when I had faith working for me.

But when people say, "I believe I'm *going* to get my healing," that's not faith; that's not present tense.

I said, "Thank You, dear Lord Jesus, for my healing! I believe that my heart is well; I believe that my paralysis is healed! I thank You for the healing of my body!"

A few minutes can seem like a long time, but I believe I must have praised God in that vein for about ten minutes. Although I didn't look at a clock, I must have spent ten minutes thanking Him that my heart was well and my body was healed!

However, almost immediately, Satan challenged me. Yes, he will contest you on every inch of the ground you take from him. He will try to fight you every step of the way.

Immediately the devil said to me, "You're a pretty-looking thing. You claim to be a Christian and now you've gone to lying."

Any other time the devil would have denied that there is a hell or a lake of fire, but this time the devil said to me, "Don't you know that the Bible says that all liars shall have their part in the lake which burneth with fire and brimstone?"

"Yes," I said, "I know that, Mr. Devil." (You see, I knew that was the devil speaking because anything that brings doubt or discouragement is from the enemy.) I continued, "Yes, I know that, Mr. Devil, but I didn't lie."

He said, "Yes, you did. You said you were healed and you're not. Now feel your heart."

I was in such a habit of feeling for my heartbeat that I unconsciously reached to feel it. When I realized what I was doing, I slapped my hand and said, "Don't you do it. Don't you do it."

Immediately I said, "Mr. Devil, I did not say anything about how I looked or felt. I said I *believe* I am healed. I *believe* I am. I *believe* I have received the answer to my prayer. And if you say that I really don't believe it, you're lying. Besides that, you're a liar anyhow, because Jesus said you were" (John 8:44).

I said, "When Jesus Christ, the Son of God, was on the earth, He said, *What things soever ye desire, when ye pray, believe that ye receive them, and ye shall have them'* (Mark 11:24). Now Jesus said it, and what He says is so; I believe that. If I believe it, then I'll have it. I believe Him right now."

Then I said, "If you want to argue and fuss about it, you go argue with Jesus. I didn't say it anyway. He said it." That put a stop to the devil speaking his doubt and unbelief to me.

I went back to praising God, thanking Him for the answer—thanking Him for my healing. I had been praising Him for about ten minutes, when on the inside of me, in my spirit, I heard these words: "Now you believe you are healed. But healed people—well people—don't have any business being in the bed at this time of day. They need to be up."

I said, "That's right! Yes, Lord, that's right. I'm going to get up. Praise God, I'm going to get up."

You see, now I was in faith. I was believing and taking God at His Word. Believing faith is *having* by faith what you asked God for. Believing is taking a step of faith. And to be in faith, you have to take steps of faith because faith requires corresponding action.

In my case, I had been bedfast, and I needed to get up out of bed. That was the corresponding action I needed to take in order to act in faith. I didn't look better. I didn't feel better. And I didn't have any feeling from my waist down. If I had gone by feelings, I'd have to say I wasn't healed because I was still partially paralyzed. But I knew I'd been healed regardless of how I felt. I pushed myself to a seated position in bed. Then with my hands I pushed my limbs and feet off of the bed, and twisted my body around so that I was sitting on the edge of the bed. My feet fell down on the floor like a couple of chunks of wood.

I knew my feet were down there on the floor. I couldn't feel them, but I knew they were there because I could see them. The devil was trying to fight me every inch of the way. Negative thoughts were coming to my mind, just as fast as a machine gun fires bullets.

The devil said, "You can't walk, and you know you can't. You're not healed, and you know you're not. You're lying about it, and you'll fall right here on the floor, and you'll have to lie there."

Then the devil continued, "Don't you know, it hasn't been thirty days since you last fell out of bed,

and you had to lie there forty-five minutes until your oldest brother came in, picked you up, and put you back in bed. Your grandmother is old, and your mother is sickly. They can't lift you."

I only weighed eighty-nine pounds, but I was just as tall as I am now. Then the devil said, "None of the neighborhood men are home, and your oldest brother has gone back to Oklahoma. You'll just have to lie there on the floor until 5 o'clock this afternoon, until your grandpa comes in from work, and then he'll have to put you back in bed."

But you know the best way in the world to put the devil in his place is to just completely ignore him. The Bible says, *"Neither give place to the devil"* (Eph. 4:27). I ignored him, and just simply acted like he hadn't said anything.

I grabbed ahold of the bedpost, but my knees wouldn't function. My limbs wouldn't function, so with my arms around that bedpost, I just hung there, sagging at the knees.

As best I could, I lifted one hand a little bit, and said, "Thank God, I'm healed. I wanted to declare in the Presence of Almighty God and the Lord Jesus Christ and the angels of Heaven, and in the presence of the devil and evil spirits, that the Word of God is true. I believe I'm healed. I believe it!"

That old room started spinning because, you see, I'd been lying flat on my back for sixteen months. The floor seemed to be where the ceiling was just minutes before, and I could see the chest of drawers moving as that room seemed to spin around and around. Everything was just spinning. I just shut my eyes and held onto that bedpost. In a few minutes I could tell everything had quit spinning.

I opened my eyes and everything was in place. I said it again, "Thank God, according to the Word I'm healed. I believe that." Then for the first time in many months I felt something. Feeling actually returned to me. It seemed to start in the top of my head, and went down over me, like you might take oil or something warm and pour it over someone's head.

For example, if you poured a lot of oil on someone, it would just run down over the whole body. This feeling, like warm oil being poured on me, went down all over my body. And when it got to my waist, feeling came, as that warm oil went down and out the end of my toes. Every nerve in my limbs was reactivated, and I felt like two million pins were sticking me in my limbs.

Then I just simply felt normal. My paralysis was gone. I said, "I'm going to walk now," and I did. And I've been walking ever since!

That is when I first learned what it means to have faith and to act on my faith. Here's what I'm saying to you. Believing you receive before you have it is not only true for exercising faith for your healing, but faith also comes into operation that way in receiving the baptism of the Holy Ghost, too, or any other petition from God.

It's true that in receiving the baptism of the Holy Spirit, God gives the believer an initial *evidence* that he is filled with the Spirit—tongues. However, the person still must believe he receives the Holy Spirit *by faith* before he has the evidence of speaking with tongues. So the principle of faith is the same: believing you have received before you have (Mark 11:24).

The Faith Principle Works In Any Area of Receiving

Seeing the truth of this principle of faith also helped me in receiving the baptism of the Holy Spirit later on. When I saw what the Word of God says on the subject of the baptism of the Holy Ghost, because I knew this principle of faith, I didn't stop and say, "I wonder if I have enough faith to get the Holy Ghost?" Or "Oh, if only I had enough faith, I could receive the Holy Ghost."

I had now learned the secret of faith, the principle of faith, and so I acted on that. I just simply said, "I'm going to go down to the Full Gospel preacher's house right now and receive the Holy Ghost."

I went down there and knocked on the preacher's door and said to him, "I came down here to get the Holy Ghost."

Immediately he said, "Wait and seek for it in the service tonight."

I said, "It won't take me very long to receive." If you are a believer, it won't take you very long either, if you'll just reach out and receive this gift of the Holy Ghost that has already been provided to every believer (Acts 1:8; 2:38–39).

Changing Hope to Faith to Receive the Holy Spirit

I was holding a meeting in Pomona, California, in 1950, and there was an eighty-three-year-old man who came forward to receive the Holy Spirit. I learned that he had been seeking the Holy Ghost for fifty years.

In fact, he said to me, "Brother Hagin, my wife received the baptism of the Holy Ghost in the revival fifty years ago here in Los Angeles at the old Azusa Street mission."

He went on to say, "Some people have said that everyone who went there got the Holy Ghost, but I went through that whole meeting for three years, three services a day. I was in every one of those services. I sought the Holy Ghost every time, and I didn't receive."

I knew the second time I laid my hands on him, in my spirit by the revelation of the Holy Spirit, just exactly what his trouble was. He was *hoping* to receive the Holy Spirit. He wasn't in faith. But I also saw that I wouldn't be able to get him to accept that. He wouldn't have believed that.

Sometimes you can tell what's wrong with folks, but just because you know what is hindering them, that doesn't always mean they are ready to receive it. They've got to understand and know it also for themselves.

I'd had a revelation about this man's situation, but I knew I wouldn't be able to get him to see it until he saw the truth of it for himself in God's Word.

But he came day and night, and I began to teach the Word. I taught on the difference between hope and faith. Finally, the truth dawned on him. (It's a strange thing to me that he heard me teach for about a week and didn't get it. He had to hear it over and over again. That's the reason I keep teaching certain truths over and over again. Folks don't get it just because you say it once.)

After about ten days, this eighty-three-year-old man came to me at the close of one of the morning meetings (I'd already taught on faith the first week, but I was going over the same teaching again the second week). He said, "Brother Hagin, you know, I just caught it this morning. I see now why I haven't received. I have never believed. I've just been hoping for fifty years that I'd get the Holy Ghost."

I said, "I knew that, Brother. I knew it the second time I laid hands on you and prayed. The Holy Spirit revealed that to me, but I also knew I wouldn't be able to get you to see that. I also knew if you'd keep coming to the services, you'd eventually see it for yourself.

"Now," he said, "you're going to have to give me a little more time."

"That's all right," I said, "take all the time you need."

He said, "You know I've been on this road for fifty years, and it's going to take me a little while to get stopped, turned around, and headed back in the right direction."

I said, "That's all right, Brother, just take all the time you need, but keep on coming to the services."

"Oh," he said, "we'll be here every service, day and night."

I said, "All right, keep coming and when you get that hope changed into faith, I'll know it, and you'll know it. Then you will receive the baptism in the Holy Spirit."

About three days later on a Friday night after we had dismissed, this man came up to the pastor and me, and said, "Brother Hagin, I wonder if I could get you brethren to lay hands on me. I've changed my hope into faith. I'm ready now to receive the baptism in the Holy Ghost. I'm ready!"

I said, "Are you expecting to receive?"

"Yes," he said, "just put your hands on me and I'll receive right away."

That pastor and I just laid our hands on him, and almost immediately his hands were in the air and he was talking in tongues! This man had been *hoping* for fifty years that he'd get the Holy Ghost!

Hope: A Good Waiter, but a Poor Receiver

Friends, hope is a good waiter, but a poor receiver. Too many times when it comes to prayer, folk say, "Well, I'm a-hoping-and-a-praying. I'm praying and hoping." Did you ever hear that? Do *you* say that?

Correct yourself if you do! Next time you say it, correct yourself, and say, "Stop that." Because that's not faith!

You also hear folks say, "Well, all we can do is pray and hope." If that's all you are doing, you're defeated already.

I remember several years ago I was preaching for a pastor in the state of Texas, and was staying in the parsonage with him and his wife. I believe that pastor was the world's worst to say, "I'm hoping and praying." He'd say that to me a half dozen or a dozen times a day. "I'm hoping and praying," or "I'm praying and hoping."

What astounded me was that he sat in every service where I taught on the difference between hope and faith, and it just ran off him like water off a duck's back. It was amazing!

That's the reason I know you have to just keep going over and over these things, because for

example, this man sat right there in the service and didn't get it.

One day I was with him alone, and he said, "Brother Hagin, I want you to pray with me about something, please."

I said, "All right, what is it?"

He said, "There's a Christian businessman here who wants to give me the equity in a cabin on a lake, along with a few acres of land. He only owes $900 on it and he said I could pay that monthly, or he'd pay it off and I could pay him back without interest. However, his wife had objected a little, and he asked me to give him thirty days to work that out."

This pastor wanted me to pray with him that everything would work out with this businessman.

The pastor said, "I'm just hoping and praying that it'll work out."

I had already preached meetings for this particular minister, and he still hadn't gotten the difference between hope and faith.

When he said, "I'm just hoping and praying," I spoke up and said, "Well, Brother, if that's all you're doing, you're wasting your time."

I didn't say this to be smart about it, and for a minute there I didn't know what he was going to do. We were traveling in his car when I said that. He batted his eyes, and I thought for a minute he was going to drive us off the road!

Then he said, "You know, that's right!"

He added, "Yes, that's right."

Then he said, "I had started to say, 'I'm wasting my time and God's too.' But actually I'm not wasting God's time because He didn't even hear me to begin with. I'm just wasting my own time!"

To make a long story short, this pastor changed his hope to faith. And in the end, he received the acreage and the cabin because he quit hoping and started believing!

You see, it's faith that gets the job done! And faith is *now*. The Bible says, *"NOW faith is the substance of things hoped for"* (Heb. 11:1). Hope is a good waiter, but a poor receiver. Hope won't get the job done, but faith will! By faith you can receive whatever God has promised to you in His Word, whether it be salvation, healing, the baptism in the Holy Spirit, or whatever it is you need from God.

Questions for Study

1. Hoping does not get the job done. What does?

   _____

   _____

2. Why isn't it God's fault if our prayer doesn't work?

   _____

   _____

3. What is the blessed hope of the Church?

   _____

   _____

4. What two things must you start doing for your faith to work for you?

   _____

   _____

5. A person can't believe beyond _____.

   _____

   _____

6. When are you supposed to believe you receive your petition?

   _____

   _____

7. Complete the phrase, "hope is a good _____, but a poor _____."

8. What will happen if you are just hoping and praying?

   _____

   _____

9. When is faith?

   _____

   _____

10. How can you receive whatever God has promised to you in His Word?

   _____

   _____

Chapter 4

What Faith Is—Part 2

Now faith is the substance of things hoped for, the evidence of things not seen.

—Hebrews 11:1

Faith gives substance to things hoped for. You see, hope doesn't have any substance. But faith gives substance to those things you are hoping for. In other words, what God is saying here in Hebrews 11:1 is that faith is taking hold of the unseen realm of hope, and bringing it into the realm of reality.

Faith, we know, grows out of the Word of God, for Romans 10:17 says, *"So then faith cometh by hearing, and hearing by the word of God."*

Another translation of Hebrews 11:1 says, "Faith is the warranty deed, that the thing for which you have fondly hoped is at last yours." Our text says faith is the *evidence* of things not seen.

By way of illustration, you might *hope* for finances to meet a particular obligation, but *faith* gives you the assurance that you'll have the money when you need it. Also, you might hope for physical strength to do a job or a task set before you, but *faith* says, *"the Lord is the strength of my life; of whom shall I be afraid?"* (Ps. 27:1). In other words, faith says the same thing the Word of God says.

Unbelief is really taking sides against God's Word. The sad thing about it is, there are so many believers who are talking doubt and unbelief, and who are taking sides against the Word of God. Then these same believers wonder why God's Word doesn't work for them.

God's Word won't work for you if you take sides against it. If you want God's Word to work for you, you must side in with it.

But what is faith—real Bible faith? One of the best ways to find out what something *is*, is to find out what it *isn't*. Then when you find out what it *isn't*, you can see more clearly what it *is*. Let's follow that approach in these lessons on the subject of faith.

Faith Is Not Hope

First, faith is not hope. We discussed that in our last lesson. *Faith is not hope!* Yet when I pray for folks and ask them, "Will you be healed?" or "Will you be filled with the Holy Ghost as I lay hands on you and pray?" many times they say, "I sure hope so, Brother Hagin."

I always answer, "As long as you are only hoping, you won't receive from God because you receive from Him by *faith*, not by *hope*."

Others will say, "God, I *want* to be healed." In order to show them that *wanting* something from God isn't enough, I often say, "You might *want* a new Cadillac, but that doesn't mean you're going to get one."

You see, just wanting something from God won't get the job done. If just wanting something from God was all it took to receive from God, we'd all have it made. We would receive instantly. But faith that receives from God isn't *hoping or wanting*. The only kind of faith that gets the job done is the Bible-kind of faith which believes God and acts on what it believes.

You'll not receive from God because you hope. Nowhere in the Bible does God say that when we pray, we shall receive what we hope for. But God's Word does say in Mark 11:24, *"What things soever ye desire, when ye pray, BELIEVE that ye receive them, and ye shall have them."*

Jesus also said, *"all things, whatsoever ye shall ask in prayer, BELIEVING, ye shall receive"* (Matt. 21:22). Jesus didn't say whatever you ask for in prayer, hoping, you shall receive. He said, *"whatsoever ye shall ask in prayer, BELIEVING, ye shall receive"* (Matt. 21:22).

If you want to know whether you are really believing God or if you are just hoping, I can tell you how to tell the difference. Hope is always future tense, because hope always looks to the future.

For instance, the Church of the Lord Jesus Christ does have a blessed hope of Jesus' return. But that is future. The coming of Christ, the resurrection of the saved dead, the rapture of the saints, is all future tense. But if you are seeking healing, it's not in the future that you want to be healed. You want to be healed right now, especially if you're hurting very badly.

If you're seeking the Holy Spirit, it's not in the future that you want to be filled with the Spirit; it's now. As long as you put off believing you receive the blessing, the blessing will be in the future and it will stay in the future. But now is when you want whatever God has promised you in His Word.

Faith for Salvation, Not Hope

For example, if it is salvation a person wants, it's not in the future that he wants to be saved. That may be too late. Yes, I've talked to men in days gone by about the salvation of their souls, and I've had many say to me that they hoped to be saved. I say with tears that some of those men are now in hell. They left this world unsaved because salvation that's based only on hope never comes to fruition.

If you were talking to someone about salvation and the condition of his soul, and he said he hoped to be saved, you would tell him what the Bible says, wouldn't you? You would tell him that salvation isn't based on hope, but it is based on faith.

This is what the Bible tells us about salvation.

EPHESIANS 2:8

8 By grace are ye SAVED through FAITH.

JOHN 6:37

37 . . . him that cometh to me I will in no wise cast out.

ROMANS 10:13

13 For whosoever shall call upon the name of the Lord shall be SAVED.

ROMANS 10:9–10

9 That if thou shalt CONFESS with thy mouth the Lord Jesus, and shalt BELIEVE in thine heart that God hath raised him from the dead, thou shalt be saved.

10 For with the HEART man believeth unto righteousness; and with the MOUTH confession is made unto salvation.

You would tell a person seeking salvation what the Word says and endeavor to get him to act on the Word right then. Yet when it comes to receiving the infilling or the baptism of the Holy Ghost, or healing for our body, or an answer to prayer, it seems that we just sort of stumble over the same stumbling stone; people aren't always taught faith to receive— they are taught hope and that won't get the job done.

In other words, we *hope* God hears our prayer. We *hope* to be healed. We *hope* to receive the Holy Ghost. Someone said, "I just believe I'll get my petition sometime." That's *hope*. That person may be calling it *believing*, but it's still hope, because it's future.

Notice our text: *"NOW faith is . . ."* (Heb. 11:1). Or we could read it, *"Now faith IS. . . ."* That is present tense. Remember, if it is not *now*, it is not faith.

Faith is present tense. Hope is future tense. Even though you say you believe, if you're putting the answer off into the future, then you are not believing, you are hoping.

That's the reason the Word isn't working for you. So get your believing in the right tense; get it in the present tense. Some people are always believing that God is going to do something for them, sometime in the future. But faith believes that He has done something, and is doing something right now.

Even when it comes to healing, many people say, "Brother Hagin, I don't understand why I haven't received my healing. I know God promised to heal me."

But actually, God has not promised to heal you at all. Some people say, "Doesn't the Word of God say, *'Himself TOOK our infirmities, and BARE our sicknesses'* [Matt. 8:17]. Isn't that a promise?"

No, that isn't a promise. That is a statement of fact that simply tells us something that has already happened. Many times we call those scriptures and others like them promises, but actually, they are statements of fact. They are telling us of our provisions in Christ—what Jesus has already provided for us. That is a *fact*.

1 PETER 2:24

24 Who his own self bare our sins in his own body on the tree, that we, being dead to sins, should live unto righteousness: by whose stripes ye WERE healed.

Someone asked, "Doesn't that scripture promise me healing?" No, that scripture doesn't promise you healing. It tells you that healing belongs to you in Christ. I've found this out, that as soon as I can get people to quit *hoping* to be healed and to quit seeking healing and start believing they receive their healing, immediately they are healed.

Faith Is Present Tense

I was preaching many years ago in the state of Oklahoma, and in one of my services a woman was brought to the service who hadn't taken one single step in four years. She was an older woman, in her seventies, and the doctors said that she would never walk another step again. Her knees had just simply worn out and wouldn't function properly, and they couldn't carry her weight. Sitting with no exercise, she had grown quite large.

When it came time for the healing line, they brought this woman forward and sat her down on the altar. I came and knelt in front of her and laid my hands on her knees and prayed.

Then I said to her, "Now, Sister, arise and walk in the Name of the Lord Jesus Christ." That dear woman did her best to get up; but all the time (and I'm not making fun of her) she was crying and praying, "Oh, dear Jesus, please heal me. Lord, I know You promised to heal me. You know what a burden I've been to my family, and I can't do one thing for myself. Dear Lord, please heal my knees; please heal my limbs; please let me walk. Oh, please, please."

I said, "Wait a minute, Sister. Wait a minute," but instead of listening, she just got louder.

I said the second time, "Wait a minute, Sister. I have a word for you. I can help you." But instead of listening, she just got louder and louder.

The third time I said, "Wait a minute, Sister. Wait a minute. I can help you." But instead of listening, she was becoming almost hysterical.

Then I just took hold of her shoulders and shook her, and said, "I command you to shut up in the Name of the Lord Jesus Christ." She stopped and looked up at me, rather startled, and the congregation put the brakes on me.

Did you know a congregation can put the brakes on you? I don't care who you are, when the people put the brakes on, you can't do anything. For instance, people put the brakes on Jesus in His hometown of Nazareth, and He couldn't do much there in the way of miracles or healings. The Bible says so.

MARK 6:5

5 And he [Jesus] **could there do no mighty work, save that he laid his hands upon a few sick folk, and healed them.**

Notice it didn't say He wouldn't do any mighty works, it said He *couldn't* do any mighty works.

The Greek reads that Jesus laid His hands on a few folks with minor ailments. In other words, the only ones God healed in Nazareth under the ministry of Jesus were a few people who had minor ailments. Why? Mark 6:6 gives us the answer: *"And he* [Jesus] *marvelled because of their unbelief."*

Well, this congregation put the brakes on me, and before I could do anything, I knew I had to get the brakes off. If I couldn't get the brakes off, then I wouldn't be able to do anything. If people could only recognize that, what a difference there would be in our services and in our churches.

So I knew I had to work on the congregation before I could go back to the woman in the wheelchair and help her. Some folks thought I was being rude to this woman, or getting smart with her, and some of them spoke right out and said so.

I said to them, "Now I want to ask you a question. If someone asked you directions to a certain place, but instead of following your directions, you saw that they mistakenly went the wrong way, wouldn't you try to stop them or flag them down and try to get them straightened out? If you knew they didn't know where they were going, wouldn't you try to get them going in the right direction?" They all agreed that they would.

I said, "All right, this woman was on the wrong road. She wasn't on the road to healing. She was on the wrong road, and all I did was just flag her down. Now I have her attention."

When I explained that, most of the people in the congregation took the brakes off, and I felt a release in the spirit so I could go back and minister to the woman.

I said, "Now, Sister, did you know you are healed?"

She looked up at me, her eyes got big, and she said, "Oh, am I?"

"Yes," I said, "you are healed, and I can prove it to you by the Bible." So I got my Bible, opened it to First Peter 2:24, handed it to her, and said, "Would you read this verse aloud please?"

She read, *"Who his own self bare our sins in his own body on the tree, that we, being dead to sins, should live unto righteousness: by whose stripes ye were healed."*

I said, "Read that last clause again."

And she read, *"by whose stripes ye were healed."*

I said, "I want to ask you a question. Is 'were' past tense, present tense, or future tense?"

She said, "It's past tense."

Then I said, "If you *were* healed by Jesus' stripes then you are healed, aren't you?"

"Yes," she said, "I am."

I said, "Will you do what I tell you to do?"

"Well," she answered, "I will if it's easy."

"This is the easiest thing you ever did in your life. Just lift your hands and look right up to heaven, and begin to praise God because you *are* healed, *present tense*. Praise Him because you *are* healed, not *going to be* healed; you are healed."

She just looked up, and as a little child, she said, "Dear Lord Jesus, I'm so glad I'm healed."

She hadn't walked a step yet. She had no evidence of healing whatever, but she said, "I'm so glad I'm healed. I'm so thankful, dear Lord Jesus. You know how tired I got sitting around all those four years. Thank God, my knees are well and my limbs are healed. I'm so thankful."

Then I said to the congregation, "Let's thank God with her because she is healed—not *going to be* healed—but because she is healed." You see, faith is present tense, not future tense. You've got to get your believing in the present tense for things to work for you. Most of the crowd raised their hands and praised God with her because she was healed.

Some probably said, "She's not healed. She hasn't walked a step yet." But don't you remember what our text said, *"faith is the . . . EVIDENCE of things not seen"* (Heb. 11:1). If you're going to wait till you see something before you believe it, then that's not faith at all. That's leaning to the evidence of your senses.

After I told the congregation to praise God with this woman, I turned to the woman and said, "Now, Sister, arise and walk in Jesus' Name." Immediately that woman jumped off that altar like a sixteen-year-old and walked and leaped and ran and praised God!

We had to get that woman's believing in the right tense. The Word won't work for you unless you get it in the right tense. As long as you're struggling to receive healing, for example, and you believe you're going to get it sometime in the future, you are not in faith. If it's future tense, that's hope. Faith says, "It's mine. I have it now."

Faith Is of the Heart, Not the Head

Then we need to realize that faith is of the heart and not of the head. I used to have a sermon I preached when I was a young denominational preacher called, "Head Faith vs. Heart Faith."

I was reading John Wesley's books and found that he had a better expression for head faith than I had. He called it "mental assent." So I adopted his expression. Wesley said, "People mentally agree that the Bible or the Word is true, but they don't believe it from their heart."

So when it comes to receiving the Holy Ghost, healing, or any answer to prayer, Christians might ask, "What's the difference between heart faith and mental assent? How can I tell whether I'm really believing from my heart or just mentally agreeing that the Word of God is so?"

If you are only mentally agreeing, you will say you believe that the Bible is true, but you don't believe it is true for you. You conclude by saying, "I believe the Bible is true, but I don't have my petition, and I don't understand why." But faith says, "It's mine. I have it now." Faith believes the Word and acts on the Word of God.

People come in the healing line in my meetings for healing or the baptism in the Holy Ghost, and say, "Brother Hagin, I know all these scriptures you have given are true. But can you tell me why I can't get healed?" or "Can you tell me why I can't get the Holy Ghost?"

I always say, "Yes, I surely can." They look at me and their eyes get big.

I respond, "It's because you just said you can't. The Bible says, *'out of the abundance of the heart the mouth speaketh'* (Matt. 12:34), and you just got through telling me why you can't get your answer to prayer—because you said you can't. You said that because you *believe* you can't get your answer, and as long as you *say* you can't and *believe* you can't, you can't. But just as soon as you start believing you can receive from God and you believe you receive whatever it is you need, you will get your answer."

Turn Your Faith Loose by Saying What You Believe

Then I also say to some concerning healing, "Why don't you just act on the Word? When are you going to start acting like God's Word is true? Faith is an action; it is acting like God's Word is true."

There is always some way you can act on God's Word even if it is only thanking and praising Him that He has heard you. And if you believe God's Word is true, you should act like it is true. Did you know it doesn't matter how much faith you have, if you don't put your faith into action, there won't be any results?

ACTS 14:7–9

7 And there they [Paul and Barnabas] **preached the gospel.**

8 And there sat a certain man at Lystra, impotent in his feet, being a cripple from his mother's womb, who never had walked:

9 The same heard Paul speak: who stedfastly beholding him, and perceiving that HE HAD FAITH TO BE HEALED.

Now I want you to get the picture. That man at Lystra is sitting there. He hasn't walked a step, yet he has faith to be healed—the Bible says so.

Every believer has faith to be healed, but you have to act on your faith or turn your faith loose for it to work for you. The Bible tells you how to put your faith in action in Mark 11:23.

MARK 11:23

23 For verily I say unto you, That whosoever shall say unto this mountain, Be thou removed, and be thou cast into the sea; and shall not doubt in his heart, but shall believe that those things which he saith shall come to pass; he shall have whatsoever he saith.

You turn your faith loose by saying what you believe. Faith can't be released out of your heart toward God without your saying what you believe. Faith simply won't work without an expression or action.

Nowhere in the Bible do you ever find that faith is released apart from an action. Faith that is only in your heart will never bring a healing to your body or the infilling of the Holy Spirit or an answer to prayer. No, faith in your heart will not do it. But faith in your heart released through your lips will!

Jesus said, *"Whosoever shall SAY unto this mountain, Be thou removed, and be thou cast into the sea; and shall not doubt in his heart, but shall believe that those things which he saith shall come to pass; he shall have whatsoever he saith"* (Mark 11:23).

Notice this impotent man in Acts 14:8. He's crippled, and he has faith. Paul perceived that the man had faith. It wasn't Paul's faith that Paul perceived. No, the man himself had faith to be healed. He got faith from what he heard Paul preach. Paul knew that faith without action or works is dead.

Paul also knew he was going to have to get the man to act on the faith that he had. Acts 14:10 says, "[Paul] *Said with a loud voice, Stand upright on thy feet. And he leaped and walked."* When Paul said, "Stand upright on your feet," and the man mixed action with his faith, he leaped and walked.

If you want to help someone get healed, if you want to help someone receive the Holy Ghost, or if you want to help someone get an answer to prayer, let me tell you what to do. There are two things that you have to work on: the believing part and the *action* part.

If you act without faith, nothing will happen—it won't work. And if you believe without action, nothing will happen—it won't work. However, when faith and action are combined, then the Word works.

Sometimes folks say to me, "Oh, Brother Hagin, you just make it too easy for people to get healed." Or they say, "You just make it too easy for people to get the Holy Ghost."

I always say, "No, it wasn't me that put healing or receiving the Holy Spirit on a gift basis, it was God. It wasn't me who made it easy, it was the Father who made it easy. I didn't put it on a gift and faith basis, God did."

You know, for God to be able to help us, we have to keep our hearts and minds open to His Word. Faith is just as easy as the Word of God says it is, because God's Word does not fail.

Questions for Study

1. If you want God's Word to work for you, what must you do?

   _____

   _____

2. What is the only kind of faith that gets the job done?

   _____

   _____

3. Even though you say you believe, if you're putting the answer off into the future, then what are you doing?

   _____

   _____

4. Why were a few people who had minor ailments the only ones God healed in Nazareth under the ministry of Jesus?

   _____

   _____

5. Faith is an _____; it is acting like _____ _____ _____ _____.

6. How do you turn your faith loose?

   _____

   _____

7. What happened in Acts 14 when the lame man mixed action with his faith?

   _____

8. What two things do you have to work on if you want to help someone get an answer to prayer?

   _____

   _____

9. What will happen when you act without faith or believe without action?

   _____

   _____

10. What do we have to do for God to be able to help us?

    _____

    _____

Chapter 5

What Faith Is—Part 3

Now faith is the substance of things hoped for, the evidence of things not seen.

— Hebrews 11:1

A modern translation reads, "Faith is giving substance to things hoped for." We need to realize that it is our faith that gives substance to the things we hope for. If we're going to wait until we get something before we'll believe we have it, we're too late and it won't work. It's your faith that gives substance to the things you desire or hope for.

We see this truth throughout the Bible, in the Old Testament as well as in the New Testament. In the Old Testament, we have a number of scriptural illustrations that very clearly give us the same thought as found in Hebrews 11:1.

For example, when Israel came into Canaan land and came up against the city of Jericho, God told the Israelites exactly what to do. But in order to enjoy the victory God had promised, they first had to believe they received God's Word to them and act upon it. Their acting upon the Word was their faith in action. They were to march around the walls of Jericho one time a day for six days, and on the seventh day, they were to march around the city seven times. Then when the musical instruments sounded, they were to shout (Joshua 6:3–5).

I want you to notice that the children of Israel shouted or acted on their faith while the walls were still standing. Anyone can shout when the walls are down; it doesn't take any faith to do that. But their faith gave substance to God's Word to them. And when they acted on their faith, God's promise became a reality and those walls came down (Joshua 6:20).

Faith Is Active

We need to realize, friends, that's what faith is. *Faith is acting upon God's Word.*

So many people, however, are waiting for answers to prayer to just come to them. For example, when it comes to receiving healing or the infilling of the Holy Ghost, too often people just wait for something to happen with a passive faith instead of an active faith. But if you need finances, for example, and you're just waiting for something to turn up, nothing will turn up but more bills to pay!

I met someone in Colorado several years ago. He wasn't working and he had a wife and five children, but he was just "trusting" God for something to turn up. Of course nothing ever did turn up because he wasn't in faith. He had been at that church a year, and the church had been taking care of them.

You see, this man was waiting for something to turn up, but nothing ever did turn up because he needed to get busy and put action to his faith.

God will help you meet your financial obligations, but from the natural standpoint, you have a part to play, and you can't just stay at home and expect something to come to you. You can pray and believe God, but then you must act on your faith by actively looking for a job, and something will happen.

The same is true from the spiritual standpoint. Too many folks are waiting for something to come to them. But it won't come to them as long as they are just passively waiting for God to do something for them. No, they must get busy and act on God's Word.

New Testament Example of Active Faith

I want to give you an illustration from the New Testament which demonstrates what faith is. Let's look at a passage of scriptures in Luke 5.

First, we have the story in Luke chapter 5 of the man who was brought by four friends to Jesus (Luke 5:18–25). Jesus was in a house teaching and they could not get in because of the crowd. The man was bedfast—he had palsy—so they took the man up on the roof and let him down into the room where Jesus was. The scripture says, *"And when he [Jesus] SAW their faith, he said unto him, Man, thy sins are forgiven thee. . . . Arise, and take up thy couch, and go into thine house"* (Luke 5:20, 24).

Some ask, "Just whose faith was it that got the man healed?" The Bible says, "When Jesus saw *their* faith." That's plural. That includes all of them. It was not only the faith of the four men who brought the man with palsy in, but it also included the faith of the sick man on the bed too.

The man who was bedfast demonstrated that he had faith because how many bedfast people would let someone take them up on top of a house and let them down through the roof!

We also know that the man who was bedfast had faith because when Jesus said to him, "Rise up," he wasn't any better. He was lying there just as help-less as he ever was. Instead of trying to get up, he could have said, "Why, Lord, didn't you see them carry me in here? I can't possibly get up. You'll have to heal me first."

But, no, when Jesus said, "Rise, take up thy bed and walk," the man with the palsy began to move, and when he did, healing was the result. If he had refused to act on the Word of the Master, he would not have received healing; but because he acted on what Jesus said, he did receive his healing.

Acting on God's Word Brings Results

There is a real spiritual lesson for us here. When we act on God's Word, that's faith. And when we're in faith, we will receive answers to prayer. If we fail to act on God's Word, just waiting for something to come to us first before we'll believe, we will not receive what we need from God.

I remember several years ago, a friend of mine told me of a service in which a woman evangelist ministered in the early days of Pentecost. This woman evangelist was ministering to four people in wheelchairs. All she said to them in a very quiet tone was, "Rise and walk in Jesus' Name," and they all got up and walked except one.

The one who was left sitting there in a wheel-chair, said, "I can't walk."

The woman evangelist said, "The others couldn't walk either, but they did."

The woman in the wheelchair answered, "I know they did; but I can't. I haven't walked in years. I can't walk." The evangelist had to walk away and leave her sitting there.

You see, when these others started to act on the Word that was spoken to them, the result was forth-coming. When you act on what God's Word says or on what the Holy Spirit may speak to your heart, then results are forthcoming, because that's faith.

You Can't Receive From God Without Faith

There was a woman in one of the churches where I pastored who was in a wheelchair. She had arthri-tis and the doctor had told her some years before that her body would become stationary and she wouldn't be able to move. He said she would have to become bedfast or stay in a wheelchair and her body would be locked in that position. In other words, her body would be locked either in a prone position or in a seated position.

She and her husband never missed a service, whether it was a weekday meeting, a Sunday serv-ice, or a revival meeting. They were always there. I could pray for that woman for any other ailment and she would always get healed, but she never asked me to pray for her arthritis.

This bothered me, as there were several people in the church who had been healed of very serious condi-tions. Some of the people would say about this woman, "Maybe it's not God's will to heal her." But I knew it was God's will because it's His will to heal everyone.

That doesn't mean that Christians aren't going to Heaven because they don't get healed. It just means that they are robbed of a blessing while on this earth.

One afternoon, a small group of church people gathered together and we went to this woman's house to pray with her. As we prayed, I saw exactly what God would have me do.

I said to everyone, "Move away from her," and I went to the opposite side of the room from her (we were in a large room). I said, "Watch, and don't any-one touch her. Stay away from her."

Then I pointed my finger at her and said, "Now, Sister, arise and walk in the Name of Jesus Christ."

I'm a witness to the fact as well as everyone else who was present there that day that an unseen power lifted her out of that chair and she just sat up in mid-air away from the chair. She could move her arms, and she reached down for that wheelchair. When she did that, she just fell back into it.

The moment she did that, by the unction of the Holy Spirit I said without thinking, "Sister, you don't have a bit of faith, do you? You don't believe you'll ever be healed of this arthritis, do you?"

She spoke up immediately and said, "No, Brother Hagin, I don't. I'll die and go to my grave with it." And she did.

You see, you can't receive from God beyond actual faith. Do you know what would have happened if she had cooperated with God and with His power that was upon her? If she had cooperated, she would have begun to walk; she would have been healed right then.

The Holy Spirit Prompts, But You Must Respond

Too many people think that God's healing power is just going to move on them and make them do something whether they want to do it or not, or whether they cooperate with His power or not. No, that would not be the Holy Spirit; that would be an evil spirit. Evil spirits use force, and they try to drive a person. But the Holy Spirit urges, prompts, or gives you a gentle push, and then it's up to you to respond; it's up to you whether or not you obey.

I was conducting a meeting in a town in Texas, and a woman there had written to a friend to come down to the meetings to receive the Holy Ghost. She came, and after being in two of our services, she came forward to receive the Holy Ghost. I laid my hands on her and prayed and the Holy Ghost came upon her, but she wouldn't respond.

I knew exactly what was wrong with her, but sometimes you can't tell people what's wrong because you know they aren't ready to receive from you. I laid hands on her again and the same thing happened. Still, she didn't respond. I knew it would take some time to get her to see where her trouble was and it was getting late, so I just turned the service back to the pastor.

After the meeting when I walked out of the church and across the parking lot to go to the parsonage, I noticed this woman sitting in her car. She looked so disappointed. I asked the Lord to let me help her. The Holy Spirit instantly showed me how to help her. I went to her car and opened my Bible to Acts 2:4 and handed it to her and asked her to read the verse of scripture aloud.

She read, *"And they were all filled with the Holy Ghost, and began to speak with other tongues, as the Spirit gave them utterance."*

I said to her, "Sister, who does that scripture say did the speaking in tongues?"

She said, "Well, it says the Holy Ghost did."

So I had her read it again and finally on the fourth time, she was beginning to catch on. So she read slowly, *"And they were all filled with the Holy Ghost, and began to speak"* (Acts 2:4).

Astonished, she said, "Why, *they* did the speaking." She took my Bible out of the case and looked at it. She said she thought maybe I had a different Bible than she did, but it was the same Bible.

"You know," she said, "I always thought that the Holy Ghost did the speaking." The Lord had already shown me that was what hindered her from receiving.

Then I said to her, "Now let's read several other scriptures so you can see it's not just one isolated passage that reads that way." I had her read Acts 10:44–46.

ACTS 10:44–46

44 While Peter yet spake these words, the Holy Ghost fell on all them which heard the Word.

45 And they of the circumcision which believed were astonished, as many as came with Peter, because that on the Gentiles also was poured out the gift of the Holy Ghost.

46 For they heard THEM speak with tongues, and magnify God.

"Oh," she said, "I see it."

I said, "That's two witnesses. Let's get three. Turn to Acts 19:6: '*And when Paul had laid his hands upon them, the Holy Ghost came on them; and THEY spake with tongues, and prophesied.*'"

She said, "You know, Brother Hagin, if they'd called me in to be a witness in court and the lawyer asked me who did the speaking in tongues, I would have said the Holy Ghost does. And I would have thought I was telling the truth."

I asked, "Now I want to ask you a question. When I laid my hands on you a while ago, did the Holy Ghost come upon you? Did the power of God come upon you?"

She replied, "Absolutely."

I said, "I want to ask you another question. Did your tongue want to say something that wasn't English?"

"Why," she said, "it was all I could do to keep from it."

I said, "You're not supposed to keep from it; you're supposed to cooperate with the Holy Ghost. When the Holy Ghost gives you utterance, *you* must have faith to act and speak out that utterance. You're not supposed to keep from yielding to the Holy Ghost. You are supposed to yield to Him!"

Some people think they're supposed to fight against that urge to speak in other tongues just as long as they can, and finally, they will be overpowered by the Holy Spirit.

This woman hadn't understood that faith is cooperating with God. When she saw that she had to yield to and cooperate with the promptings of the Holy Spirit, she immediately began to speak in tongues.

Sometime ago I talked to a fellow who had been tarrying to receive the Holy Spirit for some fifteen years. As I visited with him, he said, "You can't tell me one thing about *tarrying*! I know all about seeking God." He knew all about tarrying, but there is a difference between tarrying and receiving!

Act on God's Word!

Another evangelist friend of mine said in one of his meetings that he was in a church early one evening praying, when a man came and shook hands with him and said, "You know what?"

Of course, the evangelist responded, "No, what?"

The man said, grinning as though he were proud of the fact, "I've been seeking the Holy Ghost for nineteen years."

The evangelist said, "You haven't done any such thing. Jesus said, 'They that seek shall find' (Matt. 7:7). If you'd been seeking, you would have found by now. All you've been doing is just hanging around the altar."

It seems that all in the world many people are doing is just hanging around the altar. It's time to quit hanging around the altar and start acting on the Word of God. Faith is acting on God's Word. Faith is an act; it's taking God at His Word.

Faith Is Cooperating With God

I was in one church where a man had been burned over the lower part of his body and it had left him unable to walk. He just scooted his feet along on the floor. We were having a healing service, and through a gift of the Holy Spirit, the Lord told me to have everyone who had something wrong with their bodies from their hips down to come up first in the healing line.

About twelve people came forward. This man who had been burned was the first one in line. I waited until they were all down front before I told them what else God had told me to tell them to do.

I came up to this man and asked, "Can you run?" It took him so much by surprise that he said, "Oh, my God, no! I can't even walk, much less run."

Then I said, "Well, the Lord told me to tell you to start running."

This man didn't even give it a second thought; he just turned around and started scooting up the aisle just as fast as he could. The third time he came around the aisles, the Spirit of the Lord came on me and I jumped off the platform, grabbed him by the hand, and ran around that building with him.

When we got back to the front, he was walking—not scooting—but walking normally! He was perfectly healed!

If I had not been able to get him to act and cooperate with the Holy Ghost, I couldn't have helped him.

Faith, you see, is acting on God's Word, doing whatever He says to do in the Word or whatever He may say to us to do by the Holy Spirit.

To show you how much of a miracle this was, let me relate what happened as a result of that man's healing. The next night in the service there were two elderly gentlemen who responded to the invitation to be saved. Both were white-haired gentlemen and they looked so much alike I thought they were twins. I found out later that they were brothers; one was seventy-four and the other was seventy-two.

One of the men in the church told me that I would be interested in hearing their testimonies of why they came to church that night. These men were next-door neighbors to the burned man who had gotten healed the night before.

These brothers had seen the man out working in the yard. They thought he must have crawled out to his yard, but in a few minutes they saw him stand up, straight and well, and walk to his house. They hurried over to see what had happened. He told them of his healing and what the Lord had done for him. They both came to the service and got saved, and one of the gentlemen was filled with the Holy Ghost. The miraculous power of God convinced those fellows of the reality of Jesus the Savior and Healer!

Besides the man who had been burned and had been healed, there were eleven other people in that line. One by one, as they ran, they were healed. When we came to the last woman, I said, "Sister, are you ready to run?"

"Oh, Brother Hagin," she said, "I can't. I can't."

"The rest of these folks couldn't run either, but they did," I said.

"Yes, but I know I can't," she said.

I said, "All I know to do is just to tell you what the Lord told me."

So after she turned around and scooted up the aisle a few steps, I said, "Turn around here, Sister." She turned around.

I continued, "You didn't want to do that, did you? You resented those instructions from the Lord and everything inside of you rose up against what He said, didn't it?"

She replied, "It sure did."

"You go sit down then," I said. "I can't help you."

God can't help folks who won't cooperate with Him. But I want you to get this fact, friends. Faith is giving substance to things hoped for. Faith will eventually bring into reality what you have hoped for.

If You Believe, You Will Act

Years ago, in a vision concerning my ministry, Jesus gave me the best definition of faith. He told me about a particular situation that if I had believed His Word, I would have acted on what He had told me to do. Immediately I realized I had doubted what He had told me by not acting on it. So the best definition of faith is this: IF YOU BELIEVE, YOU WILL ACT.

That also relates to God's Word. If we believe God's Word, we will act as though it's true. Faith is giving substance to the things hoped for. Because I did not act on what Jesus had said to me by the Holy Spirit in that first phase of my ministry, I did not have any substance in my ministry. But in the second phase of my ministry, I acted on what Jesus said, and my faith gave it substance.

Act on Your Faith for Healing

People want healing for their bodies, and I can tell them just exactly how to get it. We find the answer to how folks can get healed in Acts 14.

ACTS 14:8–10

8 And there sat a certain man at Lystra, impotent in his feet, being a cripple from his mother's womb, who never had walked:

9 The same heard Paul speak: who stedfastly beholding him, and perceiving that he had faith to be healed,

10 Said with a loud voice, Stand upright on thy feet. And he leaped and walked.

Paul perceived that this impotent man had faith to be healed; yet the man was still sitting there crippled until he acted on his faith. The real truth is, every believer has faith to be healed.

Someone said, "If sick folks have faith, they're going to be healed."

Oh, no, that's wrong, because you can't find anywhere in the Bible where it says, "If you just have faith, you'll be healed." But the moment you begin to act on the faith that you do have, your faith will work and you will be healed. Yes, the devil will contest you every inch of the way. But if you keep on acting in faith, you will be healed.

Act on Your Faith for Receiving the Holy Spirit

The same principle is true of receiving the Holy Ghost. For example, after the Day of Pentecost, folks were always asked, "Have you received the Holy Ghost?" (Acts 19:2). They didn't ask, "Has God *given you* the Holy Ghost?"

God is not going to give you the Holy Ghost. As far as God is concerned, He has already given you the Holy Ghost. It is up to you to receive Him. *Receiving* is something you do.

If you can't get people to receive and act upon God's Word, there isn't any way you, or even God, can help them.

Some say, "I wish it was as simple and as easy as you make it sound." Well, it is! If it isn't, then I'm a liar, and so is Jesus, and so is the Bible because Jesus said that the Holy Ghost is a Gift (Luke 11:13; James 1:17). The Bible says, *"and having received of the Father the promise* [gift] *of the Holy Ghost . . ."* (Acts 2:33).

Just how hard is it to receive a gift?

Suppose someone asked me for my Bible, and I said, "Here it is." As I handed my Bible to him if he fell off the seat and began to beat the floor and cry and say, "Oh please, Brother Hagin, please, please give the Bible to me." People would think he was crazy. They would wonder why in the world he didn't just reach out and take it.

My brother and sister, spiritual things are just as real as material things. God offers you a Gift—the Holy Spirit. You don't have to fall down and start beating the floor and praying, "Oh, dear God, please, You know I want the Holy Spirit."

No, that's a combination of works and unbelief. God said, "Here is the gift of the Holy Ghost. If you are born again, you can receive that gift now. You don't have to wait. You're ready now to receive the Holy Ghost."

Faith comes by hearing and hearing by the Word of God (Rom. 10:17). You've heard the Word. Faith is *acting* on the Word that you've heard. It is *you* who must act on the Word, so get ready and act *now*.

36

Questions for Study

1. Give one Old Testament illustration that clearly gives the same thought concerning faith as found in Hebrews 11:1?

   _____

   _____

2. In the battle of Jericho, when did the children of Israel shout or act on their faith?

   _____

   _____

3. When you have financial obligations and are praying and believing God, what is one thing you can do to <u>act</u> on your faith?

   _____

   _____

4. Give one illustration from the New Testament which demonstrates what faith is.

   _____

   _____

5. In Luke 5:18–25, what happened when the man with palsy began to move?

   _____

   _____

6. What is the result when folks won't cooperate with God?

   _____

   _____

7. Because faith gives substance to things hoped for, what will faith eventually do?

   _____

   _____

8. What is the <u>best</u> definition of faith?

   _____

   _____

9. What happens when you begin to <u>act</u> on the faith you have?

   _____

   _____

10. How does faith come?

   _____

   _____

Chapter 6

What Faith Is—Part 4

Now faith is the substance of things hoped for, the evidence of things not seen.

—Hebrews 11:1

Moffatt's translation reads, "Now faith means that we are confident of what we hope for, convinced of what we do not see." Another modern translation of the New Testament reads, "Faith is giving substance to things hoped for."

Oh, if I could just get that over to people! But most people want to have the substance of the thing they hope for, so they can see, feel, or know it from the physical standpoint before they start believing they have received it. But your faith gives substance to the thing that you hope for when you believe you have received your petition before you have it.

In other words, what the Bible is saying is simply this: Faith is taking hold of the unseen realm of hope and bringing it into the realm of reality. We know, of course, that faith grows out of hearing the Word of God (Rom. 10:17). And through these lessons, we have already learned that faith is not hope and hope is not faith. Faith says, "I *have* it now." Hope says, "I *will* get it sometime." Faith is present tense; hope is future tense.

Agreeing Mentally With God's Word, Is Not Believing With the Heart

John Wesley, the founder of the Methodist church, said that many people who are in the church are not really saved. They have just mentally subscribed to certain truths. They have agreed that certain things are true *in their minds*, but not in their hearts. Wesley was referring to head faith versus heart faith for receiving salvation or the new birth; but the same is true concerning healing, receiving the baptism of the Holy Spirit, or an answer to prayer.

Many times people who are agreeing mentally with God's Word think that all the time they are really believing. I'll show you how you can tell the difference.

Faith says, "It's mine. I have it now."

Mental assent says, "I know I should have it, but for some reason or other I don't get it."

Those folks who are mentally agreeing with what the Word says are not believing; they're mentally assenting. They are agreeing mentally that the Word

is true, but they are not appropriating God's promises for themselves. Many times people call hope, *believing*. But hope is not believing and believing is not hope.

People who only mentally assent to God's Word may say, "I believe that I am going to get my healing." That's still not faith, that is hope. People call that believing, but it isn't believing; it is hope because it is in the future tense. I often hear people say, "I believe I will get the Holy Ghost sometime," or "I believe I'm going to get my healing," or "I believe God is going to heal me sometime." That's not believing; that is hope.

Hope won't work for receiving from God. It is faith that receives from God. God doesn't say He is going to give you the Holy Ghost or heal you *sometime* or at some future date. God doesn't say that one single time in His Word.

For example, God gave the Holy Spirit to the Church on the Day of Pentecost (Acts 2:1–4). All believers need to do is receive Him. And our healing was bought and paid for by the stripes of Jesus and by His redemptive work on the cross (Isa. 53:4–5; Matt. 8:17; 1 Peter 2:24). What we as Christians must do is accept or appropriate by faith what God has already provided for us.

"Well," someone said, "God *promised* in His Word to heal me." No, there is no place in God's Word where He promised to heal anyone. God tells us that healing is bought and paid for and that it already belongs to us. It is up to us to appropriate that healing.

Thomas' Faith vs. Abraham's Faith

Now I want to go a step further and show you the difference between head faith and heart faith. Let's look at John 20:25–29.

JOHN 20:25–29

25 The other disciples therefore said unto him, We have seen the Lord. But he [Thomas] said unto them, Except I shall see in his hands the print of the nails, and put my finger into the print of the nails, and thrust my hand into his side, I will not believe.

26 And after eight days again his disciples were within, and Thomas with them: then came Jesus, the doors being shut, and stood in the midst, and said, Peace be unto you.

27 Then saith he to Thomas, Reach hither thy finger, and behold my hands; and reach hither thy

hand, and thrust it into my side: and be not faithless, but believing.

28 And Thomas answered and said unto him, My Lord and my God.

29 Jesus saith unto him, Thomas, because thou hast seen me, thou hast believed: blessed are they that have not seen, and yet have believed.

ROMANS 4:17-21

17 (As it is written, I have made thee a father of many nations,) before him whom he believed, even God, who quickeneth the dead, and calleth those things which be not as though they were.

18 Who against hope believed in hope, that he might become the father of many nations, according to that which was spoken, So shall thy seed be.

19 And being not weak in faith, he considered not his own body now dead, when he was about an hundred years old, neither yet the deadness of Sarah's womb:

20 He staggered not at the promise of God through unbelief; but was strong in faith, giving glory to God;

21 And being fully persuaded that, what he had promised, he was able also to perform.

Can you see any difference between Abraham's faith and Thomas' faith? Decidedly, yes! Thomas said, "I won't believe unless I can see the print of the nails and see the wound in his side" (John 20:25). Jesus said, *"because thou hast seen me, thou hast believed: blessed are they THAT HAVE NOT SEEN, and yet have BELIEVED"* (v. 29).

Then look at Abraham who *"calleth those things which be not as though they were"* (Rom. 4:17). Which faith is Bible faith? Of course, Abraham's faith is, because our text in Hebrews 11:1 says, *"Now faith is the substance of things hoped for, the evidence of things NOT SEEN."*

Abraham is mentioned in Hebrews chapter 11 as having faith which pleased God (Heb. 11:8–12). Abraham's faith was based on *"being fully persuaded that, what he* [God] *had promised, he was able also to perform"* (Rom. 4:21). Abraham believed God and he believed God's promise.

Bible Faith

So here's a little formula for the faith that pleases God. You can make this Bible faith work for you. It is the same faith that Abraham used and it worked for him because it is faith that is based on what God has said.

1. Have God's Word for what you desire to receive from God.

2. Believe God's Word.

3. Consider not the contradictory circumstances.

4. Give praise to God for the answer.

Follow these four steps and you'll always get the desired result because these are four certain or sure steps to deliverance, healing, answered prayers, or whatever it is that you are seeking from God.

Then notice Thomas' faith. Thomas' faith was *not* based upon what God said: Thomas' faith was based upon what his own physical senses told him. For example, Thomas said he would not believe unless he could *see.*

So many people say, "When I *see* it or when I *feel* it then I'll *know* I *have* my petition." But that's not Bible faith. That's natural human faith and any sinner already has that kind of faith. You see, real faith in God is based upon the Word of God. Real faith in the Word says, "If God says it's true, it is." Believing God is believing His Word!

I like something Smith Wigglesworth said. He said, "I can't understand God by feelings. I can't understand the Lord Jesus Christ by feelings. I can understand God the Father and Jesus Christ only by what the Word says about them. God is everything the Word says He is." Wigglesworth went on to say, "We need to get acquainted with the Lord Jesus Christ through the Word."

Too many people try to get acquainted with God through feelings, and when they feel good, they think God has heard them. But if they don't feel good, they think He is not hearing them. Their faith is based on their feelings, but my faith is based upon God's Word.

If God's Word says He hears me, then I know He hears me because He said so, and His Word cannot lie. In other words, if my faith is based upon my feelings, then I am just using a natural human faith. I'm trying to get spiritual results with natural human faith, and I cannot do that. I have to use scriptural faith, Bible faith, and believe God's Word. And if my faith is based upon the Word of God, then I believe the Word regardless of evidences which would satisfy my physical senses.

Too many people are trying to get Abraham's blessing with Thomas' faith, and that just won't work. We who are believers have the Abraham kind of faith because Galatians 3:29 says, *"And if ye be Christ's, then are ye Abraham's seed, and heirs according to the promise."* And Galatians 3:7 says, *"Know ye therefore that they which are of faith, the same are the children of Abraham."* We have the Abraham kind of faith. We're not trying to get it; we have it.

An Example of Walking by Sight Instead of by Faith

At one place where I was holding a meeting, there was a woman minister who had come forward in the healing line time after time and never got her healing. The pastor asked me why. He said she was well-known in that area and there were other people who weren't responding for healing because they felt if she couldn't get her healing, they couldn't either.

So I asked the Lord to help me. If I couldn't get this woman to see where she was missing it and what faith is, at least I wanted the Lord to help me show the people in the congregation what faith is. The Lord told me I wouldn't be able to get her to see it, but to use her as an example so the rest of the congregation could understand what faith is.

When I came to her in the healing line, I prayed for her. When I finished, she began to feel the place on her body where she was sick. Immediately she said, "No, I haven't gotten it yet. Pray again." So I prayed again, and when I finished, she began to do the same thing.

Finally I said, "I'll pray for you one more time and then you can go sit down." When I got through praying the third time, the Lord told me exactly what to do to help the congregation. By this time she had gone up the aisle back to her seat, and I called her back down to where I was standing.

I said, "Sister, I want to ask you a question."

She said, "All right, go ahead!"

I said, "When are you going to start believing you are healed?"

"Well," she said, "when I get healed."

I asked, "What in the world would you want to believe it then for? You would know it then."

She said, "Say that again."

I made this statement to her four more times and she never did get it. But the majority of the congregation did, and afterwards, many of them came into the healing line and were healed.

You see, she was trying to grasp that truth with her mind, but you can't, because your mind can't grasp things in the spiritual realm. But if you listen to your spirit, there's something that responds on the inside of you because your heart knows it's so.

Divine Healing Is Spiritual Healing

Anyone can believe what he can feel, hear, or see. In the natural realm as human beings, we operate in the physical realm most of the time. And in the natural realm you do have to walk by sight. But I'm talking about when it comes to Bible things; when it comes to spiritual things, we *don't* walk by sight. In the supernatural realm we walk by faith, not by sight (2 Cor. 5:7).

God's healing is spiritual healing. If medical science heals, it heals through the physical. But when God heals, He heals through the spirit.

Spiritual healing—divine healing—is received from God the Father the same way the new birth, which is a rebirth of our spirits, is received.

Salvation Is a Spiritual Rebirth

You see, when you are born again, it is not your body that is born again, for you still have the same body you always had. You know the Bible says, *"Therefore if any man be in Christ, he is a new creature"* (2 Cor. 5:17).

That verse is not talking about your body being made new. The new birth doesn't change the physical man. The new birth changes the spirit man on the inside. After you get saved, the man on the inside is to dominate the physical man, and you will have to do something with your own body (1 Cor. 9:27). But it is the man on the inside, the inner man, that is born again.

The new birth is the rebirth of the human spirit. Jesus said, *"That which is born of the flesh is flesh; and that which is born of the Spirit is spirit"* (John 3:6). When a person is born again, you can't tell just by looking at him what's happened to him on the *inside*. But in the process of time, it'll show up on the *outside* too.

When a person is born again, you can't tell at the moment just what has happened on the *inside* of him, because the new birth is a rebirth of the human spirit. But if that person walks in the light of what he has, it'll show up on the outside.

We've been fooled many, many times by people who have come to the altar. They pray and cry and jump and hug others and act so happy, but then you never see them anymore. All the time we really thought they had received something. But many times it was just an emotional experience, but not the new birth.

Then there are other people who come to be saved and who aren't emotional at all. In fact, just by appearance, you might wonder if they got anything at all. They're not even down at the altar long enough, you may think, to receive anything from the Lord.

But many of these folks become very outstanding Christians during their lifetime.

You see, what happens is our faith many times is based upon our physical senses. Now I certainly believe in feelings, but I put feelings last when it comes to faith and prayer.

God's Word comes first. Faith in God's Word comes second. And feelings come last. Too many people turn it around and put feelings first, faith in their feelings second, and the Word of God last. But those people will never be a success in anything.

Divine healing comes the same way as the new birth. It comes through our spirit. It doesn't always show up immediately on the outside. Heart faith is Bible faith. The Bible says, "... *with the heart man believeth* ..." (Rom. 10:10). *Your heart is your spirit,* and healing begins in your spirit. It begins on the inside of you and works to the outside.

Receiving the Holy Spirit Is a Spiritual Reality

Whether you realize it or not, the same thing is true about receiving the Holy Spirit. Receiving the Holy Spirit is a spiritual experience and not a mental or physical experience. Actually, we may call receiving the baptism in the Holy Ghost an experience, but it's much more than that.

In the new birth, the Holy Spirit comes to dwell in your spirit and your body becomes the temple of the Holy Ghost (1 Cor. 3:16; 2 Cor. 6:16). Then in the baptism of the Holy Spirit you are filled to a greater measure with the Holy Spirit so that you may live in the power of God to bless others (Luke 24:49; Acts 1:5,8).

The only reason your body becomes the temple of the Holy Ghost is that your body is the temple or house of your own spirit, and the Holy Spirit is dwelling in your spirit. You cannot contact God with your mind. God is not a mind. Then again the Bible says, "God is not a man" (Num. 23:19), which means that He is not a physical being. He is a Spirit (John 4:24).

Now again, God is not "spirit" like some people think of "spirit." He is a divine Spirit Being. You see "spirit" to many people just means an influence in the atmosphere somewhere. But God is a divine Personality. You can't contact God with your mind and you can't contact God with your body. You contact God with your spirit for He is a Spirit Being.

This is exactly where many miss it when it comes to receiving the Holy Ghost: They try to receive the Holy Ghost mentally or they try to receive the Holy Ghost physically. They are wanting a physical experience, but it is a spiritual experience. The only physical part of receiving the Holy Spirit is speaking in tongues; that is, the Holy Spirit will give you utterance, but you must yield to the Holy Spirit and speak out the utterance He gives. The utterance the Holy Spirit gives you comes out of your spirit. But you yield to the Holy Spirit and do the speaking.

Paul says in First Corinthians 14:14, "*For if I pray in an unknown tongue, my spirit prayeth, but my understanding is unfruitful.*" The *Amplified Bible, Classic Edition* reads, "*For if I pray in an [unknown] tongue, my spirit [by the Holy Spirit within me] prays.*" In other words, it's the Holy Spirit within you who gives you the ability to speak with other tongues.

Many times when it comes to receiving from God, it is difficult to get people out of the mental realm, for they must receive from God in the spiritual realm first. Whether people realize it or not, many people are trying to reach out with their minds and mentally receive the Holy Ghost.

When I see people trying to mentally receive the Holy Spirit, I have to keep working with them and telling them, "No, you're trying to receive the Holy Spirit mentally. You can't do that." People cannot receive the Holy Ghost through mental effort. In fact, when they are trying to receive, their minds must be quiet and stayed on Jesus.

Fleshly Demonstration Is Not Necessary in Receiving the Holy Spirit

Then again, in receiving the Holy Spirit, it is not necessary for a physical display to take place either. I do not care a thing in the world about physical appearances or actions being displayed when I lay hands on someone to receive the Holy Spirit. What is important is spiritual actions—that is, Bible-based actions. People need to receive the gift of the Holy Ghost that God has already freely given by *faith*.

I've heard people working at the altar say to those seeking the Holy Spirit, "Holler louder so God will hear you." If God heard people because they hollered louder, then we ought to put a microphone in front of them so they could holler even louder. Then God would be sure to hear them!

What does teaching people things like this accomplish? It leaves people with the impression that it's *physical* action to which God responds. But God responds to *faith* (Heb. 11:6).

Then again, I've heard people tell folks, "You have to raise your hands higher so God will hear you."

If God heard you because you raised your hands higher, then it would be even better if you could get on top of the church building and raise them up. Do you see how ridiculous that sounds?

Doing things such as hollering louder and raising your hands up higher are just physical action and they won't necessarily produce any lasting spiritual result.

If people do receive the Holy Spirit under such conditions—basing their faith on outward, fleshly demonstrations instead of on the Word of God—as soon as the feelings subside, they will say, "Maybe I didn't receive after all. I sure thought I did. I had a wonderful experience, but now I'm not sure."

But my brother and sister, receiving the Holy Spirit is not just an experience. It is more than that. It is receiving the Holy Spirit, a divine Personality. The Holy Spirit is a Person, the third Person of the Godhead. And He comes to make His home in the believer's spirit.

JOHN 14:16
16 And I will pray the Father, and he shall give you another Comforter, that he may abide with you for ever.

Receive the Holy Spirit, Then Speak With Tongues

The Holy Spirit comes in to live and dwell in you, and then you must learn to respond to Him. And when you receive the infilling of the Holy Spirit, He will give you utterance, but you are to respond to Him by doing the speaking. Many people fail here because they base their faith on physical evidence. In other words, they're not going to believe they have received the Holy Ghost until they speak with tongues. That's wrong. They must believe they have received the Holy Spirit, *then* He will grant the utterance.

People who believe that, have the cart before the horse. You believe and receive the Holy Ghost first, *then* you speak with tongues as a result of having received. Some don't understand that, and that's the very thing that hinders many from receiving.

As I minister to people to receive the Holy Spirit, I tell them, "Believe that you receive the Holy Ghost and *then* speak in tongues. You don't speak in tongues first and then receive the Holy Ghost."

Acts 2:4 says, *"And they were all filled with the Holy Ghost. . . ."* If you stop reading there, it just says they were all filled. But keep reading: *". . . they were all filled with the Holy Ghost, and* [THEY] *began to speak with other tongues."* (v. 4). *They* began to speak with other tongues *after* they were filled.

That's the very area where many folks stumble and miss it. They think they're going to speak in tongues and *then* believe they have the Holy Ghost. But, you've got to believe it *first*. You receive Him *first*.

If people seeking the Holy Ghost would put everything out of their minds including all the preconceived ideas they have collected over the years about the Holy Ghost and just go to the Word and study, it would be so easy to say with their mouths from their hearts, "I receive the Holy Ghost now by faith."

Nowhere do you have the manifestation or the answer and then the faith. No, you believe first, and then you have the manifestation or the answer.

Don't Try God's Word—Believe and Act on It!

God's Word works for everyone—if the person will only *believe* it—not *try* to believe. The Word won't work if you just try it or hope it will work. No, it's believing faith—apart from physical circumstances—that gets the job done. We walk by faith and not by sight when it comes to the baptism of the Holy Ghost, healing, an answer to prayer, as well as receiving anything else from God.

In the natural we do have to go by our senses. For example, if you are crossing the street and your eyes tell you there are cars coming, you need to have enough sense to wait until the cars pass before you proceed to cross the street! In things in the natural realm, you have to walk by natural faith—faith in your sight, faith in your smell, or faith in your feelings. Therefore, there are many areas in which we have to walk by faith in our physical senses.

But, you see, many people are trying to believe God with their physical senses or with natural, human faith. And if their physical senses tell them their prayer hasn't been answered, then they believe their physical senses, instead of the Word of God.

But what do your physical senses have to do with the Bible? God's Word is so whether you feel like it is or not. God's Word is so whether it looks like it is so or not. God's Word is true all the time regardless of your feelings. No matter what the circumstances, God's Word is still true.

I can't teach faith any plainer than that. That's as plain as faith gets: put your faith in what the Word says rather than in what your senses tell you. If you can't understand faith yet, you just keep reading these lessons and studying God's Word. As you do, eventually your mind will be renewed with the Word and the light will come to you.

Questions for Study

1. If faith says, "It's mine. I have it now," what does mental assent say?

   _____

   _____

2. Which faith is Bible faith: Thomas' faith or Abraham's faith?

   _____

   _____

3. What was Abraham's faith based on?

   _____

   _____

4. What is a four-step formula for the faith that pleases God?

   _____

5. What was Thomas' faith based on?

   _____

   _____

6. What two scripture references tell us that believers have the Abraham kind of faith?

   _____

   _____

7. As human beings, what realm do we operate in most of the time?

   _____

   _____

8. The new birth is the _____ of the _____ spirit.

9. What two things should come before your feelings?

   _____

   _____

10. What can you do if you can't understand faith yet?

    _____

    _____

Chapter 7

What It Means to Believe With the Heart—Part 1

For WITH THE HEART man believeth unto righteousness; and with the mouth confession is made unto salvation.

—Romans 10:10

I want you to notice the words in this verse, *"For with the heart man believeth."* It's with the heart that man believes.

MARK 11:23

23 For verily I say unto you, That whosoever shall say unto this mountain, Be thou removed, and be thou cast into the sea; AND SHALL NOT DOUBT IN HIS HEART, but shall BELIEVE [in his heart] that those things which he saith shall come to pass; he shall have whatsoever he saith.

I want you to notice the phrases in both of these verses of scripture pertaining to believing with the heart. From these scriptures we can see that it's with the heart that man believes.

The Heart of Man Is the Spirit of Man

To further explain what it means to believe with the heart, we must understand that the heart of man is the spirit of man. Man *is* a spirit; he *has* a soul; and he *lives* in a body.

I don't know about you, but for years I had been eagerly searching for a satisfactory explanation for what it means to believe with the heart. Now you understand this, of course, that the word "heart" used in the scriptures we just mentioned is not referring to the physical organ that pumps the blood through our bodies and keeps us alive. That would mean we are to believe God with our bodies!

No, the word "heart" does not refer to the human physical organ of the body. You couldn't believe with your physical heart any more than you could believe with your physical hand or finger.

The word "heart" is used to convey a thought. Notice how we use the word "heart" today. We talk about the heart of a tree. What do we mean? We mean the center, the very core. We talk about the heart of a subject. What do we mean? We mean the most important part of that subject—the very center of it—the main part of it around which the rest revolves.

And when God speaks of the human heart, He is speaking about the main part of man, the very center of man's being, which is his *spirit*. Man *is* a spirit; he *has* a soul; and he *lives* in a body.

1 THESSALONIANS 5:23

23 And the very God of peace sanctify you wholly; and I pray God your whole SPIRIT and SOUL and BODY be preserved blameless unto the coming of our Lord Jesus Christ.

The Apostle Paul said, *"I pray God your whole spirit . . . soul . . . and body. . . ."* Notice that Paul started with the very heart of man, his spirit. When God speaks of the heart, He means the human spirit. You will find that many times the words "heart" and "spirit" in the Bible are interchangeable.

We know that man is a spirit because he is in the same class as God. Man is made in the image and the likeness of God (Gen. 1:26). And Jesus said, *"God is a Spirit"* (John 4:24). It is not your physical man that is like God, for the Bible says that God is not a man (Num. 23:19). Remember that there is an inward man and there is an outward man.

Jesus said to Nicodemus in John chapter 3, *"Except a man be born again, he cannot see the kingdom of God"* (John 3:3). Nicodemus was operating in the natural realm, and he could only think in terms of the natural, so he asked Jesus, *"How can a man be born when he is old? can he enter the second time into his mother's womb, and be born?"* (John 3:4). Notice how Jesus answered him.

JOHN 3:6

6 That which is born of the flesh is flesh; and that which is born of the Spirit is spirit.

The new birth is a rebirth of the human spirit. Notice what Paul said in Romans 1:9, *"For God is my witness, whom I serve with my spirit in the gospel of his Son. . . ."* Also, notice what Jesus said to the woman at the well in Samaria.

JOHN 4:24

24 God is a Spirit: and they that worship him must worship him in spirit and in truth.

The words "in spirit" in the phrase, "worship him [God] *in spirit* and in truth" refers to the human spirit, not the Holy Spirit. You see, you cannot contact God with your body and you cannot contact God with your mind. You can only contact God with your spirit; therefore, you must worship him from your spirit or heart.

ROMANS 2:28–29

28 For he is not a Jew, which is one outwardly; neither is that circumcision, which is outward in the flesh:

29 But he is a Jew, which is one inwardly; and circumcision is that of the HEART, IN THE SPIRIT, and not in the letter; whose praise is not of men, but of God.

In this passage, the "heart" of man and the "spirit" of man are used interchangeably. Romans 2:29 says, *"circumcision is that of the heart, in the spirit. . . ."* That is referring to the human spirit. Your heart, according to this text, is your spirit.

Now read First Corinthians 14:14: *"For if I pray in an unknown tongue, my SPIRIT prayeth, but my UNDERSTANDING is unfruitful."* Notice in this passage that the Bible makes a distinction between the spirit of man and the understanding or mind of man.

Your spirit is not your mind. And your mind is not your spirit. I heard someone say sometime ago that your mind is actually your spirit. But, no, your mind is not your spirit! Anyone who speaks in tongues ought to know that, because you don't speak in tongues out of your head. You know where those tongues come from; they come from down inside of you—from your innermost being—from the Holy Spirit in your spirit.

Now look at First Corinthians 14:15: *"What is it then? I will pray with the SPIRIT, and I will pray with the UNDERSTANDING also."* In other words, Paul was saying that the spirit of man is distinct and separate from man's mind or understanding.

The Inward Man vs. the Outward Man

Now let's read some other scriptures. I want to simply get you conscious of the fact that you are a spirit, that you *have* a soul, and that you *live* in a body.

HEBREWS 12:18–23

18 For ye are not come unto the mount that might be touched, and that burned with fire, nor unto blackness, and darkness, and tempest,

19 And the sound of a trumpet, and the voice of words; which voice they that heard intreated that the word should not be spoken to them any more:

20 (For they could not endure that which was commanded, And if so much as a beast touch the mountain, it shall be stoned, or thrust through with a dart:

21 And so terrible was the sight, that Moses said, I exceedingly fear and quake:)

22 But ye are come unto mount Sion, and unto the city of the living God, the heavenly Jerusalem, and to an innumerable company of angels,

23 To the general assembly and church of the firstborn, which are written in heaven, and to God the Judge of all, and to THE SPIRITS OF JUST MEN MADE PERFECT.

2 CORINTHIANS 4:16

16 For which cause we faint not; but though our OUTWARD MAN perish, yet the INWARD MAN is renewed day by day.

The Bible makes a distinction between the inward man and the outward man. The outward man is the body, and the inward man is the spirit. The inward man is not the soul. The inward man, or the spirit, *has* a soul, but the inward man is not the soul.

1 CORINTHIANS 9:27

27 But I keep under my body, and [I] bring it into subjection: lest that by any means, when I have preached to others, I myself should be a castaway.

The inward man, the spirit, is the real man. Notice Paul said, *"I keep under my body . . ."* (1 Cor. 9:27). I want you to notice something. If the body were the real man, Paul would have said, "I keep myself under. I bring myself into subjection." But Paul calls his body "it."

He said, *"I keep under my body and [I] bring IT into subjection"* (1 Cor. 9:27). "I" is the man on the inside; the inward man that's been reborn. Paul said, *"I do something with my body. I bring it into subjection."*

You see, the man we look at on the outside is not the real man. It's just the house we live in.

Present Your Body; Renew Your Mind

ROMANS 12:1–2

1 I beseech you therefore, brethren, by the mercies of God, that ye present your bodies a living sacrifice, holy, acceptable unto God, which is your reasonable service.

2 And be not conformed to this world: but be ye transformed by the renewing of your mind, that ye may prove what is that good, and acceptable, and perfect, will of God.

There is something in these verses of scripture that astounded me when I saw it. I had been preaching for about twenty years when I first saw this, and it came as a shock to me. Here Paul is writing a letter to the Roman Christians. He wasn't writing to sinners. He wrote in Romans chapter 1, *"To all that be in Rome, beloved of God, called to be SAINTS"* (Rom. 1:7).

He is writing to men and women who have been born again and filled with the Holy Ghost. And yet he says that Christians need to do something with their own bodies and their minds.

That really came as a shock to me that here were people who were saved and filled with the Holy Ghost, yet their bodies and minds hadn't been affected. Can you see that?

So, you see, the new birth is not a rebirth of the human body or the mind, but it is a rebirth of the human spirit. And the infilling of the Holy Ghost is not a physical experience or a mental experience, but it is a spiritual experience.

Because your body was not born again in the new birth, you will have to do something with your body. You will have to present it to God as a living sacrifice. And you will have to do something with your mind. You will have to get your mind renewed with the Word. This is something that *you* do, not God. God gives you eternal life; God offers you His spirit; but God doesn't do anything with your body. If anything is done with it, *you* will have to do it.

Someone said, "But I can't." As long as you take sides against God and against His Word and you say you can't, then of course, you won't be able to do anything. But the Bible says that you are to present your body unto God (Rom. 12:1). That means you *can* do it. In fact, no one else can do it for you. *You* present your own body unto God.

Then the Bible says, *"be ye transformed by the renewing of your mind"* (Rom. 12:2). Our minds are to be renewed with the Word of God. That comes through reading and meditating on the Word. But, God also put teachers in the Church to teach people the truth and help people renew their minds. I dare say that your minds have begun to be renewed through these lessons. Have you become conscious of the fact that you are really a spirit, that you *have* a soul, and that you *live* in a body?

Man Is a Spirit Being

The spirit of man is the heart of man. We know that man is a spirit. We know that as a spirit being, man is in the same class with God. He has to be, because he is made in the image and likeness of God (Gen. 1:26; John 4:24). Man is not an animal. You know some folks would have you believe man is just an animal. But if man is just an animal, it wouldn't

be any more wrong to kill a man and eat him than it would be to kill a cow and eat it! But we know that's not true.

Man has a physical body that he is living in, all right, but he is not an animal, and he is more than just mind and body. Man is spirit, soul, and body. He *is* a spirit, he *has* a soul, and he *lives* in a body. That is what makes man different from animals.

You see, one thing some of the false cults teach is that in Genesis, in the Hebrew language, the Word of God speaks of the souls of animals. We've never really defined spirit, soul, and body of man in Christiandom as we should have. And so many adherents of these cults say animals have souls just as much as people do, so when a person is dead, he is dead just like a dog is dead.

It is true that animals do have souls, but they are not spirit beings like we are. You see, there is nothing in animals that is like God. But God took something of Himself—His Spirit—and put it in man. God made the body of man out of the dust of the earth, but He breathed into man's nostrils the breath of life (Gen. 2:7).

Now that doesn't mean that God is a human and that He breathes as we do in order to stay alive. The word "breath" there, or "ruach" in the Hebrew means *breath, wind, or spirit*, and is translated "Holy Spirit" many times in the Old Testament.

God is a Spirit, so He took something of Himself, which is spirit, and put it into man. The minute He did, man became a living soul. Man wasn't alive until then, but then man became a living soul. We could say that when man became a living being is when man became conscious of himself and his own existence because his body was dead without the spirit.

Animals do have a soul because the soul is the mind, will, and emotions. Animals do have a certain amount of mental, emotional, and volitional qualities, but it is all based upon the physical, and when the physical is dead, it is all over. But our souls—our emotional, mental, and volitional qualities—are not based upon the physical, but upon the spirit because when the body is dead, these qualities still exist.

Lazarus and the Rich Man: Man's Spirit and Soul After Death

Let's look at a passage in Luke 16 that gives us some insight regarding man as a spirit being. This passage also shows us that man's spirit and soul separate from his body after physical death.

LUKE 16:19–22

19 There was a certain rich man, which was clothed in purple and fine linen, and fared sumptuously every day:

20 And there was a certain beggar named Lazarus, which was laid at his gate, full of sores,

21 And desiring to be fed with the crumbs which fell from the rich man's table: moreover the dogs came and licked his sores.

22 And it came to pass, that the beggar died, and was carried by the angels into Abraham's bosom: the rich man also died, and was buried.

Now the beggar died and the angels (angels are ministering spirits) carried him, that is, his spirit, away. His spirit was the real person. Let's continue reading.

LUKE 16:23–26

23 And in hell he [the rich man] **lift up his eyes, being in torments, and seeth Abraham afar off, and Lazarus in his bosom.**

24 And he cried and said, Father Abraham, have mercy on me, and send Lazarus, that he may dip the tip of his finger in water, and cool my tongue; for I am tormented in this flame.

25 But Abraham said, Son, remember that thou in thy lifetime receivedst thy good things, and likewise Lazarus evil things: but now he is comforted, and thou art tormented.

26 And beside all this, between us and you there is a great gulf fixed: so that they which would pass from hence to you cannot; neither can they pass to us, that would come from thence.

Verse 22 says, *"the rich man also died, and was buried."* The rich man's body was put in the grave, but the Bible says that in hell he lifted up his eyes.

At that time, Abraham's body had been in the grave for years, and yet the Bible says the rich man saw Abraham (Luke 16:23). Also the rich man recognized the beggar, Lazarus. Therefore, we can conclude that in the spirit realm, man looks very similar to what he looks like in this life. In other words, people can be recognized in Heaven; you can know who they are.

LUKE 16:24–25

24 And he cried and said, Father Abraham, have mercy on me, and send Lazarus, that he may dip the tip of his finger in water, and cool my tongue; for I am tormented in this flame.

25 But Abraham said, Son, remember that thou in thy lifetime receivedst thy good things, and likewise Lazarus evil things: but now he is comforted, and thou art tormented.

You see, man is a spirit; he has a soul; and he lives on this earth in a body. In Heaven, man's soul is still intact. He can still remember things, and he still has emotions (the soul is made up of the mind, will, and emotions) because we read in Luke 16:27 and 28 that the rich man was concerned about his five brothers who were still alive on the earth, and he wanted to warn them.

The 'Building' of God—Our Bodies

2 CORINTHIANS 5:1

1   For we know that if our EARTHLY HOUSE OF THIS TABERNACLE [man's body] **were dissolved, we have a building of God, an house not made with hands, eternal in the heavens.**

The Bible is saying here that the body of man was made with hands, but the inward man, the spirit of man, was not. Therefore, when our body is put in the grave, we still have a "building of God"—our spirit—not made with hands, and we shall live eternally in the heavens (2 Cor. 5:1). Notice what Paul says in verses 6 through 8.

2 CORINTHIANS 5:6–8

6   Therefore we are always confident, knowing that, whilst we are at home in the body, we are absent from the Lord [We are at home in our bodies because our bodies are our fleshly homes down here on the earth; our bodies are not the real us—they are just the houses we live in]:

7   (For we walk by faith, not by sight:)

8   We are confident, I say, and willing rather to be absent from the body, and to be present with the Lord.

Who is going to be absent from the body? We are—the real us—the spirit man on the inside of each of us as Christians. We're going to be absent from the body here on earth one day, but we will be present with the Lord.

The Bible talks of the inward man as being the real you. All of these scriptures prove that statement.

We know that God is a Spirit; we know that Jesus became a man, for Jesus was God manifested in the flesh living in a human body. We know that Jesus took on a physical body, and when He did, He was not less God than He was before He had a physical body.

We also know that man leaves his physical body at death and likewise, when he does, he is no less man than he was when he had his physical body. That is also proven by the story of the rich man and Lazarus in Luke chapter 16.

I Went to Hell

I don't know about you, but I've always been interested in the spirit realm because I died and went to hell as a teenager on the bed of sickness, and I've preached about it, giving my testimony many times. That happened on April 22, 1933, Saturday night at 7:30 p.m., in the south bedroom of 405 N. College Street in the city of McKinney, Texas.

Just as Grandpa's old clock on the mantlepiece struck 7:30, my heart stopped beating within my bosom, and I felt the circulation cut off way down at the end of my toes all the way up to my heart. I had the sensation of just leaping out of my body.

I knew I was out of my body, and yet I was not less man then, than I was when I was in my body. I began to descend, and I went down, down, down, like I was going down into a pit or a cavern or a well.

I looked up and I could see the lights of the earth way above me (for the earth puts off a certain amount of light). The farther down I went, the darker it became, until finally, darkness totally encompassed me round about—darkness darker than any night man has ever seen in this life. It was a darkness that seemed to be so dense that if you had a knife you could cut a piece of it out, as if it were a solid mass.

The farther down I went, the hotter it became and the more stifling it became. My mind, my soul, was intact. I thought of my life, and my entire past came up before me, in my mind.

As I descended, I could see fingers of light playing on that wall of darkness. All the time I was still going down, down, making a descent. And in a few moments, I came to the bottom of a pit and I saw what caused the light to play against the wall of darkness. In front of me I saw giant orange flames crested by a white hot flame. I came to the gate—the entrance—the portals of hell itself.

There was a creature of some kind that met me when I got to the bottom of the pit. I never looked at him, although I knew he was by my side, for my gaze was riveted to hell itself. I intended to put up a fight if I could, to keep from going into that awful place, and so I paused, never coming to a complete stop. I paused momentarily, and when I did, this creature by my side took me by the arm.

All the time this was happening, my physical body lay on the bed back in the bedroom in McKinney, Texas. But, you see, there is a spiritual body and that spiritual body has arms and legs and eyes and ears—all the features that the physical body has. That's why the rich man in Luke 16 said, *"I am tormented in this flame"* (Luke 16:24).

The rich man was possessed with all his faculties. He *saw* Lazarus with his eyes and recognized him. Actually, when I was in hell, I couldn't tell any difference in myself between the physical and spiritual man except for the fact that I could not contact the physical realm, and that I wasn't living in the physical realm; I was in the spiritual realm.

Paul expressed this in Second Corinthians 12.

2 CORINTHIANS 12:2
2 I knew a man in Christ above fourteen years ago, (whether in the body, I cannot tell; or whether out of the body, I cannot tell: God knoweth;) such an one caught up to the third heaven.

Paul told how he had been caught up into Paradise and heard, *"unspeakable words, which it is not lawful for a man to utter"* (2 Cor. 12:4).

Most Bible scholars agree that Paul was talking about his own experience. Paul said, in effect, "I don't know whether I was in my body or out of my body." I know what Paul meant by that because in my own experience, as far as I was concerned, I couldn't tell either.

As that creature took me by the arm to escort me into hell, there was a Voice that spoke from far above the blackness, above the earth, and above the heavens—from the throne room of God. I don't know what the Voice said. It was the sound of a man's voice, a male voice, and I could hear it as it boomed and echoed down through that shaft of darkness from Heaven above.

I don't know what the Voice said because the words weren't spoken in English; it was a foreign tongue to me. But it was the Voice of God. When He spoke those words (I suppose He spoke from six to nine words), that whole region of the damned shook and quivered, just like a leaf in the wind. Then that creature took his hand off of my arm and there was an unseen power just like a suction, an irresistible pull to my back, that began to pull me back away from the entrance of hell, back to the shadows of that shaft of darkness.

Then that irresistible unseen power pulled me back up to earth. I came up head first. I came up on the porch outside the south bedroom where my body lay dead. I knew for just a second that I was standing on the porch. Then I went right through the wall because, you see, material things have no effect on spiritual things. And I went back inside my body; I just seemed to leap inside my body like a man would put his foot into a shoe.

I realized as soon as I got inside my body that I could contact the physical realm again. And I said to my grandmother, who had held my head in her lap and bathed my face with a cool, damp cloth, "Granny, I'm dying."

She said, "Son, I thought you were dead. I didn't know you were coming back."

I said, "I'm going again, and I won't be back next time."

And that same incident of descending into hell happened three times. Each time I did come back. As my spirit left my body and I descended into the lower regions into hell, that same Voice spoke and I was brought back to earth. It was the Voice of God.

When I began to descend the third time, I began to scream out to God, "God, I belong to the church." No answer came as I said those words, for it will take more than church membership to miss hell and make Heaven. Jesus said, *"Ye must be born again"* (John 3:7). Certainly, I believe in joining a church, but it is not church membership that will save a person; it is being born again.

As I came out of that horrible pit the third time, my spirit began to pray. My physical voice picked up the prayer as I entered back into my body the third time. I prayed so loudly that neighbors could hear me.

I began to call upon God, that He would have mercy upon me, a sinner, and that He would forgive me for my sins and cleanse me from all unrighteousness. I accepted Jesus as my Savior and confessed Him as my Lord. I felt so wonderful, as if a heavy burden had rolled off of my chest. (For a detailed account of this experience, see Kenneth E. Hagin's book *I Believe in Visions*.)

I looked at the clock and saw that it was twenty minutes before eight o'clock. That was the very hour I was born again due to the mercy of God.

I Went to Heaven

Then about four months later, on August 16, 1933, at 1:30 in the afternoon, I knew I was again dying. I was in the last throes of death. So I said to my youngest brother, who was standing by my bed, "Pat, run and get Mama quick. I'm dying. I want to tell her good-bye." And he ran out of the room like a shot!

Just as Mama came into the room, I had the same sensation of leaving my body as I had had before,

except I was saved now. I leaped out of my body and when I left my body, this time I began to *ascend*. I didn't go down this time; I went up!

We lived in an old-fashioned house with a high ceiling and I got up to about where the roof of the house should have been—I must have been about sixteen or eighteen feet above the bed. I was fully conscious. I knew everything that was going on.

When I got up that high, I stopped ascending, and I just seemed to stand there. When I stopped, I looked down into the room and I saw my body (not me, my spirit, but my physical body) lying there on the bed, and I saw my mother stooped over me with my hand in hers.

Mama told me afterwards that I had her hand in a death-like grip. But, you see, I had left my body; therefore, I couldn't tell her good-bye. Then I looked up and heard a Voice. Again, I didn't see anyone, but I heard a Voice and again it was a male voice. I do not know whether it was Jesus, whether it was an angel, or who it was, but I know it was an emissary of Heaven.

This time the Voice did not speak in a foreign tongue, but spoke in English. And here's what the Voice said: "Go back, go back, go back. You can't come yet. Your work on earth is not done."

And when He—whoever it was—said that, I began to descend and I came back into my body. And when I got back inside my body, I said, "Mama, I'm not going to die now." She thought I meant I wasn't going to die that minute, but I meant that I wasn't going to die then at all, but live and do the work and the will of God!

I lay there bedfast exactly twelve months, almost to the day, before I received my healing. For even though it was the will of God for me to live, God couldn't make an exception of me. In other words, I had to receive my healing, like anyone else does by faith, and it took me twelve months to see the truth of God's Word concerning healing.

After this experience, I lay on that bed for months and months, waiting for God to heal me, and He didn't do it. And if you're waiting for God to heal you, He's not going to do it. You're just wasting your time because God is waiting for *you* to receive what He has already freely given.

If you will begin reading the Word and meditating on it, you'll begin to appropriate your healing and receive that which God has already wrought for you, and you will receive your healing.

Can you see why I have been so interested in the subject of faith and healing? Too many times theories are taught instead of facts from the Bible. But I'm teaching something that *works*—God's precious, holy Word.

Here is what I am trying to get over to you (and I know this from experience as well as from the Bible). When a man dies, he leaves his physical body, and he is no less man then, than he was when he was in his physical body. It was that way with me; it was that way with the rich man in Luke 16; and it was that way with Lazarus in Luke 16.

Physical Death Is Separation From the Body

Also, we can see from the following scriptures that when a man dies, he leaves his physical body.

2 CORINTHIANS 5:8

8 We are confident, I say, and willing rather to be ABSENT FROM THE BODY, and to be PRESENT WITH THE LORD.

PHILIPPIANS 1:21–24

21 For to me to live is Christ, and to die is gain.

22 But if I live in the flesh, this is the fruit of my labour: yet what I shall choose I wot not.

23 For I am in a strait betwixt two, having a desire to DEPART, AND TO BE WITH CHRIST; which is far better:

24 Nevertheless to abide IN THE FLESH is more needful for you.

Paul said, *"For to me to live is Christ, and to die is gain. . . . Nevertheless to abide in the flesh is more needful for you"* (Phil. 1:21, 24). He also said, *"yet what I shall choose I wot not"* (v. 22). The Bible is saying that when a believer dies, he leaves his physical body, and he goes to Heaven to be with the Lord.

Friends, we can only understand God and the things of God through His Word. And we cannot know God through our natural human knowledge and through our minds. God is only revealed to man through the spirit. When I say the "spirit" I'm not referring to the Holy Spirit. I mean that we know God through *man's* spirit. It is the spirit of man that contacts God, for God is a Spirit (Prov. 20:27; John 4:24).

We know that spiritual things are just as real as material things. God is just as real as though He had a physical body, yet He doesn't. He is a Spirit.

Jesus has a physical body now—a flesh and bone body—but not a flesh and blood body (Luke 24:39). You remember that after Jesus' resurrection, He appeared to the disciples and they thought they were seeing a spirit or a ghost. But Jesus said, *"handle me, and see; for a spirit hath not flesh and bones, AS YE SEE ME HAVE"* (Luke 24:39).

Also, in John chapter 21, Peter and some of the others had gone fishing. They had fished all night and had caught nothing. The next morning they saw Jesus on the shore, and He spoke to them. They caught so many fish *"they were not able to draw it for the multitude of fishes"* (John 21:6).

Then they came to the shore, and Jesus had fish there on the fire and He ate with them (John 21:9–15). Jesus had a physical body then, a resurrected flesh and bone physical body because His disciples saw Him and He broke bread with them.

The Spiritual Realm Is Real

Jesus with His physical body now in Heaven is not more real than the Holy Spirit or God the Father is real. God is a Spirit. Some people think God is some sort of an impersonal influence. No, God *is a Spirit*. That does not mean that He doesn't have a shape or a form in the spiritual realm because He does. For example, the Bible says that angels are spirits, or spirit beings, and yet angels have a form or a spirit body.

For example, there was an incident in the Old Testament in which a man's eyes were opened to behold the angels of God and the chariots of fire round about.

The king of Syria warred against Israel, and in his bedchamber he would tell his servants the battle plan. But God would reveal the battle plan to Elisha, and he would warn the king of Israel.

The king of Syria found out about it, and besieged the city where Elisha was. Elisha's servant was afraid and said to Elisha, *"Alas, my master! how shall we do?"* (2 Kings 6:15). Elisha answered his servant, *"Fear not: for they that be with us are more than they that be with them"* (2 Kings 6:16). And Elisha prayed and asked God to open the eyes of his servant (2 Kings 6:17).

Elisha wasn't talking about his physical eyes but his spiritual eyes. When the eyes of his spirit were opened he saw angels of fire, horsemen of fire, and chariots of fire all around about the city (2 Kings 6:14, 17). And sometimes, as God wills, angels have the ability to take a form or appearance in the natural realm where you can see them, but not always.

The Bible says, *"the Lord spake unto Moses face to face, as a man speaketh unto his friend."*

(Exod. 33:11), indicating what kind of relationship they had. So we know God has a face, although Moses didn't actually see God's face, for God said to Moses, *"Thou canst not see MY FACE: for there shall no man see me, and live"* (Exod. 33:20). God said, *"I will put thee in a clift of the rock, and will cover thee with my hand while I pass by: And I will take away mine hand, and thou shalt see my back parts: but my face shall not be seen"* (Exod. 33:22–23).

I'm saying this to show you that God is a Spirit; yet He is no less real because He is a Spirit than He would be if He had a physical body. Jesus with His physical body is now in Heaven (Heb. 1:3), but He is not more real than the Holy Spirit or the Father is real. Spiritual things are just as real, even more real than material things. That is what I'm trying to get over to you.

The Hidden Man of the Heart Is the *Real* Man

The same thing is true with the "hidden man of the heart," as the spirit man is called in First Peter 3:4. Your spirit man on the inside is actually the "real you," for it is the part of you that is eternal.

Notice that word "heart" again. The inward man, your spirit, is called the hidden man. He is the man of the heart; the man of the spirit. The hidden man is hidden to the physical or the natural man. The natural man doesn't necessarily want to submit to the inward man (Rom. 8:7), but the inward man—the spirit man is the real man on the inside.

Actually believers need a new psychology, which goes beyond the mere study of the mind of man. We ought to call it spiritology because psychology only deals with the operation of the human mind through the physical senses. Psychology books have to be constantly changed because they are based on natural human knowledge and theories. Spiritology, on the other hand, would be the study of the human spirit. In Romans 7:22 the spirit is called the "inward man." This inward man or the "hidden man" in First Peter 3:4 gives us God's definition of the human spirit.

The real man is a *spirit*; he has a soul; and he lives in a body. With his spirit, man contacts the spiritual realm. With his soul he contacts the intellectual and emotional realm. And with his body he contacts the physical realm.

Questions for Study

1. When God speaks of the human heart, what is He speaking about?

   _____

   _____

2. What two words in the Bible are often used interchangeably?

   _____

   _____

3. You can only contact God with your _____.

4. When you speak with tongues, where do those tongues come from?

5. Because your <u>body</u> was not born again in the new birth, what do you have to do with it?

   _____

   _____

6. What makes men different from animals?

   _____

   _____

7. What can we conclude from the fact that in Luke 16:23, the Bible says the rich man saw Abraham and recognized the beggar Lazarus?

   _____

   _____

8. If you're waiting for God to heal you, why isn't He going to do it?

   _____

   _____

9. If you begin reading and meditating on God's Word, what will begin to happen to you?

   _____

   _____

10. The real man is a _____; he has a _____; and he lives in a _____.

Chapter 8

What It Means to Believe With the Heart—Part 2

For with the HEART man believeth unto righteousness; and with the mouth confession is made unto salvation.

—Romans 10:10

The Heart of Man

Notice particularly the words, *"For with the heart man believeth."* It's with the heart that man believes. Now when God speaks of the human heart here, He is not speaking of the physical organ, that great pumping station that pumps blood throughout your body and keeps your physical body alive. He is actually speaking of the human spirit which is the very center of man's being.

You remember in previous chapters, I talked about the spirit or the heart of man as being the real man. Man *is* a spirit; he *has* a soul; and he *lives* in a body.

I remember as a youngster, I heard a man speak; he called it preaching but actually he only gave an intellectual discourse because it wasn't preaching. What he was talking about wasn't New Testament; it wasn't the Word of God.

In the course of his so-called sermon, he began to poke fun at those of us who believe in old-fashioned, Bible-based, heart-felt salvation. He used the term "heart" literally and said if a man had a "change of heart," that means he would have heart trouble and he would die! This man actually said that this "change of heart" would kill a person because then his blood wouldn't flow right! He mistakenly thought man was just mind and body. But man is more than mind and body. He *is* a spirit; he *has* a soul; and he *lives* in a body.

We know that man was created in the image and the likeness of God (Gen. 1:26). That means man is in the same class with God. Man has to be in the same class with God, otherwise he wouldn't be able to worship God in spirit and in truth. Jesus said, *"God is a Spirit"* (John 4:24). And then Jesus said, *"they that worship him must worship him in spirit and in truth"* (v. 24).

We know from our last lesson that your spirit is not your mind. Your mind is part of your soul. The soul is comprised of your mind, your will, and your emotions. Anyone, particularly Full Gospel people, ought to know what the spirit of man is, because

when you speak with tongues, you speak out of your heart or out of your spirit. So to believe God with your heart means to believe God with your spirit—the real man or the inner man.

Hidden Man of the Heart

1 PETER 3:4

4   But let it be the hidden man of the HEART, in that which is not corruptible. . . .

Notice the word "heart" again. Notice also that Peter says, *"the hidden MAN of the heart"* (1 Peter 3:4). Peter used the words "hidden man" because, really, the spirit or the heart is the real you. The body is not the real you; it is just the house you live in.

Remember Paul said in First Corinthians 9:27, *"I keep under my body, and [I] bring IT [the body] into subjection: lest that by any means, when I have preached to others, I myself should be a castaway."*

If your body were the real you, Paul would have said, "I keep myself under. I bring myself under subjection." But he said, *"I keep my body under. I bring it under subjection."*

In First Corinthians 9:27, "I" is the man on the inside. It is the "hidden man of the heart" in First Peter 3:4. It is the spirit—the real man, or the inner man. The "hidden man of the heart" is called that because he is hidden to the natural man or to the natural mind.

The Inward Man

ROMANS 7:22

22 For I delight in the law of God after the inward man.

In Romans 7:22, the spirit of man is called the "inward man." So this inward man and the hidden man gives us God's definition of the human spirit. Remember the real man *is* a spirit; he *has* a soul; and he *lives* in a body (1 Thess. 5:23).

With our spirit we contact the spiritual realm; with our soul we contact the intellectual and emotional realm; and with our physical being we contact the physical realm.

You can't contact God with your mind. You can't contact God with your body. You can only contact

God with your spirit. And God contacts and communicates with you through your spirit.

Certainly, you know that when you hear the Word of God preached, you hear it with your physical ears and it goes through your natural mind before it goes into your heart or your spirit. Can you remember as a sinner how the Word of God affected you on the inside, in your spirit? The Holy Spirit through the Word, spoke to your heart or your spirit. You heard the Word with your physical ears, but it affected your spirit.

That explains something for us. First Corinthians 2:14 says, *"But the natural man receiveth not the things of the Spirit of God."* Another translation reads, "The natural man or the natural mind *understands* not the things of the Spirit of God." The rest of that verse reads, *"for they are foolishness unto him: neither can he know them, because they are spiritually discerned"* (1 Cor. 2:14).

The Word of God is of the Spirit of God, and the Bible says the Word of God is foolish to the natural mind. The reason the Word of God is foolish to the natural mind is that you don't understand the Bible with your head; it is spiritually understood. You understand the Bible with your heart or your spirit.

That's the reason you can read certain verses over and over again and not understand the meaning. Then one day you can be reading along, and suddenly you see the truth of a particular verse of scripture, and you say, "Why didn't I ever see that before?" Well, you just then understood it with your heart.

The Revelation of God's Word in Your Heart

You see, you've got to get the revelation of God's Word in your heart. That's the reason we have to depend upon the Spirit of God to open and unveil the Word to us.

For example, just because a preacher brings forth a Bible truth, people don't necessarily understand it immediately. It's very difficult sometimes to get people to see some truths from the scriptures because they sometimes try to figure it out with their minds, instead of with their spirits. We have to depend upon the Spirit of God to unveil and unfold the Word to people.

As a young boy, I lay on the bed of sickness for months. Most of the time I tried to figure out how to act on Mark 11:24 and get results. Mark 11:24 says, *"What things soever ye desire, when ye pray, believe that ye receive them, and ye shall have them."*

In the first place, the devil told me that scripture doesn't mean what it says. Well, if it doesn't mean what it says, then Jesus told a lie about it! But Jesus doesn't lie.

The devil told me, "Now that scripture doesn't mean what things soever ye desire naturally or physically or materially, like healing. [You see, I desired healing.] That just means what things soever ye desire *spiritually.*"

I am sorry to say, I listened to the devil at first. I decided I would send for my pastor and ask *him* what Mark 11:24 meant. So I asked my grandmother if she would contact the pastor of the church where my mother and I were members.

My pastor promised to come, but he never showed up. I wept about it when he didn't come because I had great confidence in him, and I was so sure he would know what Mark 11:24 meant. But after I got healed and went back to the same church, I found out what he believed. He didn't believe Mark 11:24 meant what it said at all. Thank God he never showed up!

You see, it was a good thing he didn't come to see me, because at that time I would have believed whatever he would have said. When he found out I did believe Mark 11:24 meant what it said, he commented, "The poor boy stayed in bed so long it affected his mind."

Wouldn't it be wonderful if we could get some more minds affected like that, because as soon as my mind was "affected"—as soon as I believed those words in Mark 11:24 spoken from the lips of Jesus— my paralysis left me! As soon as my mind was "affected," my heart condition left me. Praise God! I was healed and raised up from the bed of sickness!

When my pastor didn't come to see me as I lay there bedfast, my grandmother finally said, "I'll walk over to the north part of town and see another minister who is a pastor in the same kind of church you and your mother belong to." I had great confidence in this minister too.

She walked to that part of town and asked him if he would come to see me, and he said he would. Thank God, he never showed up either! He believed just like the first minister believed.

But I wept when he didn't come. I am thoroughly convinced now, however, and have been for a long time, that God may have stopped those fellows from coming to see me because He knew I would have believed what they said.

But as I lay on that bed, I was still trying to understand Mark 11:24 with my mind, and Satan was still doing his best to talk me out of the notion of believing that Jesus meant what He said in that verse. Finally my aunt, who belonged to another church, said that her pastor would come to see me. I was thrilled about that because I had gone to Sunday School there before and had met the pastor. I didn't much believe that he would come either, but one day I heard the sound of his voice at the front door.

I couldn't see too well and most of the time I couldn't hear too well, but the minute I heard the voice at the front door, I knew it was he. My heart sort of leaped within me for joy as he came in.

Only one person was allowed in the room at a time to visit me. The doctors wouldn't allow anyone else in, so no one else came in with him. I couldn't see more than a few inches away from my face, but I could hear him coming. As he stooped over my bed, his face suddenly came into focus, and I felt him put my hand in his.

I was partially paralyzed and my tongue wouldn't work right. My throat was partially paralyzed, too, so it would take me some time to say whatever I wanted to say, and then sometimes I would say it backwards. I was trying to ask this pastor to get my New Testament and read Mark 11:24 and tell me if it meant what it said. Isn't that strange that you should have to ask someone whether or not Jesus meant what He said?

I was struggling, trying to get those words out, and if he would have waited long enough, I would have eventually spoken them out! But before I could say what I was trying to say, he just patted the back of my hand and put on a professional tone of voice and said, "Just be patient, my boy. In a few more days it'll all be over."

Well, I got an answer, all right! And I want you to know, spiritually speaking it was dark in that room after he said that. The pastor laid my hand down on my breast and turned around and walked out. I never did get out an intelligible word!

This pastor put out the only light—the only beam of hope—I had, just like you'd turned the light out in a room. Then he went into the other room to talk to my family. As a usual thing, I couldn't hear very well, but I think the devil must have let me hear extra well that day. The pastor went into the other room and my family gathered around him, and I could hear him pray.

He said, "Our Father, we pray that you would help this grandmother and grandfather who are about to be bereaved of this grandson."

Something rose up inside of me. I couldn't holler it out loud, but I was sort of like the little mischievous boy who had to stand in the corner of the class room. The little boy said, "I may be standing up on the outside, but on the inside I'm sitting down." And so, on the inside I just yelled out, "I ain't dead yet!"

And then this pastor prayed, "Dear God, bless this dear mother. Prepare her heart for this hour of darkness that's about to overtake her."

On the inside of me I hollered again, "I ain't dead yet!" And the pastor left.

After that incident, I just lay there on that bed for about a month without even reading the Bible. That pastor had just knocked all the props out from under me and had put out all the lights. And so for a little more than a month, I didn't even look at the Bible.

But finally when I did, I turned to Mark 11:24 and said, "Dear Lord Jesus, I'm coming off this bed of sickness. And if I don't get off this bed, it'll be because the Son of God told a falsehood, and I'll just have to tell people to throw the New Testament away."

But I still lay there for eleven more months before I came off that bed. I thought about Mark 11:24, and I meditated on it. I'd pray, and many times I was sure that God had healed me. Then I'd look at my body and feel for my heartbeat, and I still wasn't well.

As I said, the Word is *spiritually* understood. The Word is by the inspiration of the Spirit of God, for holy men of old wrote as they were moved by the Spirit of God (2 Tim. 3:16; 2 Peter 1:21).

On the second Tuesday of August 1934 at about 8:30 in the morning as I meditated on that scripture, I finally saw what Mark 11:23 and 24 said. The light came. It was as though someone had turned on a light inside of me.

And in my ministry I keep teaching people about the truth of this scripture over and over. Yet I know they'll have to understand it with their spirits in order to see the truth of it. But I must keep teaching about Mark 11:23 and 24 because the more you teach a truth, the more folks will eventually catch on to it.

I can tell when the truth of that scripture dawns on them, for their eyes kind of light up. Some of the rest of the folks who have not yet seen it just sit there and I can tell that they don't understand.

Believe and Receive—Then Have!

However, I notice all the time in my ministry, as I preach on the subject of faith, folks just keep catching on!

When Jesus said, *"What things soever ye desire . . . ,"* He meant just exactly what it said (Mark 11:24). And when Jesus said, *"when ye pray . . . ,"* He meant the *very moment* you pray. You are to believe you receive whatsoever things you desire the *moment* you pray.

Jesus said, *"BELIEVE that ye RECEIVE them, and ye shall HAVE them."* In common, everyday language, Jesus said, "You've got to believe you've got your answer before you get it!"

When the light of this scripture first dawned on me, I immediately said, "Why, Lord, I see what I've got to do. I must believe while I'm still lying here flat on my back that my paralysis is healed, not going to be healed, but healed now."

You see, many people say, "I believe God's *going* to heal me." That's not New Testament believing. I ought to know! I stayed bedfast for an entire year believing that, and I never got anything.

I continued talking to the Lord, "I've got to believe that my heart is well while my heart is still not beating right."

Now notice what it said, *"believe that ye receive them, and ye shall have them"* (Mark 11:24). Most folks want to have their petition first, and *then* believe they've got it. But you've got to believe it *first*; *then* you'll have it.

Someone said, "I don't understand that." I told you that you can't understand the Bible with your head. The things of the Spirit of God are foolishness to the natural mind, and the Bible is of the Spirit of God. The scriptures are *spiritually* discerned. You have to grasp or understand the truth of the Word with your *spirit*.

As I said, the moment I saw the truth of Mark 11:24, I began to act upon the Word. There is always some way you can act on the Word. The only way I could act on it at the moment was to raise my hands and praise God for His Word, and thank Him for my healing.

I said, "Thank God, I believe. I believe that my paralysis is healed. I believe my body is well." And, of course, the moment I said that, the devil challenged me.

You see, I am showing you what it means to believe with your heart. To believe with your heart means *to believe with your spirit*. It means to act in faith on God's Word regardless of what you feel or see.

After I began to act on Mark 11:24, immediately the devil challenged me. He said, "You're a pretty looking thing, claiming to be a Christian, and now you've gone to lying."

You see, in our natural minds we don't understand the things of the Spirit of God. For instance, in order to act on Mark 11:24 and get results, we say in effect, "I *believe* I receive." And Jesus said, "If you believe you receive what things so ever you desire, then you shall have them" (Mark 11:24).

Believe *first* that you receive your petitions and you *shall have* them.

MARK 11:24 (AMPC)

24 For this reason I am telling you, whatever you ask for in prayer, believe—trust and be confident—that it is granted to you, and you will [get it].

When are you going to get what you desire? *After* you trust and are confident that it *is* already granted to you. Do you see that? Too many people want to get what they desire first, and *then* they're going to believe they've got it. But Jesus said that you've got to believe you've received what you desire from God, and then you'll have it. That is the simplest way to put it—that is faith.

God's Word Is Faith Food

To believe with the heart means to believe with the spirit—the inward man. How does our spirit get faith that our intellect cannot obtain? Through reading and meditating on the Word. Jesus said in Matthew 4:4, *"Man shall not live by bread alone, but by every word that proceedeth out of the mouth of God."*

Jesus is speaking here of spiritual food. He is using the natural human idea—bread—to convey a spiritual thought. The Word is spirit and faith food.

The Word of God is to the spirit of man what natural food is to the body of man.

Our spirits become filled with assurance and confidence as we meditate in the Word.

For many years, I walked by faith for our finances, for all my physical needs, and while our children were small, for all of their physical needs too. After our children grew up, they had to use their own faith.

I know that the Word of God is the food that builds the spirit of man. The Word of God is the food that makes our spirits strong and that gives us quiet assurance and confidence.

We know that to believe with the heart is to believe with the spirit, the real man, or the inner man. Actually, to believe with the heart means to believe apart from what your physical body may tell you or what your physical senses may tell you.

You see, the body, the physical or outward man, believes in what he sees with his physical eyes or in what he hears with his physical ears or in what his physical feelings tell him.

But the man on the inside—the spirit or the heart of man—believes in the Word regardless of seeing, hearing, or feeling. His believing does not depend on sense knowledge; it depends on the Word of God.

Some people are prayed for again and again and again about the same situation or circumstance. I'm not saying that you shouldn't come back and be prayed for the second time for healing if you need to. I'm saying there are folks who come for prayer for the same things again and again and again. Those folks who are prayed for again and again and do not get their healing, do not have faith in the Word.

In other words, if they do not *see* that they are healed or if they do not have some *physical evidence*, they won't believe they are healed. And that's not what the Bible teaches.

They do have a natural human faith. However, natural, human faith and heart faith are two different kinds of faith. If you will believe the Word of God first, the physical evidence will take care of itself. You won't have to worry about the physical evidence or manifestation.

Our faith must be based upon what the Word says. So then to believe with all of our heart is to believe with our spirit. To believe with all of our heart is to believe independently of our heads or of our bodies.

PROVERBS 3:5

5　Trust in the Lord with all thine HEART; and lean not unto thine own understanding [or your mind].

I think most folks practice this scripture, all right, but they practice it in reverse! They trust with all of their *understanding* and lean not to their own *heart*.

It's the same thing people do with James 1:19. They practice what James tells us in verse 19, only in reverse. In his epistle James says, *"Let every man be swift to hear, slow to speak, slow to wrath"* (James 1:19). Most of us practice that, but we practice it in reverse. We are swift to speak and swift to wrath and slow to hear. But that's not what James said.

The Bible goes on to say in Proverbs, *"In all thy ways acknowledge him, and he shall direct thy paths. BE NOT WISE IN THINE OWN EYES . . ."* (Prov. 3:6–7). What the Bible is saying is this: "Don't be wise with natural human knowledge which would lead you to repudiate or to act independently of the Word of God."

Faith Casts Down Human Reasonings

Here is the counterpart to that scripture in the New Testament.

2 CORINTHIANS 10:4–5

4　(For the weapons of our warfare are not carnal, but mighty through God to the pulling down of strong holds;)

5　Casting down IMAGINATIONS [or reasonings]**, and every high thing that exalteth itself against the knowledge of God, and bringing into captivity EVERY THOUGHT to the obedience of Christ.**

I remember when I came off the bed of sickness and I went back to high school. I was just as tall as I am now and only weighed eighty-nine pounds. They called me a walking skeleton.

One day the principal of my school called me into his office and said, "Do you think you should be coming to school? All the women teachers are just scared to death that you're going to fall down dead in the classroom. They have called your doctor, and he has told them, 'Yes, that's just what he will do.' And that is just frightening them to death. In fact, I called the doctor myself, and the doctor said you didn't have any business walking two miles to school and climbing steps. He said you were just up by willpower and that he would give you ninety days at the most to live. So do you suppose you ought to be coming to school?"

I said, "Mr. Smart, I'm not up by WILLPOWER. I'm up and going by *faith*." And I told him what the Lord Jesus Christ said when He was on earth as recorded in Mark 11:24: *"Therefore I say unto you, What things soever ye desire, when ye pray, believe that ye receive them, and ye shall have them."* I didn't argue with him about divine healing. I just talked about prayer and faith.

I continued, "Mr. Smart, I believe that I have received healing for my heart and my body, and I'm not walking by willpower, I'm walking by faith."

And do you know, that man began to weep and he said, "Son, if that is what you're doing, I wouldn't stand in your way a minute. I don't understand it myself, but if you want to come to school, you just come on. I'll just talk to these teachers and they'll have to do the best they can."

I said, "I believe I have received my healing; I believe I have what I prayed for."

"Well, Son," he said, "I wouldn't put one stone in your way. I phoned your mother and asked her if she should take you out and she told me the same thing. She said, 'No, Mr. Smart, he is not up by willpower; he's walking by faith, and his faith will hold out.'"

I said, "It will, Sir." He didn't realize it but immediately he played right into the hands of the enemy himself. He did put some stones in my way.

He said, "I'm going to talk to all of your teachers, and anytime you want to, you can go out of class for a breath of fresh air or for a drink of water. Or you can just get up and go home if you want to. I give you permission ahead of time. Just don't ask anyone anything; just do what you feel like doing."

Oh, he made it so easy to fail. But you know, if I had missed one class—if I had failed to climb those steps to the schoolhouse just one time—I would have been admitting failure and been acting in doubt and my faith wouldn't have held out.

So I didn't miss one class. And I tell you, as weak as I was by the time those afternoon classes came around, it would have been easy to miss classes; but I never missed one.

I had my worst struggles and my hardest battles in the nighttime. Whether you realize it or not, the devil is a good mathematician. After I would go to bed at night, the devil would say, "You've got just so many days left, boy. Remember what the doctor said—only ninety days."

Every night the devil would tell me how many more days I had left. And I would struggle sometimes in the nighttime for hours casting down imaginations, and that is not always easy. I remember one time I don't think I slept over an hour all night long for fighting the good fight of faith.

But, thank God, it can be done by "Casting down reasonings and every high thing that exalts itself against the Word of God, and by bringing every thought into captivity to the obedience of the Word, for Christ is the Word" (2 Cor. 10:5; John 1:14).

And so in the nighttime, I would begin to think in line with what God's Word says. And I would say, "Now, Mr. Devil, I appreciate my doctor. I appreciate him highly. I appreciate him more than any of the other five doctors. He came to my house one day and sat down by my bedside and told me the truth. He said there wasn't anything he or any other doctor could do unless a Higher Power intervened." (Actually, it isn't a matter of a *Higher Power intervening*; it is a matter of *a person believing God.*)

My doctor had told me to go down the middle of the road and stay ready to go. I appreciated him for being frank with me and for telling me the truth. So I said to the devil, "I appreciate my doctor and all he's done for me. He never charged us a penny and he would come whenever my family would call him. But I'm walking in the light of the Word; and the Word says God has heard me. And the Word says I'm healed. The Word says I *have* my healing. And I believe the Word."

Walk By the Word—Not by Sight or Feelings

Now friends, this is very important: If we want to walk by faith, *the Word must be superior to everything else and anything else.* The Word must be superior to any knowledge, whether that knowledge is ours or someone else's knowledge.

We must also remember this, that when we trust God with all of our hearts, there comes a quietness and a peace into our spirits. Hebrews 4:3 says, *"For we which have believed do ENTER INTO REST."*

For example, when God says in His Word, *"My God shall supply all your need according to his riches in glory by Christ Jesus"* (Phil. 4:19), then we just simply know in our spirits that everything we need will be supplied, and we don't worry. We have no anxiety. If we're worrying, if we have anxiety, then we're not believing. Our hearts take courage as we read the Word. As we meditate in the Word, our assurance and confidence becomes deeper.

This assurance in our spirits is independent of our human reasoning or of human knowledge. That assurance may contradict human reasoning; it may even contradict physical evidence, but to believe God with your heart means to believe apart from your body or mind anyway. I practiced this as a Baptist boy and as a Full Gospel preacher and it worked. God's Word works for you whoever you are.

I remember one night after church when I was a pastor, I had turned the lights out at the side door of my church and instead of going down the steps, I just jumped down the steps and landed in the yard.

When I jumped, I landed in a rut in the ground, and when I did, I turned my ankle, and I fell to the ground in pain. In fact, my ankle popped like a gun going off and I just knew I had broken it. When I got up, I couldn't put that foot down on the ground. I couldn't walk on it at all, so I hopped over to the parsonage on one foot.

My wife said, "What's the matter?"

And I answered, "I guess I broke my ankle. I jumped out there into a rut and is it ever hurting!" I could see that the ankle was swollen, but I didn't know whether it was broken or not. However, I *could* see it was in bad shape.

I began to recall what the Word of God says. I called God's attention to the fact that my eyes could see and that my human senses told me that my ankle could be broken and that it was seriously hurt. I could sure feel it hurting and throbbing. But I called God's attention and the devil's attention to the fact that the Word of God says that I'm healed.

I know people in the natural (even some Full Gospel folks who are always in the natural realm) will think a person is strange for believing God's Word even more than their physical senses. But remember, if you want to walk by faith, the Word must be superior to everything else and anything else.

As I put God in remembrance of His Word and stood on the Word in faith, my ankle was healed. The next day I got up and drove my car nearly one hundred miles to a meeting.

And thank God, as I've continued to follow that same principle of faith, I've continued to walk in divine health these many years.

I once heard several people telling of a certain minister's testimony. When I was at his church, I had him tell his testimony firsthand.

This minister was at a youth camp, and during their recreation time they were playing ball and he slid into third base and broke his ankle. In fact, part of the bone was sticking out through the skin. Those around him said they had better get him into town to a doctor. But one of the ministers asked him if he wanted medical help or if he wanted to receive healing from God. He said he would rather receive healing from God.

"All right," this other minister said, "you can. I've been in the Pentecostal movement since the beginning," and he began to tell him about broken bones he had seen healed. That other minister sat out there next to third base and talked to that fellow for about forty minutes and got his mind off of his ankle and his foot. Then he told him to get up, and the minute he put his broken foot on the ground, he fainted and fell to the ground.

The other minister worked to revive him and talked with him another forty minutes. He got him up on his good foot again, and when he put weight on the injured foot, he fainted and fell again.

This other minister got him revived and he said, "We're missing it somewhere." So he prayed, "God, where are we missing it?" And then he said, "Oh, I see. I see it! Now, Son, this time when you get up, don't get up on your good foot. Get up on your bad foot." As he did that in faith, it never hurt a bit and instantly it was perfectly healed!

Believing with your heart is believing independent of your sense knowledge. I tell you, some of those old timers knew what faith was. Dr. Lilian B. Yeomans had this to say in one of her books and her books are some of the finest you can read on the subject of healing: "God delights in his children stepping out over the aching void with nothing underneath their feet but the Word of God." Dr. Yeomans also said that to look to see whether God is healing you is a sin.

A certain minister once told me that he was in one of Dr. Yeomans' classes when she taught in a Bible school. She always prayed for the students in her class and had healing services in her classes. He told me, "I went up and asked her to pray for me."

She responded, "What for?" She spoke very boldly and with authority.

He replied, "I want you to pray for my cold." And she said, "*Your* cold? Well, if it's *your* cold, there's no use praying for it. You've already accepted it and you won't get any healing. Now if you want to be delivered from *the devil's* cold, all right."

He said, "That's what I mean."

She responded, "Say what you mean."

This is the reason a lot of people are defeated. They *accept* defeat and claim it as theirs. But the Word says in First John 4:4 that the Greater One is in us. He rises up in us and we know we cannot be conquered. We know because we *believe* that in our hearts!

Questions for Study

1. According to Romans 10:10, with what does man believe?

   _____

   _____

2. God is a Spirit, and according to John 4:24, how must man worship Him?

   _____

   _____

3. What is the soul comprised of?

   _____

   _____

4. Why is the spirit — the real man, or the inner man — called "the hidden man of the heart"?

   _____

   _____

5. Complete the statement: With our spirit we contact the _____ realm; with our soul we contact the _____ and _____ realm; and with our physical being we contact the _____ realm.

6. Why does the Bible say that the Word of God is foolish to the natural mind?

   _____

   _____

7. In common, everyday language, what was Jesus saying in Mark 11:24 when He said, "BELIEVE that ye RECEIVE them , and ye shall HAVE them"?

   _____

   _____

8. What happens to our spirits as we meditate in the Word of God?

   _____

   _____

9. The Word of God is the _____ that makes our _____ strong and that gives us quiet assurance and confidence.

10. If we want to walk by faith, what must be superior to everything else and anything else?

    _____

    _____

Chapter 9

How to Turn Your Faith Loose—Part 1

For with the HEART man believeth unto right-eousness; and with the mouth CONFESSION is made unto salvation.

—Romans 10:10

For verily I say unto you, That whosoever shall say unto this mountain, Be thou removed, and be thou cast into the sea; and shall not doubt in his heart, but shall believe that those things which he saith shall come to pass; he shall have whatsoever he saith.

—Mark 11:23

In the *last* two lessons we talked about the first part of Romans 10:10—about what it means to believe with the heart.

Now let's look at the latter part of this verse: *"With the mouth CONFESSION is made unto salvation."*

Four Kinds of Confession

You will find four kinds of confessions spoken of in the New Testament. Let's examine these closely because there is much confused thought in regard to the subject of *confession.*

The Jews' Confession of Sin

First, there is the teaching of John the Baptist and Jesus' teaching to the Jews which was *the confession of their sins.*

MARK 1:4–5
4 John did baptize in the wilderness, and preach the baptism of repentance for the remission of sins.

5 And there went out unto him all the land of Judaea, and they of Jerusalem, and were all baptized of him in the river of Jordan, CONFESSING THEIR SINS.

MARK 1:14–15
14 Now after that John was put in prison, Jesus came into Galilee, preaching the gospel of the kingdom of God,

15 And saying, The time is fulfilled, and the kingdom of God is at hand: repent ye, and believe the gospel.

The Confession of the Sinner Under the New Covenant

Second, there is the *confession of the sinner under the New Covenant.* Jesus made a very important statement in the New Testament in John 16:7–11 concerning the sinner under the New Covenant.

JOHN 16:7–11
7 Nevertheless I tell you the truth; It is expedient for you that I go away: for if I go not away, the Comforter will not come unto you; but if I depart, I will send him unto you.

8 And when he is come, HE WILL REPROVE THE WORLD OF SIN, and of righteousness, and of judgment:

9 Of sin, BECAUSE THEY BELIEVE NOT ON ME;

10 Of righteousness, because I go to my Father, and ye see me no more;

11 Of judgment, because the prince of this world is judged.

Notice Jesus said, *"Of sin, because they believe not on me"* (v. 9). Jesus tells us that the sinner will be convicted by the Holy Spirit of but one sin, and that is the sin of rejecting Jesus: *"because they believe not on me [Jesus]"* (John 16:9).

How many times we've insisted that the sinner confess all the sins he's ever committed in order to be saved. Actually, the sinner *couldn't* confess all the sins he's ever committed. He couldn't even think of everything he's ever done that was wrong. No, the main confession the sinner must make is the Lordship of Jesus.

ROMANS 10:9
9 That if thou shalt confess with thy mouth the Lord Jesus, and shalt believe in thine heart that God hath raised him from the dead, thou shalt be saved.

The Believer's Confession of His Sins

The third confession in the New Testament is the *believer's confession of his sins when he is out of fellowship with God* (1 John 1:9). That broken fellowship many times may cause sickness, because in James the Bible said, *"Confess your faults one to another, and pray one for another, THAT YE MAY BE HEALED"* (James 5:16).

The Believer's Confession of Faith

The fourth kind of confession spoken of in the Bible is the *confession of our faith in the Word, in Christ, and in God the Father.* These are the four kinds of confessions that we are going to discuss in this chapter.

It is important that we make the distinction here between the confession of sins of the Jews under the Old Covenant to whom Jesus and John the Baptist were talking, and the confession of sins of the sinner under the New Covenant who has never met Christ.

MATTHEW 3:5–6

5   Then went out to him [John] **Jerusalem, and all Judaea, and all the region round about Jordan,**

6   And were baptized of him in Jordan, CONFESSING THEIR SINS.

Here is the picture of God's covenant people confessing their sins and being baptized by John. This is not Christian baptism. Jesus had not yet died and risen. John did not baptize in the Name of the Father and the Son and the Holy Ghost; he only baptized in the Name of the Father. These were Jews under the Law, and under the Old Covenant, before Jesus' death, burial, and resurrection.

In Acts 19:18 we read, *"And many that believed came, and confessed, and shewed their deeds."* These were Gentiles or non-Jewish Christians. It doesn't say what they confessed, but it is evident that they were believers who were confessing their sins of practicing magical arts.

But now I want you to notice something. They were not confessing these sins in order to get saved. They were already saved. These Gentile Christians didn't confess these sins, nor did they give up these practices in order to get saved. The Bible says they were already saved. But you see, after they were saved, those sins and wrong practices were easier to confess.

So many times people have gotten the cart before the horse. For example, they tell sinners, "You are going to have to quit this, and you are going to have to quit that in order to be saved." But actually, the sinner must accept the Lordship of Jesus, and then those other things will take care of themselves.

Salvation Not Based on What You Give Up

A Foursquare missionary told me that through his denomination, in just a span of a few years in the 1950s in Brazil, 268,000 people were saved and nearly 100,000 were baptized in the Holy Ghost, with the evidence of speaking with other tongues. In one year's time, these particular missionaries built more than one hundred churches. That's revival, especially when you realize that ninety-nine percent of the people to whom they were preaching were Roman Catholic.

This missionary said to me, "I spent seven years in Brazil as a missionary where we had a little mission station. Our highest attendance in Sunday School was only thirty-seven, and after seven years of that I came home discouraged.

"Then I went back to Brazil, and I began to give some time to God's Word and to fasting and prayer. Fasting also gave me more time to wait upon God in prayer. As I waited on God, I didn't preach *against* anything; I didn't tell people what they had to give up in order to be saved. I just began to preach what the Word says."

The missionary continued, "The Catholics had one song about the blood of Jesus, so we adopted this as our theme song and started tent meetings. When the Brazilian people, who were largely Catholic, heard us singing this song, they thought we were Catholic and they came to the tent meeting by the droves. They would ask us if we were Catholic and we would say, 'Yes, but not Roman Catholic.'"

The missionary explained, "After all, we are Catholic in the sense that we believe there is just one Church. The word 'catholic' means *general, or universal Christian church.* There is but one Church, the Church of the Lord Jesus Christ. I just didn't say *Roman* Catholic! But because we preached the Word and didn't preach against anyone's religion or what people had to give up, we saw people saved by the droves."

This missionary said, "For example, I remember one woman in her early sixties came to me after she was saved and had received the Holy Ghost, and said she wanted to talk to me. She said, 'Since I've come here and have been filled with the Holy Ghost, I just can't get anything out of Mass. In fact, I hardly ever go anymore. I think I'll just quit altogether. What do you suggest?'"

The missionary answered, "I don't have any suggestions. Just follow your own convictions and let the Lord lead you."

He said, "A few days later she told me she had just stacked up all those icons, and had thrown them in the trash can, and had quit going to Mass. She said, 'I think I'll come over and join your church.'

"I replied, 'You are welcome if the Lord leads you that way.'"

The way this missionary handled this situation was much better than trying to tell this woman what to do; he allowed her to be led by the Holy Spirit Who is her Guide (John 16:13).

I believe we would do a lot better if we just used a little wisdom in some of these areas. We don't need to fight anyone, nor tell people what they have to give up; we just need to preach the Word and tell them what to believe and confess—that Jesus is Lord!

I remember back in 1942, I read an article in *The Pentecostal Evangel* about a minister who had won many Roman Catholics to Christ here in America. Many were wanting to know his technique, so his testimony was printed in this periodical.

He said, "In the first place, I never tell people they are wrong about anything. It does no good to argue over religion. You are just wasting your time."

Then he said, "I just find some place where I can hook up in agreement with people. I get their attention by telling them I believe in Mary more than they do. They don't understand that and they want it explained to them."

He said, "I turn to the Book of Acts and I show them that Mary went to the upper room and was filled with the Holy Ghost. I tell them, 'I followed Mary up there to the upper room, and I've been filled with the Holy Spirit, speaking with tongues too.'"

He said, "Just as soon as Catholics see that Mary was baptized in the Holy Spirit, they are ready to receive that experience too! I don't tell them they are going to have to be saved first; I just tell them to get on their knees, and they don't mind kneeling, so we pray. I have them pray the sinner's prayer first and then I pray them right on through to the baptism in the Holy Ghost with the evidence of speaking with other tongues!"

This missionary used wisdom, didn't he? The Bible says we need to be as wise as serpents and harmless as doves (Matt. 10:16). He didn't preach to people what they had to give up in order to get saved; he just preached Jesus to them.

At the last church I pastored, I visited a couple's home, and the wife was saved, but the husband wasn't. So I invited him to church. He said, "No, I'm not going," although he had gone to church some before. But he was so antagonistic, I thought maybe I had said or done something that displeased him, so I apologized.

He said, "Oh, no, Brother Hagin, it isn't you. I didn't mean it that way. I'll tell you why I'm not going to church. When I go to church I get under conviction."

I said, "That is what we want you to do."

He said, "My wife just this morning at the table asked me why I didn't give up this and that and get saved. She doesn't know it, but for weeks at a time I have given up those things, and I always go back to them. I've tried it and there's no use in my coming to church. I just can't seem to give those things up."

The Confession the Sinner Makes

However, the real truth about it was that he didn't have to give up anything or quit anything in order to get saved. In Romans 10:9, it tells us how to get saved. It says, *"If thou shalt CONFESS WITH THY MOUTH THE LORD JESUS, and shalt believe in thine heart that God hath raised him from the dead, thou shalt be saved."*

Notice it says, *"That if thou shalt CONFESS"* (Rom. 10:9).

This is the real confession the sinner makes. He has served Satan. He is guilty of only one sin in the sight of God and that is the sin of rejecting Jesus Christ as Savior and Lord. Therefore, God demands that the sinner confess the Lordship of Jesus Christ. This is real repentance. This is real faith.

To demand that a sinner confess his sins before God can make him a new creature is just as sensible as it would be for the governor of a state to say to a prisoner behind bars, "I'm going to parole you, if you will confess that you are in prison." The fact that a prisoner is in prison is a self-evident fact.

And it is a self-evident fact that the sinner is a child of the devil. The thing that the sinner *must* confess is the Lordship of Christ. He must confess Jesus as His Savior in order to be saved. He must let Jesus dominate his daily life. Confessing the Lordship of Jesus is the very heart of the gospel.

Once a person is born again, God will deal with him about the things he needs to change and will give him the power to change them.

Now notice again the phrase, *"thou shalt confess with thy mouth the Lord Jesus . . ."* (Rom. 10:9). In other words, there must be a vocal confession by a person of the Lordship of Jesus—his lips must frame the words. That confession is not only for his own sake, but it is for the sake of those unsaved people in the world around us, and it is for the benefit of

Satan, declaring that you are no longer under his dominion (Eph. 1:19–21).

I remember many years ago I was preaching in Dallas in a Full Gospel church, and one man said to me, "Brother Hagin, I wish you could pray with a man who has been coming to our early morning prayer meetings. The men in our church meet to pray before they go to work each day, and this man has been coming five days a week for six months and is still unsaved. I think you could help him."

Since the men worked during the day, of course, they couldn't come to the day services, so I agreed to have a teaching class on Saturday nights for several weeks just for the men. On the first night, I was introduced to this man they wanted me to help. He had his Bible with him.

The moment I looked at him, I knew by the Holy Spirit exactly what was wrong with him. There were a few testimonies while everyone was getting settled, and then I said to this man, "Get up and testify and confess that you are saved."

That startled him and he looked around and stammered and stuttered and finally said, "Well, I'm not saved yet."

I said, "I know it. You've got your Bible there in your hand. Open it to Romans 10:9 and 10 and read that aloud." And he read the following verses:

ROMANS 10:9–10

9 That if thou shalt confess with thy mouth the Lord Jesus, and shalt believe in thine heart that God hath raised him from the dead, thou shalt be saved.

10 For with the heart man believeth unto righteousness; and with the mouth confession is made unto salvation.

I said, "Read that last clause again."

And he read, *"and with the mouth confession is made unto salvation"* (v. 10).

I said, "Certainly you can't be saved until you *confess*. And it is with the mouth that confession is made unto your salvation. Now stand and confess that you are saved."

"Well," he said, "I don't *feel* like I'm saved."

I said, "Certainly, you don't. You can't feel something that you don't have, and you can't have it until you confess it."

He said, "Well, I don't much believe I want to do that."

I said, "If I understand it correctly you've been coming to this church and praying for six months."

He said, "Yes, I sure have. I've wept and cried and have repented and called upon the Lord up and down these aisles for six months."

"All you lack," I said, "is standing on this verse. That's why I want you to stand up and confess that you are saved."

"No, I don't much believe I will," he said.

Then I actually startled myself (I sometimes do things by the Spirit of God that startle me). Before I knew it, the Spirit of God motivated me, and I found myself pointing my finger at him and saying, "I command you to stand and confess your salvation in the Name of the Lord Jesus Christ."

I spoke with such anointing and authority that he got up from there immediately and looked around about half-scared.

He said, "Well, I do believe these verses, that Jesus died for my sins and that He was raised from the dead. God raised Him up for my justification, so I just take Him as my Savior and confess Him as my Lord." Then he sat down real quickly.

To get the attention away from him, I had another man testify. Several others testified and I looked back over at this man and his face was just lighted up like a neon sign in the dark.

"Now," I said, "stand up and testify."

This time I didn't have to ask the second time. He leaped up to his feet and shouted and said, "You know, when I said that, something happened down inside of me."

I said, "Sure something happened on the inside of you. Eternal life was imparted to your spirit."

You see, with the mouth confession is made unto salvation (Rom. 10:10). That is the confession that the sinner is to make.

MATTHEW 10:32–33

32 Whosoever therefore shall CONFESS ME before men, him will I confess also before my Father which is in heaven.

33 But whosoever shall deny me before men, him will I also deny before my Father which is in heaven.

I want you to notice that in the new birth—in receiving eternal life—there must be public confession. Public confession is really making the break with the world. It is a change of lordship; it defines our position. The confession of the Lordship of Jesus puts us immediately under Jesus' supervision, care, and protection.

Satan was once our lord, but we changed lords. When we take Jesus as our Savior and confess Him, Jesus becomes our Lord. Jesus becomes our Head and Master. So let's hold fast to the confession of the Lordship of Jesus.

He is my Lord. Is He your Lord? Not only confess Jesus' Lordship to yourself, and not only confess it to the devil, but Jesus also said to confess it before men: *"Whosoever therefore shall confess me BEFORE MEN"* (Matt. 10:32). So confess the Lordship of Jesus before others too.

The Believer Confessing His Sins

Notice that the third kind of confession that is spoken of in the New Testament is of the believer confessing his sin when he has broken fellowship. In Psalm 137 we see a type of broken fellowship.

PSALM 137:1–4

1 By the rivers of Babylon, there we sat down, yea, we wept, when we remembered Zion.

2 We hanged our harps upon the willows in the midst thereof.

3 For there they that carried us away captive required of us a song; and they that wasted us required of us mirth, saying, Sing us one of the songs of Zion.

4 How shall we sing the Lord's song in a strange land?

In Psalm 137 we see that Israel had sinned. They were carried away into captivity in Babylon. They could remember Zion, of course. Their harps were hung on the willows and when their enemies asked for a song, they cried, *"How shall we sing the Lord's song in a strange land?"* (Ps. 137:4). This is a picture of broken fellowship.

Friends, we as Christians lose our testimony the moment we sin. Sin always puts the light out.

Faith has no song when fellowship is broken!

1 JOHN 1:3–10

3 That which we have seen and heard declare we unto you, that ye also may have FELLOWSHIP with us: and truly our FELLOWSHIP is with the Father, and with his Son Jesus Christ.

4 And these things write we unto you, that your joy may be full.

5 This then is the message which we have heard of him, and declare unto you, that God is light, and in him is no darkness at all.

6 If we say we have FELLOWSHIP with him, and walk in darkness, we lie, and do not the truth:

7 But if we walk in the light, as he is in the light, we have FELLOWSHIP one with another, and the blood of Jesus Christ his Son cleanseth us from all sin.

8 If we say that we have no sin, we deceive ourselves, and the truth is not in us.

9 If we confess our sins, he is faithful and just to forgive us our sins, and to cleanse us from all unrighteousness.

10 If we say that we have not sinned, we make him a liar, and his word is not in us.

Notice that the word "fellowship" is mentioned four times in these verses. Read these verses carefully and go over them again and again. They are not written to sinners. Don't ever use these verses in praying with a sinner; they don't belong to him.

These words are written to the believer. (First, as a warning against broken fellowship.) Second, these scriptures show the believer the way back into fellowship. If we say we have fellowship with the Lord and yet we walk in darkness, the Bible says we lie and do not tell the truth (1 John 1:6).

In other words, God is saying that if I'm out of fellowship and I declare that I am spiritually all right, I'm not telling the truth because I'm not all right with God. If I say I have not committed sin, and yet my fellowship with God is broken, then my faith is feeble.

Then God says if I confess my sins, He is faithful and just to forgive my sins and to cleanse me from all unrighteousness (1 John 1:9). It is important not to take verses of scripture out of their setting. Some people take verse 10, which says, *"If we say that we have not sinned, we make him a liar, and his word is not in us,"* out of its setting. Don't take that verse out and try to apply it to everyone. This verse is talking about the person who has been born again but who is out of fellowship with God and won't admit it.

Let me say this, friends. If you've sinned, you know it. And if you don't know it, for goodness' sake, don't be trying to drag up something to condemn yourself with. When you are always looking for something to condemn yourself with, you are robbing yourself of faith. If you sin you know it. The minute you sin, you know it on the inside of you; and if you don't know it, then you need to get saved.

Christians have a "monitor"—the voice of our conscience—on the inside of each of us, and it lets us know when we've done wrong. If you miss the mark and mess up in some way, don't wait to repent; stop right then and say, "Lord, I missed it. Please forgive me."

He'll do it, and then you can just keep walking in fellowship. *"If we confess our sins, he is faithful and just to forgive us our sins, and to cleanse us from all unrighteousness"* (1 John 1:9). If I confess my sins once, that moment He forgives me and I can stand in His Presence as though I had never sinned.

Once you confess a sin, don't keep confessing the same sins over and over again because that only builds weakness, doubt, and sin-consciousness into your spirit. If you confessed your sin once, God forgave you and He forgot it, so you need to forget it. God forgave you and He forgot it, so you need to forget it. God has no memory of your sin once you truly repent and ask for forgiveness.

ISAIAH 43:25

25 I, even I, am he that blotteth out thy transgressions . . . and will not remember thy sins.

Once you repent and ask forgiveness, God does not have any memory of the sin that broke your fellowship. Since God has no memory of it, then why should you have memory of it? That isn't the Holy Spirit or God who is condemning you. That is Satan trying to take advantage of you; and if Satan can keep you thinking about that sin, he has you at a disadvantage.

The thing you must do is refuse to think upon that sin any longer. If you continue to condemn yourself once you have asked for forgiveness, your faith will be throttled and held in bondage.

PSALM 103:1–3

1 Bless the Lord, O my soul: and all that is within me, bless his holy name.
2 Bless the Lord, O my soul, and forget not all his benefits:
3 Who FORGIVETH ALL THINE INIQUITIES; who healeth all thy diseases.

I hear Christians say, "I don't know if God will hear me or not when I pray." People come wanting me to pray for them. They don't know whether God will hear them or not because they have sinned and they have failed.

But if they have repented, God doesn't remember that they've done anything wrong!

ISAIAH 43:25

25 I, even I, am he that blotteth out thy transgressions for mine own sake, and will not remember thy sins.

ISAIAH 1:18

18 Come now, and let us reason together, saith the Lord: though your sins be as scarlet, they shall be as white as snow; though they be red like crimson, they shall be as wool.

PSALM 103:12

12 As far as the east is from the west, so far hath he removed our transgressions from us.

Can't you see with what confidence, faith, and boldness we can come to Him?

Someone said, "How does God forgive and wash my sins clean?" I don't know how He does it, but, thank God, He does it! You can't figure God out. He's too big! Let's just rejoice in the truth.

So many people have talked themselves right out of faith. There's no need for that. If we have sinned and have asked God to forgive us, then He did and He forgot it and we should too.

What I'm saying is this: The believer must be willing to forgive himself just as the Father God is willing to forgive him. Many people have robbed themselves of faith because they are not willing to forgive themselves. They hold themselves in a state of condemnation and it robs them of their faith.

JAMES 5:14–15

14 Is any sick among you? let him call for the elders of the church; and let them pray over him, anointing him with oil in the name of the Lord:
15 And the prayer of faith shall save the sick, and the Lord shall raise him up; and IF HE HAVE COMMITTED SINS, THEY SHALL BE FORGIVEN HIM.

I have used this scripture for years in preaching divine healing, trying to get through to people that it is God's will to heal them. But most of us have never really read that last clause: *"and if he have committed sins, they SHALL BE forgiven him."*

However, a short time ago, I was praying about a certain man and I knew this man was involved in sin. In fact, I knew that he just kept stumbling over the same sin, doing the same thing again and again. As I was praying about this fellow, I said to the Lord, "I don't know about this fellow. After all, he's committed the same sin over and over again."

As I said this, the Lord said to me, "In the first place, do you think that I would require and ask you to do something that I wouldn't do?"

I said, "Why, no, Lord, certainly not."

The Lord continued, "Didn't you ever read in My Word where Peter said, *'Lord, how oft shall my brother sin against me, and I forgive him? till seven times?'"* (Matt. 18:21). Then I understood what the Lord meant.

The Lord said, "I said to Peter, 'Not up to seven times, but seventy *times* seven.'" (That is four hundred and ninety times!)

Then Jesus said, "Would I require you to do something that I wouldn't do?"

I said, "No, that would be unjust, and You're not unjust."

"Well," the Lord said. "I'll forgive the man; you go ahead and pray with him."

Then sometimes we may think about a person, "Yes, he's done wrong; he's going to reap results of his wrongdoing. In fact, he's sick now because he's done wrong." And sometimes broken fellowship *will* cause sickness. But the Word of the God says, *"and if he have committed sins, they shall be forgiven him"* (James 5:15).

I'll be honest with you, the revelation of that gave me fresh encouragement to be able to help others because I've seen too many people talk themselves right out of faith due to condemnation about the past. They think they are going to lie there on the bed of sickness because they have failed and sinned. But, oh, thank God, the Bible says, *"the prayer of faith shall save [or heal] the sick, and the Lord shall raise him up; and if he have committed sins, they shall be forgiven him"* (James 5:15).

There is healing in forgiveness. Can you see that? That's almost too much for us humans to comprehend sometimes, but thank God for His grace. His grace is beyond our human comprehension.

I remember sometime ago I was preaching at a convention and in the day service I was teaching along this line. The district superintendent of a particular denomination said to me, "You know, Brother Hagin, there was a time when I wouldn't have agreed with what you are teaching. But I remember before I became superintendent we were working in a new church we had built and we only had one man in the church. The women were carrying the burden and doing what they could to keep up the payments on the building. The only man in the church was the owner of a business. He was financially better off than anyone else in the church, but the most he ever gave was about a dollar a week. We needed his support so terribly."

The superintendent continued, "About two o'clock one morning the telephone rang and it was this man on the line. He said to me, 'Just before closing time yesterday I broke my ankle. The man next door is here with me and I was talking to him about healing. He's Roman Catholic but he told me he thought if I would call you and have you come and pray for me, God would heal me.'

"Well," this district superintendent said, "there I was. I was just sure God wouldn't heal this fellow because he was so unfaithful and stingy. In fact, I felt like saying to him, 'Brother, God's not going to heal you,' and then just hanging up on him. But I couldn't do that.

"So I got dressed and went over to his house and went in, and he introduced me to the Catholic man. The Catholic man told me that he believed God could do anything. Before I realized what was happening, I was kneeling at the foot of that bed, laying hands on the man's ankle, which was in a cast, and I was declaring, 'God heal him now in the Name of Jesus Christ!' And I knew in my spirit he was healed.

"I stood there and watched as that man cut his cast off and jumped out of bed on that ankle and instantly walked!"

The district superintendent said, "That night I couldn't sleep." *How come God healed him?* I kept wondering. Then I remembered, *'the Lord shall raise him up; and if he have committed sins, they shall be forgiven him'* (James 5:15). God knew more about the man and his situation than I did. I knew the fellow had prayed and had asked God to forgive him because I heard him doing that while I was praying for his ankle. I heard him praying, 'Dear God, forgive me of every wrong.'"

Isn't it wonderful that God is merciful? This superintendent continued his story, "About that time, I left that church. The church continued to grow, but the war came and about half the people moved away. So it looked as though the district office was going to have to make the payments on the property. But this man stepped forward and said, 'I'll make the payments.' During the war, he paid more than $4,000 on that property.

"Several years after the war, the church finally paid the mortgage off and they invited me down for the burning of the mortgage papers. I said to the church board, 'You ought to pay this man back, because after all he has put a lot of money into this property, and I understand you have quite a bit on hand financially.'

"This fellow replied, 'No, I'll just be happy with about half that much.' Then he told the church secretary, 'When you make that check out, just make it out to the home missions department for this district.'"

This superintendent told me, "I sincerely repented for acting the way I did about having to go and pray for that man."

You see, friends, it makes all the difference in the world whether we look at things the way the Word of God says, or the way we think things should be. Oh, when we can see things God's way, what a big difference it makes! *If he have committed sins, they shall be forgiven him* (James 5:15).

When you understand the Bible, you can understand why God does things the way He does. You can understand why and how things work many times. Let me finish this lesson with a scripture found in Hebrews.

HEBREWS 10:1-4

1 For the law having a shadow of good things to come, and not the very image of the things, can never with those sacrifices which they offered year by year continually make the comers thereunto perfect.

2 For then would they not have ceased to be offered? because that the worshippers once purged should have had no more conscience of sins.

3 But in those sacrifices there is a remembrance again made of sins every year.

4 For it is not possible that the blood of bulls and of goats should take away sins.

This passage of Scripture tells of the failure of the blood of bulls and goats under the Old Covenant to take away sins. The blood of bulls and goats could only cover sins. Those animal sacrifices still left the sin in the heart of man. And with the sin was sin consciousness.

But God, in our redemption in Christ, has redeemed us from sin consciousness. Once we have asked forgiveness for our sins, we don't ever have to remember them again.

HEBREWS 9:14

14 How much more shall the blood of Christ, who through the eternal Spirit offered himself without spot to God, PURGE YOUR CONSCIENCE from dead works to serve the living God?

1 JOHN 1:9

9 If we confess our sins, he is faithful and just to forgive us our sins, and to CLEANSE US from all unrighteousness.

If you sin, and you repent and confess your sin to God, you should have no more remembrance of it. God doesn't, so why should you? Then you can see with what confidence we can come before God in prayer and know with a *certainty* that He hears us.

Questions for Study

1. What are the four kinds of confessions spoken of in the New Testament?

   _____

   _____

2. What is the main confession a sinner must make?

   _____

   _____

3. What may be caused by a believer's broken fellowship with God?

   _____

   _____

4. Why did John baptize only in the Name of the Father?

   _____

   _____

5. What one sin is the sinner guilty of?

   _____

   _____

6. What is the very heart of the Gospel?

   _____

   _____

7. Once a person is born again, what will God do with him?

   _____

   _____

8. What is another name for the "monitor" that Christians have on the inside of them to let them know when they've done wrong?

   _____

   _____

9. Why shouldn't you keep confessing the same sins over and over again?

   _____

   _____

10. What will happen to your faith if you continue to condemn yourself once you have asked for forgiveness?

   _____

   _____

Chapter 10

How to Turn Your Faith Loose—Part 2

For with the heart man believeth unto righteousness; and with the mouth confession is made unto salvation.

—Romans 10:10

For verily I say unto you, That whosoever shall say unto this mountain, Be thou removed, and be thou cast into the sea; and shall not doubt in his heart, but shall believe that those things which he saith shall come to pass; he shall have whatsoever he saith.

—Mark 11:23

We have covered lessons on what it means to believe with the heart. Now we are going to learn how to *activate* our faith—or how to turn our faith loose.

Believing Plus Confessing Equals Activated Faith

Notice the latter part of Romans 10:10: *"with the mouth confession is made UNTO. . . ."* The text says that with the mouth confession is made unto salvation. But that's not only true concerning salvation, it is true concerning anything else you receive from God. Everything you receive from God comes the same way—through *faith*.

For example, it's with the *heart* that man believes when it comes to receiving healing, and it's with the *mouth* that confession is made unto healing.

It is with the *heart* that man believes when it comes to receiving the baptism of the Holy Spirit, and it is with the *mouth* that confession is made unto this Pentecostal experience.

Whatever it is that you receive from God, it is done the same way—through faith. Faith is activated by *believing* with your *heart* and *confessing* with your *mouth*.

Notice the text in Mark 11:23.

MARK 11:23

23 For verily I say unto you, That whosoever shall SAY unto this mountain, Be thou removed, and be thou cast into the sea; and shall not doubt in his heart, but shall BELIEVE [that is, BELIEVE in his heart] **that those things which he SAITH shall come to pass; he shall have whatsoever he SAITH.**

One day as I was reading that verse and meditating on it, the Holy Ghost brought to my attention that in this text Jesus mentions *believing* one time, and He mentions *saying* three times. Then the Lord said to me, "You will have to do three times as much preaching about the *saying* part as you do about the *believing* part. Folks are not missing it primarily in the *believing* part; they are missing it in the *saying* part."

You have to say with your mouth what you believe in your heart if the Word is to work for you. Nowhere in the Bible does it teach that if you just believe in your heart, you'll get an answer. But it does teach that if you *believe* with your heart and *say* what you believe with your mouth, whatever you want from God's Word shall come to pass in your life. Romans 10:8–10 also shows us this faith principle.

ROMANS 10:8–10

8 But what saith it? The word is nigh thee, even in thy MOUTH, and in thy heart: that is, the word of FAITH, which we preach;

9 That if thou shalt CONFESS with thy MOUTH the Lord Jesus, and shalt BELIEVE in thine HEART that God hath raised him from the dead, thou shalt be saved.

10 For with the HEART man BELIEVETH unto righteousness; and with the mouth CONFESSION is made unto SALVATION.

Now notice in verse 8 that the word of faith must be in your mouth as well as in your heart for faith to work for you. If the Word is only in your heart, it won't work. But when faith is in both your heart *and* in your mouth, thank God, your faith will work!

Right Thinking, Believing, and Confessing

Romans 10:10 says, *". . . with the MOUTH confession is made unto. . . ."* In this lesson, I want to discuss right *thinking* and right *believing* and right *confessing*. What you *think* and what you *believe* will affect your confession—what you *say*.

If your thinking is right, your believing will be right because what you meditate on will eventually get down into your heart. And you will begin to believe what you have been meditating upon. If your believing is right then your confessing will be right. But if any one of the three is wrong—your thinking, your believing, or your confessing—then all three of them will be wrong.

God has given us His Word to get our thinking straightened out. And when we think in line with God's Word, our believing will be right. When we are believing right, then what we say with our mouths will be right.

The Positive Side of Confession

I'm sure of this one thing: Very few Christians have actually realized and recognized the place that confession holds in the scheme of things. And it is to be regretted that whenever we use the word "confession," folks invariably think of confessing sins, weaknesses, and failures. That is the negative side of confession, but there is a positive side. And the Bible has more to say about the positive side of confession than it does about the negative side.

'Confession' Defined

The dictionary says that "to confess" means *to acknowledge* or *to own up to* or *to acknowledge faith in*. It also means *to make confession of one's faults*. But remember, one definition is *to make confession of one's faith* or to acknowledge faith in God's Word.

If we just live on one side of this confession subject—the negative side—and constantly confess our faults and failures, and that's all we ever confess, then we are going to grow to be lopsided in our Christian life. This will build weakness and sin and failure-consciousness into our spirits.

Actually, Christianity is called "The Great Confession." Confessing is actually three things:

1. Confession is stating something we believe.

2. Confession is declaring something we know to be true.

3. Confession is proclaiming a truth we've accepted wholeheartedly.

In other words, your confession is a proclamation of what you know to be true. Your confession states what you believe. Your confession declares something you know. And your confession proclaims a truth you have accepted wholeheartedly.

What Are We to Confess?

The major problem for us in this area is to know *what* we are to confess. Our confession needs to center around these principal truths:

1. What God has done for us through Christ in His plan of salvation.

2. What God has done in us by the Word and the Holy Ghost in the new birth and the infilling of the Holy Ghost.

3. Who we are to God the Father in Christ Jesus.

4. What Jesus is presently doing for us at the right hand of the Father where He ever lives to make intercession for us.

5. What God can accomplish through us, or what His Word will accomplish through us as we proclaim it.

Confessing Who We Are *in Christ*

People ask me about methods of studying the Bible, and I suggest to believers everywhere I go that they read through the New Testament, primarily the epistles which are written to the Church, and underline with a red pencil or write down the scriptures that have the expression "in Him," "in Christ," or "in whom," referring to Jesus.

The moment you find these scriptures, begin to confess that this is who you are and what you have. If you'll do that, I'll guarantee you that before many days, life will be different for you.

I'm going to give you a few sample scriptures to get you headed in that direction. Then you will have to find the rest on your own because we couldn't cover all of them (there are approximately 133 or 134 of them). When you find these scriptures, begin to confess that they are a reality in your life.

I will cover a few scriptures that we should confess of who we are in Christ. We should confess these scriptures not only before God, but before the world.

New Creatures in Christ

2 CORINTHIANS 5:17

17 Therefore if any man be IN CHRIST [there's the expression "in Christ"]**, he is a NEW CREATURE: old things are passed away; behold, all things are become new.**

What a revolutionary truth this scripture is for the Church to teach, believe, and confess! We are new creatures in Christ Jesus. We are *not* just forgiven sinners. We are *not* poor, weak, staggering, sinning, "barely-getting-along" church members. That is *not* who we are. We are *new creatures*, created by God in Christ Jesus.

Paul said, writing to the Church in Ephesus, that we are created by God in Christ Jesus (Eph. 2:10). Therefore, we are new creatures created in Christ Jesus with the life of God, the nature of God, and the ability of God in us.

Second Corinthians 5:17 has always been one of my favorite scriptures and I believe one reason for that is when I was raised up off the bed of sickness, I began to tell everyone everywhere I went that I was a new creature in Christ Jesus.

I was a young seventeen-year-old Baptist boy, but I never had the problems that so many young people have had and do have. That's simply because I was quick to tell everyone, "I am a new creature in Christ," and I was quick to witness and to testify of my salvation. You see, the more you talk about the new birth, the more real the new creation becomes to you because that's *who* you are and that's *what* you are.

I remember one time when I was just a young Baptist boy, preaching in the jails and on the streets and working in the church, a young fellow came up to me one night. I had gone to town and was standing on the corner when he came along and said, "Kenneth, would you do me a favor?"

I knew this fellow belonged to a church, all right. He belonged to the same kind of church I did but I'm sorry to say, if he had ever been saved, I didn't know it. And neither did anyone else, judging by the way he lived. And in talking to him, he said he had never been saved, but that he had just joined the church. (There's a difference between joining the church and being saved.)

Anyway, this young fellow said to me, "Would you do me a favor? I wouldn't ask you, but I'm already running late."

He continued, "You know my girlfriend, don't you?" I did, and I knew that he and his girlfriend were just about two of the meanest and toughest people I knew.

He said, "My girlfriend's cousin is visiting, and I promised my girlfriend that I would bring a date for her cousin, but I haven't been able to get anyone."

He added, "Her cousin is not like my girl," because he knew if she were, I wouldn't agree to the date.

He asked, "Would you come along and help me out of this jam? I'll be grateful, and I promise we won't stay very long—thirty or forty minutes at the most. Then we'll leave. There won't be any drinking or dancing, and I won't even smoke a cigarette while we're there."

I finally agreed and went along to help him out. When we got to his girlfriend's house, she introduced me to her cousin. We had barely gotten there when they started dancing, and the cousin asked me to dance. I said, "No, I don't dance."

Her eyes got big and she said, "Why not?"

I said, "Because I'm a new creature."

She asked, "What do you mean, you're a new creature?"

I said, "Well, in Second Corinthians 5:17 it says, *'Therefore if any man be in Christ, he is a new creature: old things are passed away; behold, all things are become new.'* There was a time when I was interested in things like you folks are interested in, but since then I've been made a new creature in Christ Jesus."

While that music record was playing on that player, I preached this cousin under conviction, and she began to cry. When the record stopped, the other boy and girl saw I had her under conviction, and he said, "Let's go." He was ready to take me home immediately!

I didn't care where it was, whether it was in the home, on the streets, or in school, I told everyone that I was a new creature in Christ Jesus.

Friends, if we'll confess that, it will make all the difference in our lives. I wasn't tempted by the things of the world because I constantly confessed, "I am a new creature in Christ Jesus."

In Whom We Have Redemption

Here is another "in Him" or "in whom" scripture.

EPHESIANS 1:7–8
7 IN WHOM [in Christ] **we have REDEMPTION THROUGH HIS BLOOD, the forgiveness of sins, according to the riches of his grace;**
8 Wherein he hath abounded toward us in all wisdom and prudence.

I want you to notice the first part of verse 7, *"In whom we have. . . ."* Notice the expressions "in whom" and "we have." Thank God, we are not trying to get redemption; we *have* it. We are not *going* to have it some time in the future; we have it now—present tense. What is it that we have now in Him or in Christ? *Redemption.* That means that Satan's dominion over our lives has been broken!

Satan lost his dominion over your life the moment you became a new creature. In the new birth, you received a new lord, Jesus Christ (Col. 1:13). Now Jesus Christ is to reign over your life. Satan was your lord, but now Jesus is your Lord. Romans 10:9 says, *"That if thou shalt confess with thy mouth the Lord Jesus* [or Jesus as Lord] *. . . thou shalt be saved."*

Satan's dominion ended and Jesus' dominion began the moment you were born again. *"In whom* [Jesus Christ] *we have redemption . . ."* (Eph. 1:7). From what and from whom are we redeemed? Many times people say, "Thank God, I'm redeemed from sin." That's a part of the story, but not nearly all of it.

Redeemed From the Curse of the Law

GALATIANS 3:13

13 Christ hath REDEEMED US FROM THE CURSE OF THE LAW, being made a curse for us: for it is written, Cursed is every one that hangeth on a tree.

We are redeemed from the curse of the Law. What is the curse of the Law? Go back to the Law and find out. The Law invariably refers to the first five books of the Bible, also called the Pentateuch.

As you study those five books of the Law, you will find that the curse or the punishment for breaking God's Law is threefold: It is *poverty, sickness,* and *the second death.*

Thank God, Jesus has redeemed us from the curse of poverty (Deut. 28:15–68). Did you know that? He has also redeemed us from the curse of sickness (Deut. 28:15–68). Christ has redeemed us from the curse of death—that is, spiritual death or eternal separation from God now, and physical death when Jesus comes again. We need have no fear of the second death. Hell is the home of the spiritually dead and I'm not spiritually dead and neither are you if you are born again!

Redeemed From the Curse of Poverty

Yes, you are redeemed from the curse of poverty. Some folks think that it is the will of God for a person to go through life and not ever have anything. We have heard that taught a lot in days gone by.

I'm sorry to say that when I was a young boy I didn't know any better than that myself because I didn't know my Bible any better than that. Sometimes it is easier to believe tradition than to believe the Bible. Many times, instead of actually believing the Bible, we believe what we've been *taught* that the Bible says—not what the Bible actually says.

For example, you hear people say all the time, "The Bible teaches that money is the root of all evil." The Bible doesn't say that at all! It says *the love* of money is the root of all evil (1 Tim. 6:10), and you can be guilty of that sin and not have even one dime!

You also hear people say, "I guess I must be another Job," referring to the calamities and trials of Job as recorded in the Book of Job. Some people think poor old Job went through life poverty stricken, sick, and afflicted, but he didn't. Most Bible scholars believe the events recorded in the entire Book of Job took place in about nine months' time.

When the thieves broke in and stole Job's things, he was in captivity to Satan. When the fire burned up Job's crops, he was in captivity to Satan. When the storm came and blew the house down on his children and they were all killed, Job was in captivity to Satan. When Job was smitten with boils from his head to his feet and his wife turned against him and said, "Curse God and die," Job was in captivity to Satan. But the Bible says that God *turned* Job's captivity (Job 42:10)!

In other words, you had better be careful saying you are another Job, because that implies you'll have to become one of the richest men in the world, just as Job did (Job 1:3)! You'll have twice as much as you've ever had before (Job 42:10, 12), and you'll be healed and live to a good old age, just as Job did (Job 42:16–17).

Job lived a hundred years after the calamities and trials recorded in the Book of Job. You hear folks using the expression, "as poor as Job's turkey." Well, Job's turkeys weren't poor and I can prove it to you from the Bible. In the first place, the thieves broke in and stole from Job, and if there were turkeys in the flocks of animals that he had, they wouldn't have stolen the poor ones. In the second place, when God turned Job's captivity, He gave him twice as much as he had to begin with, so Job had plenty of grain to feed them. So Job's turkeys weren't poor, and there is no need for you to be poor either!

But many of us young preachers in days gone by sat around with our eyes shut and our mouths wide open like young mocking birds, and just swallowed everything anyone would poke down us! I remember I lived in poverty for years, and you talk about being on the bottom of the barrel! I wasn't just scraping the bottom—I was under the barrel, and the barrel was on top of me!

Every time we young preachers would hear a good scripture about material or financial blessings, someone would say, "That's just for the Jews." And for years we had little enough sense but to believe it! But one day as I was reading the Bible, I read Galatians 3:13 and 14.

GALATIANS 3:13–14

13 Christ HATH REDEEMED US FROM THE CURSE OF THE LAW, being made a curse for us: for it is written, Cursed is every one that hangeth on a tree:

14 That THE BLESSING OF ABRAHAM might come on the Gentiles through Jesus Christ; that we might receive the promise of the Spirit through faith.

The Blessing of Abraham Is for All Believers

Abraham's blessing was threefold in nature.

1. It was a material or a financial blessing (Gen. 13:2,15; Deut. 28:4–5, 8, 11–12).

2. It was a physical blessing (Gen. 13:16; 17:16; Exod. 15:26; 23:25–26).

3. It was a spiritual blessing (Gal. 3:14).

In the New Testament, Third John 2 agrees that God wants us to be prosperous materially, financially, physically and spiritually.

3 JOHN 2

2 Beloved, I wish above all things that thou mayest PROSPER and be in health, EVEN AS THY SOUL PROSPERETH.

Prosperity was not just for the Jews under the Old Covenant. Third John 2 was written to believers! The Bible is our final authority. I'm sorry to say, you can't believe everything you read everywhere. You had better check up on what you read, I don't care what kind of a periodical it's found in.

For example in one periodical I was reading, a certain Bible scholar said that long life here on the earth was not a New Testament blessing. Well, I always thought the Book of Ephesians was in the New Testament, didn't you! In fact, Ephesians 6, was written to the Church at Ephesus—to believers.

EPHESIANS 6:2–3

2 Honour thy father and mother; which is the first commandment with promise;

3 That it may be well with thee, and thou mayest LIVE LONG ON THE EARTH.

Wasn't the church at Ephesus a New Testament church? And wasn't Paul preaching New Testament doctrine to them and instructing them in their rights and privileges in Christ—the blessings and provisions that belonged to them?

Paul said, *"Children, obey your parents in the Lord: for this is right. Honour thy father and mother; which is the first commandment with promise"* (Eph. 6:1–2). What is the promise? *"That it may be well with thee, and thou mayest live long on earth"* (Eph. 6:3).

Paul told the Church at Ephesus that long life belonged to them. If it belonged to the Church of the Lord Jesus Christ at Ephesus, it belongs to the Church of the Lord Jesus Christ today. If the commandment to honor our fathers and mothers is for today, then the promise—long life on the earth—is still for us today too. I believe the commandment part as well as the promise part. That promise is still to be enjoyed and practiced.

So, you see, you can't believe everything you read unless you're reading the Bible. I don't care what it is you are reading, you had better check up on it, and see if it is in line with the Word of God.

In our denomination when I was young, we were taught that material and financial blessings were just for the Jews, and we accepted that as fact. But I began studying the matter and I found that prosperity belongs to us as Christians as much as it did to the Jews under the Old Covenant.

In the first place, who are the Jews? The word "Jew" is just simply a short term or a nickname for *Judah.* The Israelites were never called Jews until after the twelve tribes split into Israel and Judah. But Judah didn't have any more promise of material and financial blessing than any of the other tribes of Israel.

The Israelites all received or inherited the blessing through their father Jacob, called Israel. Jacob inherited the promised blessing through his father Isaac. Isaac inherited the promised blessing through his father Abraham. And so it's not the Jews' blessing; it's not Israel's blessing; and it's not Isaac's blessing. It is *Abraham's* blessing.

That's exactly what our text says, *"That the blessing of Abraham might come on the Gentiles through Jesus Christ"* (Gal. 3:14). Therefore, Abraham's blessing is mine and yours.

For years I swallowed that erroneous teaching that we ought not to have anything in life, and that we ought to go through life with our noses to the grindstone. That was supposed to be characteristic of humility and piety.

But I remember when I got ahold of this truth of prosperity, I was so thrilled I couldn't sleep. Then after I got light on Galatians 3:14, other scriptures began to come to me, and the Holy Spirit said to me, "After all, didn't God put everything on the earth that's here? Didn't the Psalms say that the world in its fullness is God's (Ps. 24:1; Ps. 50:12)? Doesn't the Bible say that the gold and silver and cattle on a thousand hills are the Lord's (Hag. 2:8; Ps. 50:10)? Then for whom did God make all those things?"

The Bible says that God made the world and the fullness thereof (Gen. 1:3–27; Ps. 89:11). He created everything, then He made His man, Adam, and said, "Adam, I give you dominion over all the works of my hands" (Gen. 1:28). By saying that, God was saying He made everything for His man Adam. He gave Adam dominion over the cattle on a thousand hills, over the silver and gold, over the world and the fullness thereof. In other words, Adam was the god or the caretaker of this world.

Someone said, "Then how come the devil and his crowd have all the prosperity?" Because Adam committed high treason (Gen. 2:17; 3:6–7; Rom. 5:14). Adam sold out to the devil and Satan then became the god of this world. That is why in the New Testament, Satan is called the god of this world (2 Cor. 4:4). But Jesus, the second Adam (1 Cor. 15:45–47), came to redeem us from the hand of Satan (Eph. 1:7; Col. 1:13).

ROMANS 5:17
17 For if by one man's offence death reigned by one; much more they which receive abundance of grace and of the gift of righteousness shall reign in life by one, Jesus Christ.

The *Amplified Bible, Classic Edition* reads, *"[they] reign as kings in life through the One, Jesus Christ."*

In this scripture, the Bible says that *we* shall reign as kings in life. That means that *in* Christ we have dominion over Satan in our lives. We are to dominate, not be dominated by Satan or circumstances.

Circumstances are not to dominate you; you are to dominate circumstances. Poverty is not to rule and reign over you; you are to rule and reign over poverty. Sickness and disease are not to rule and reign over you; you are to rule and reign over sickness and disease. Each member in the Body of Christ is to reign as kings in life by Christ Jesus, in whom we have our redemption.

Heirs of Abraham's Blessing

I read something in Galatians chapter 3 along this same line which revolutionized my thinking (and it will help you too).

GALATIANS 3:29
29 And IF YE BE CHRIST'S, then are ye Abraham's seed, and HEIRS ACCORDING TO THE PROMISE.

I want you to look at Galatians 3:7.

GALATIANS 3:7
7 Know ye therefore that THEY WHICH ARE OF FAITH, the same are the CHILDREN OF ABRAHAM.

Thank God, Abraham's blessing is ours!

I tell you, when I got ahold of this truth in my heart, as conservative as I am, there in the night-time, I got so thrilled that I got up out of bed and ran around the room, rejoicing. You know, you can become so thrilled you can't be still! I get thrilled over the Word of God.

I feel sorry for some people who get thrilled and worked up emotionally over something worldly and carnal. Sometimes when I am teaching the Word, I get so thrilled with the mighty truths in it that before I know it, I'm running up and down the aisles.

Why shouldn't we be thrilled with the Word of God? When we go to a football game (and I'm not opposed to going to ball games), we get all excited and worked up over someone running down the field with a bag of wind under his arm! And no one says anything against that; it's considered all right to get excited about that.

But I tell you, Brother and Sister, when you get thrilled about the Word of God, and you get so thrilled it shows up on the outside, then, someone says about you, "He's a nut!"

But, no, we Christians have got something to be really thrilled about! Abraham's blessing is ours! That's something to be thrilled about! My heart told me it was so all the time, but it wasn't until I got my mind renewed with the Word of God that I got it through to my head.

Turn back to Deuteronomy 28. In Deuteronomy 28:15–28, the Bible lists the curse of breaking God's Law. However, in verses 1–14 the Bible lists the blessings of obedience to God. The blessings listed here are the blessings of Abraham. Notice what God says to His people.

DEUTERONOMY 28:8, 11–13

8 The Lord shall command the blessing upon thee in thy storehouses, and in all that thou settest thine hand unto. . . .

11 And the Lord shall make thee plenteous in goods. . . .

12 The Lord shall open unto thee his good treasure. . . .

13 And the Lord shall make thee the head, and not the tail; and thou shalt be above only, and thou shalt not be beneath. . . .

Remember, God was talking about material *and* financial blessings. Instead of being on the tail end, as I was at one time because of a lack of knowledge, you will be right at the head!

What else is the Bible saying in verse 13? It is saying that you'll not be on the bottom financially; you'll be on the top!

When I caught the revelation of what God was really saying in His Word, I was thrilled! After running around that room about ten times, I got back into bed and tried to sleep, but just about the time I dozed off, I raised up out of that bed shouting on the inside, although I was whispering on the outside because I didn't want to awaken anyone.

"Thank God, Abraham's blessing is mine," I whispered. I got so thrilled again I had to get up and run around the room some more. I got up the third time at four o'clock in the morning and ran around that room again. I tell you, I was so thrilled to find out that I was redeemed from the curse of the Law, the curse of poverty, sickness, and the second death. I was thrilled to know that Abraham's blessing is mine!

The Riches of the Earth Are for Us!

I want to share with you what the Lord said to me. He said, "Don't pray for money anymore. Don't pray for money because, you see, you have authority in My Name—the Name of Jesus—on the earth. After all, I put all those riches on the earth for My children."

Do you think God put cattle, silver, and gold here for the devil and his bunch? We know God loves the sinner, but does He love a sinner more than He loves His own children? No, of course not! God put the riches of the world here for His people.

God said to Israel, *"If ye be willing and obedient, ye shall eat the good of the land"* (Isa. 1:19). I know if God wants us to *eat* the best, He wants us to *wear*

the best. He also wants us to *drive* the best, and He wants us to *have* the best. Jesus came to the earth to introduce and reveal the Father to us. And Jesus is the One who said, *"If ye then, being evil, know how to give good gifts unto your children, how much more shall your Father which is in heaven give GOOD THINGS to them that ask him?"* (Matt. 7:11).

How many of you parents have the desire for your children to go through life with their noses to the grindstone, sick and diseased, never having enough to get by? There is not a one of us who wants that! In fact, I'm sure most of us have worked hard and sacrificed in order to help our children get a better education than we had, so they could make a better living than we did.

After the Lord told me not to pray for money anymore and explained why and I obeyed Him, I saw a change in my financial situation. When I would preach in churches, the pastors would say to me, "That's the biggest offering this church has ever given to an evangelist!" And the pastors didn't even make a big appeal for money to their congregations!

It was because I had discovered the key that unlocks the door to God's blessings.

Of course, seeing that my children got a better education than I had and that they were better off in other ways as well, involved some sacrifice on my part, too, because it takes a lot of money to raise children. I had two children in private school and my mother-in-law stayed at home with the children for a while when my wife and I were out on the field together.

Some weeks there wasn't any money coming in at all because the weeks we didn't work, there was no income. So, of course, some sacrifice was involved, but it didn't hurt us. We've all sacrificed to help our children. That's what Jesus meant when He said in Matthew 7:11, *"If ye then, being evil, know how to give good gifts unto your children, HOW MUCH MORE. . . ."*

God has made provision for us through Christ Jesus. The Lord had said to me, "Don't pray about finances any more. I have already put gold, silver, and cattle on a thousand hills for my man Adam, and I gave him dominion over it all. Then he committed high treason and sold it out to Satan, and Satan became the god of this world. But I, the second Adam, came to redeem mankind from the hand of the enemy and to get mankind out from under the curse."

Regarding finances, Jesus continued, "Now then, instead of praying that I would do something about your finances, because I have already made provision for you, you just simply say 'Satan, take your hands off my money.'"

Jesus said, "You just claim what you want and what you need. *You* claim it."

I responded, "Just how do I do that, Lord?"

He said, "Well, if you need $200 this week, you say, 'Satan, take your hands off my money in Jesus' Name. Father, I claim $200 this week.'"

Jesus said, "My Word says you reign in life by Christ Jesus" (Rom. 5:17).

I remember with fear and trembling I did as the Lord instructed me. Yes, God will put up with a little unbelief in you, when you're new in spiritual things. After a while, He expects more from you.

I remember the next church I went to. I said, "Lord, if I get the amount of money I need, I will know this really works, because the last time I was here, they only gave me about $60 a week for the two weeks."

I continued, "All right, Lord, I'm going to claim an amount of money which I know they will think is impossible." Then I said, "Satan, you take your hands off my money in the Name of Jesus. Father, I claim $150 this week."

You see, faith doesn't believe for the possible; faith believes for the impossible.

I was only supposed to be at that church a week, but as it turned out I was there ten days. So I said to the Lord, "Lord, I'm claiming $200 for these ten days. And Satan, in Jesus' Name, you take your hands off my money."

Up to this point in my life, I had been poverty stricken. I remember the pastor never said a word to the congregation about the offering; he just simply passed the plate and when it was over, I had $240. I had claimed $200.

After I had learned this lesson on prosperity, in the course of time I went back to the churches where I had been, and I preached prosperity to them. I can show you on my books that I got twice as much in offerings than I did the first time I was in those churches—just by using the key!

Thank God, we are not under the curse. We are not under the curse, for Jesus has set us free! For sickness we can have health. Instead of poverty we can have wealth! We have been redeemed.

As we have seen, there is a rich inheritance in Jesus Christ for us to discover in the Word of God. In Christ we have become new creatures and have been redeemed from the curse of the Law. Poverty, sickness, and spiritual death can no longer reign over us, for we reign as kings in this life by Jesus Christ!

As you meditate on these scriptural truths that we have discussed in this chapter and as you confess them to be true in your own life, you will cause these truths to become a reality in your heart and life. Believing with your heart and confessing with your mouth—*that* is how you turn your faith loose!

Questions for Study

1. How is faith activated?

   _____

   _____

2. Folks are not missing it primarily in the <u>believing</u> part. Where are they missing it?

   _____

3. According to the Bible, what will happen if you <u>believe</u> with your heart and <u>say</u> what you believe with your mouth?

   _____

   _____

4. Christianity is called "The Great Confession." Confessing is actually what three things?

   _____

   _____

5. Our confession needs to center around what five principal truths?

   _____

   _____

6. What is the threefold curse or punishment for breaking God's law?

   _____

   _____

7. What is the threefold nature of Abraham's blessing?

   _____

   _____

8. According to Ephesians 6:3, what is the promise of the commandment to honor our fathers and mothers?

   _____

   _____

9. What does faith believe for?

   _____

   _____

10. How do you turn your faith loose?

    _____

    _____

How to Turn Your Faith Loose—Part 3

For with the heart man believeth unto righteousness; and with the mouth confession is made unto salvation.

— Romans 10:10

Notice this verse says, *"with the mouth confession is made unto. . . ."* Jesus said in Mark 11:23, *"Whosoever shall SAY . . . and shall not doubt in his heart, but shall believe that those things which he SAITH shall come to pass; he shall have whatsoever he SAITH."*

You can always tell if a person is believing right by what he says. If his confession is wrong, his believing is wrong. If his believing is wrong, his thinking is wrong. If his thinking is wrong, it's because his mind has not been renewed with the Word of God.

All three of these—thinking, believing, and confessing—go together. God has given us His Word to get our thinking straightened out. We can *think* in line with God's Word; we can *believe* in line with God's Word, and we can *speak* in line with God's Word.

Don't Take Sides Against the Word

For the life of me, I have never been able to figure out how a person thinks he can get help from God apart from the Word of God. I don't understand people—I mean Full Gospel believers—who think they can get answers from God apart from His Word. *God only moves in line with His Word.* The Bible says God has magnified His Word even above His Name (Ps. 138:2)! How in the world can believers get help from God when they are actually taking sides against the Word?

You may unconsciously be taking sides against the Word through ignorance, for example. But no matter what the reason, if you are taking sides against the Word, you can't get God to work for you. He only works in line with His Word.

It is absolutely astonishing to see the attitude people have toward the Word. We should treat God's Word with the same reverence that we would treat Jesus if He were here in the natural. I don't mean we should reverence the paper and ink. I'm not talking about reverencing a physical *book*; I mean we should reverence the words in the Book; we should reverence and respect what the Word of God says.

I was preaching in a certain place once and there were several churches of the same denomination in that city. The pastors of every one of those churches had been in the services.

One day I was in the office of the church where I was ministering when the phone rang. It was one of the other pastors calling the pastor where I was holding the meeting. Even though I didn't have the telephone to my ear, I could hear every word this other pastor was saying. The one calling was complaining about the sermon I had preached the night before.

The pastor of the church where I was preaching said, "Well, it's all in the Word. I followed him, and it's in the Bible. I've been in the ministry for years, and I can read, and what Brother Hagin is teaching is in there."

The other pastor said, "I'll tell you, I've preached it my way for twenty-five years and, right or wrong, Bible or no Bible, I'm going to stay with it."

Now isn't that a sad statement! That pastor said, "Right or wrong, Bible or no Bible, I'm going to preach it *my* way," just because he had been preaching it that way for twenty-five years and did not want to change. As long as folks don't know any better, God will put up with some unbelief, much like we put up with spiritual babies. But when we as Christians come into the knowledge of the truth, then God expects us to grow up spiritually and walk in the light of the truth of God's Word.

I remember I was pastoring a church one time where we had put on a church homecoming; every former pastor was invited to come back, and certain ones were designated to speak. One of these fellows who had pastored there before and had become an official of some kind in this particular denomination was called on to speak. What he said astounded me.

He said, "I just want everyone to know that I believe every single thing about the Bible just like I did twenty or twenty-five years ago. And I want everyone to know that I haven't changed one bit in the last twenty-five years."

I thought to myself, "Yes, and he is still a baby because anyone who started preaching twenty-five years ago didn't know it all when he began." Fundamentally speaking, you can believe the same things as far as basic doctrine goes, but I've changed a lot of my ideas and ways of thinking over the years, haven't you?

Confession—Affirming, Testifying, Witnessing

As I said, *thinking*, *believing*, and *confessing* in line with the Word all go together. Now whenever the word "confession" is used, we instinctively think of confessing sin and failure, but that is the negative side of confession. That is important in its place, but as we discussed in Chapter 10, there is also a positive side of confession and the Bible has more to say about that than it does the negative side.

Confession, as we said in the last lesson, is stating something we believe. It is declaring something we know to be true, and it is proclaiming a truth we have accepted wholeheartedly. Our confession should center around several basic, scriptural truths. Let's review them again:

1. What God has done for us through Christ in His plan of salvation.

2. What God has done in us by the Word and the Holy Ghost in the new birth and the infilling of the Holy Ghost.

3. Who we are to God the Father in Christ Jesus.

4. What Jesus is presently doing for us at the right hand of the Father, where He ever lives to make intercession for us.

5. What God can accomplish through us, or what His Word can accomplish through us as we proclaim it.

God Works Through Believers to Confirm His Word

The way God works through us and in our lives is by His Word through our lips. Jesus said, "Go teach" (Matt. 28:19). Jesus commanded us to teach His Word. That is the way God works in and through us— through His Word. We are carriers of the Word. And if we don't carry the Word and give out the Word, then we aren't obeying Jesus.

God will work in our lives through His Word. For example, you are just wasting your time praying that God will save a person if someone is not going to bring the Word to him. If we could just pray and get people saved, we wouldn't have to send missionaries all over the world. We could just pray all the heathen

into the Kingdom of God. But the Holy Ghost and God only work in connection with the Word.

MARK 16:15–18, 20

15 And he [Jesus] **said unto them, Go ye into all the world, and preach the gospel to every creature.**

16 He that believeth and is baptized shall be saved; but he that believeth not shall be damned.

17 And these signs shall follow them that believe; In my name shall they cast out devils; they shall speak with new tongues;

18 They shall take up serpents; and if they drink any deadly thing, it shall not hurt them; they shall lay hands on the sick, and they shall recover. . . .

20 And they went forth, and preached [the gospel, or the Word] **every where, the Lord working with them, and confirming the word with signs following.**

What did God do as the disciples preached His Word? God confirmed His Word. God didn't do a thing until they preached the Word.

If you give the Word out, the signs will take care of themselves. *You* don't follow *signs*. *Signs* follow *the Word*.

In the last church I pastored, I became greatly concerned because there weren't enough signs following in our services. I would shut myself up in my church and would pray for days at a time, and I kept saying to the Lord, "Now, Lord, we get people saved occasionally and healed and filled with the Holy Ghost, but not a great number. There are just not enough signs following."

Finally the Lord startled me. He said, "You don't have to ask Me to confirm My Word with signs. You have been praying that I would confirm My Word and that signs would follow. But all you have to do is preach the Word and I'll do the confirming. If you'll preach the Word, the signs will follow. If the signs aren't following, then you are not preaching the Word."

I tell you, that startled me. I almost felt insulted. I said, "Why, Lord, you know I've always been a *stickler* for the Word." (You can think you are a stickler for the Word, and yet not really be, you know.)

The Lord said to me, "Check up on what you are preaching, and see to it that you preach the Word."

I want you to know, I began to examine what I was preaching, and to my utter astonishment, I found out that I was preaching about sixty percent Word, about thirty percent tradition, and about ten percent unbelief. And do you know what will happen most of the time in a situation like that? The people will listen to the tradition and the unbelief quicker than they will the Word!

I started changing my preaching, and I'll be honest with you, it took me a little while to change. Folks would many times rather hear tradition than the Word. And many of them would rather hear unbelief than the Word. I began correcting myself in the way that I said things, and sometimes in the pulpit I would just stop and say, "No, that's unbelief. I take that back." Or else I'd say, "That's tradition; I'm not going to say that because that's not right."

Some people said, "Well, we've been saying that in Full Gospel circles for thirty years."

I said, "It is still tradition, and God won't confirm that with any signs following." When I corrected myself and just started preaching the Word, then we started having signs. And I found out that the more Word I preached, the more signs we had.

Confession Is Witnessing to What You Know

Regarding confession, I have also said that you can't witness about things you don't know about. And it is what you personally know about the Lord Jesus Christ and what you are in Him that counts.

Of course, first you have to be born again before you can know Jesus. But just because you've been born again does not mean you are a successful Christian. You must also know *what you have* in Christ and *who you are* in Him. When you know who you are in Him, and when you think in line with that and believe and confess that, then there is no failure for you.

In the last lesson, I gave you some of the scriptures that contain the expression "in Him," "in whom," and "in Christ." Find all of them in the New Testament and begin to confess, "This is who I am and this is what I have in Christ." As you do, you will find that life will be different for you.

I've had people come to me and say, "Brother Hagin, I've read all those scriptures, but they don't seem real to me."

I always answer, "Have you confessed what God's Word says about you?"

One sister responded, "Well, yes, but what God's Word says about me isn't so in my life."

I said, "God says it is so."

"Yes, but I know it's not," she said.

"Well," I said, "either you or God is lying about it then. Because according to the Bible, what God says about you in His Word is so, but you say it isn't so."

I said to that woman, "If you stood right in front of your mother and called her a liar, would you feel bad? Of course you would. Well, it's no wonder you don't feel right. You're looking God right in the face and saying, 'You're a liar. Your Word is a lie; it isn't so.' You must start saying that what God says about you in His Word is so—*just* because the Bible says it is so."

This woman walked away mumbling, "Yes, but I know it's not."

How in the world can folks like that be victorious? There are some people who just won't have things in their lives as the Bible says they are. Some folks won't believe even when it happens. They just aren't going to receive the blessings of God into their lives. Some are that way about receiving the Holy Ghost too.

But it is *believing* in line with God's Word; *thinking* in line with God's Word; and *confessing* in line with God's Word that counts.

Or to say it another way, it is *affirming*, *testifying*, and *witnessing* to the truth you know of God's Word that counts.

Your confession is what puts you over and causes you to succeed in life.

Confess Your Rights and Privileges in Christ

I want to use several scriptures that do not have the words "in Him," "in whom," or "in Christ" in them, yet they do infer something about our rights and privileges in Christ.

COLOSSIANS 1:13

13 Who hath DELIVERED us from the power [authority] **of darkness, and hath TRANSLATED US into the kingdom of his dear Son:**

The word "who" in this verse refers to God. In Christ we are delivered from the power or authority of darkness.

1 JOHN 4:4

4 Ye are of God, little children, and have overcome them: because greater is he that is in you, than he that is in the world.

A companion scripture to First John 4:4 in the Old Testament is Isaiah 41:10.

ISAIAH 41:10

10 Fear thou not; for I AM WITH THEE: be not dismayed; for I am thy God: I will strengthen thee; yea, I will help thee; yea, I will uphold thee with the right hand of my righteousness.

Then in the New Testament, God says something else that agrees with the scripture we just read.

ROMANS 8:31

31 What shall we then say to these things? If God be FOR US, who can be against us?

Take these scriptures as a personal message from God to you. Remember, the Bible is God speaking to you. God said in Isaiah 41:10, *"Fear thou not; for I am with thee. . . ."* And because we as Christians are under the New Covenant, we can also say, "Thank God, He is *in* us."

That's the best reason in the world not to be afraid, because God is *with* us and *in* us. Sometimes we try to help people and we'll say, "Well, the darkest hour is just before dawn," or "Don't worry, things will be better tomorrow." But I'm glad God gives us the best reason in the world not to fear. He is *with* us and *in* us!

Did you ever notice that again and again when God sent a message to His people, He would say, "Fear thou not." He would send a message, perhaps through the prophets, and say, "Fear thou not." Also, Jesus said to Jairus when they came and told Jairus that his little daughter was dead, "Fear not, only believe" (Mark 5:36; Luke 8:50). If God just told me, "Don't be afraid," and left it at that, I might say, "I can't help it." But He said in Isaiah 41:10, "For I am *with* thee."

Can you really believe that He is *with* you and be afraid? No! Can you really believe that He is *in* you and be afraid? No! If you are afraid, it's because you are doubting Him.

"Yes," someone said, "but, Brother Hagin, you don't understand. I am so weak."

But God said, *"I will strengthen thee"* (Isa. 41:10).

"Yes, but you just don't understand. I just feel so helpless."

But God said, *"yea, I will uphold thee"* (v. 10).

Thank God, we already have the answer to every problem in the Word! But it is amazing how little the Word means to some people. We can help folks who want to be helped. But we can't do anything for those who don't want to be helped. If you beat people over the head with the truth, so to speak, that still does not help them if they don't want to be helped.

Actually, love is the greatest tool there is for helping people. Just let people see that you really love them and that you are really interested in them. That will help them more than anything.

I was reading an article in a magazine once which was written by the president of the American Medical Association. He said, "There are two things that the old country doctors, as we called them, had that the doctors today do not have: That is *consideration* for the patients and *love and sympathy*." In the article, this man said that these two qualities are the greatest healing agents we have.

I tell you, friends, I believe the same thing is true in the spiritual realm. I believe you will find that when the majority of folks who are really sincere, see what God's plan is for them and know it, they will rise to the level of it.

Another way to say this is that if you will approach any subject from the positive side and not from the negative side, you will win more folks. Preach *for* something and not against something. I am glad that God is *for* me, aren't you? *"Fear thou not; for I am with thee"* (Isa. 41:10). And in the New Testament we read, *"If God be for us, who can be against us?"* (Rom. 8:31).

Our confession should be, "God is with me." "Greater is He who is in me than he who is in the world." You can fearlessly say, "God is in me now."

You may be facing some task that seems impossible. Instead of talking about how impossible that task is, look to Him who is inside of you and say, "God is in me now." You will find that your confession of faith will cause God to work on your behalf. He will rise up in you and give you success.

The Master of all of creation is in you. You can face life fearlessly because you know that greater is He who is in you than any force that can be arrayed against you. This should be your continual confession. Now hold fast to it.

No Faith Without Confession

Let me state this: *There is no faith without confession.* There is no such thing as faith without confession! Confession is faith's way of expressing itself. Faith, like love, is of the heart or the spirit. And you know just as well as I do that there is no love without word or action.

You can't reason love into people and you can't reason love out of them because love is of the heart. Faith is of the heart or the spirit, too, and it's safe to say that there is no faith without confession. And faith, like love, *grows* with your confession.

Remember your confession does two things for you: First, it pinpoints your location. Second, it sets the boundaries of your life. You don't realize beyond what you say. If you say you can't, then you can't. You get nothing. But if you say you can, then you can. You can have what you say, whether you talk unbelief or belief. Your confession mightily affects your spirit or your inner man.

The reason the majority of Christians are weak, although they are sincere, is they have never boldly declared who they are in Christ. What they must do is find out from the Scripture how God the Father looks at them and then confess that.

These scriptures are found primarily in the epistles, as they were written to the Church. When you find those scriptures, boldly confess what the Word declares you are in Christ. As you do this, your faith will abound.

The reason faith is weak and held in bondage is that you've never dared to confess you are who God says you are.

Remember, *faith never grows beyond your confession.* Your daily confession of who the Father is to you, of what Jesus is doing for you now at the right hand of the Father, and what His mighty Holy Spirit is doing in you will build a solid, positive faith life. You will not be afraid of any circumstances. You will not be afraid of any disease. You will not be afraid of any condition. You will face life fearlessly, a conqueror.

Confession Is Made Unto . . .

You will never be a conqueror first and *then* believe you are one. No, you have to confess it first, and then you get there. The confessions of your faith will cause the desired realities in your life.

I want you to get this spiritual law, and once you understand the truth of it, it will help your spiritual growth immeasurably.

ROMANS 10:10

10 For with the heart man believeth unto righteousness; and with the mouth confession is made unto salvation.

Paul said, *"with the heart man believeth . . . and with the mouth confession is made UNTO. . . ."* Confession is made unto what? In this case, unto salvation, but it can be *unto* anything.

Take, for example, a man who wants to get saved. He has to believe in his heart that Jesus is Lord and that God has raised Him from the dead because the Word says it. Then he must confess with his mouth what he believes in his heart—that Jesus died for him according to the scriptures and that Jesus was raised from the dead for his justification. Then he must confess Jesus as His Lord with his mouth because he believes it in his heart. Then according to the Bible, he is saved.

You see, the same thing is true concerning healing or receiving the baptism of the Holy Spirit or receiving any answer to prayer. You don't go by sight or by feelings. You go by what the Word says. The Bible says to believe the Word first and then to confess the Word with your mouth, and it shall be done (Mark 11:23–24). We walk by faith and not by sight (2 Cor. 5:7). Romans 10:10 says, *"For with the heart man believeth unto righteousness; and with the mouth confession is made unto salvation* [or whatever it is you need from God's Word]."

If you can grasp that, you will understand God's law of faith. I've seen Christians get their healing or begin to speak in tongues, but they wouldn't accept it by faith, so they lost what they had. But it is with the *mouth* that confession is made unto salvation and unto *all* the blessings of God.

When you read in God's Word about who God's Word says you are and who you are in Christ and what you have, even though it doesn't seem real to you, instead of taking sides against the Word and saying, "No, that is not so for me," and making God out to be a liar, start confessing, "It *is* so!" Say, "Yes, that's mine. Whatever God says in His Word is mine!" You will find that faith's confession does create reality.

Questions for Study

1. How can you tell if a person is believing right?

   _____
   _____

2. Why can't you get answers from God apart from His Word?

   _____
   _____

3. How should we treat God's Word?

   _____
   _____

4. How does God work through us and in our lives?

   _____
   _____

5. What did God do as the disciples preached His Word?

   _____
   _____

6. What will happen if you preach the Word?

   _____
   _____

7. What must you know in order to be a successful Christian?

   _____
   _____

8. What puts you over and causes you to succeed in life?

   _____
   _____

9. In Christ, we are delivered from the _____ or _____ _____ _____.

10. What is the greatest tool there is for helping people?

    _____
    _____

Chapter 12

How to Turn Your Faith Loose—Part 4

For with the heart man believeth unto righteousness; and with the mouth confession is made unto salvation.

— Romans 10:10

We have been reading about confession: *"with the mouth confession is made UNTO. . . ."*

MARK 11:23

23 For verily I say unto you, That whosoever shall SAY unto this mountain, Be thou removed, and be thou cast into the sea; and shall not doubt in his heart, but shall BELIEVE that those things which he SAITH shall come to pass; he shall have whatsoever he SAITH.

We have been discussing right and wrong thinking, right and wrong believing, and right and wrong confession.

If our confessing is wrong, it is because our believing is wrong.

If our believing is wrong, it is because our thinking is wrong.

If our thinking is wrong, it is because our minds have not yet been renewed with the Word of God.

But dare to think God's thoughts after Him! You see, the Bible contains God's thoughts, and, of course, God's thoughts are different than man's thoughts. God says, *"For as the heavens are higher than the earth, so are my ways higher than your ways, and my thoughts than your thoughts"* (Isa. 55:9).

You know, sometimes you can say some things that the Bible says are true, and in your natural mind, it doesn't sound reasonable. But that is because your mind hasn't been renewed with the Word of God. But the Word works. It works by saying or it works by praying.

MARK 11:22–24

22 . . . Have faith in God [or, Have the God-kind of faith].

23 For verily I say unto you, That whosoever shall say unto this mountain, Be thou removed, and be thou cast into the sea; and shall not doubt in his heart, but shall believe that those things which he saith shall come to pass; he shall have whatsoever he saith.

24 Therefore I say unto you, What things soever ye desire, when ye pray, believe that ye receive them, and ye shall have them.

The *Amplified Bible, Classic Edition* reads, *"For this reason I am telling you, whatever you ask for in prayer, believe—trust and be confident—that it is granted to you, and you will [get it]."* If you trust and are confident that whatever you asked for is granted, then you are going to say, "It's mine, I have it now." That is your faith speaking.

The greatest things that will ever happen to you will occur when you move out into this faith realm of *believing* and *saying*. But the intellect and the physical senses will fight you every step of the way to keep you from moving into this realm. That's because the physical or natural mind, if it isn't renewed by the Word, wants to hold you in the natural realm.

But there is a *spiritual* realm and that is really our realm as *spirit beings*.

The Lord once said to me, "So many have barely touched that spiritual realm. Yea, ye enter into it briefly in being filled with the Spirit and speaking with tongues. Why not enter on into it? Yea, go on out, even into the deep things of Mine. For surely your every desire shall be granted and the fullness of God shall be yours to enjoy."

Wrong Thinking, Believing, and Confessing

In this lesson, let us talk for a while about *wrong* thinking, *wrong* believing, and *wrong* confessing. Then we'll bring confession back to the positive side again before we conclude.

Wrong confession, of course, is a confession of defeat, of failure, and of the supremacy of Satan. To talk about how the devil is hindering you—how he is keeping you from success, how he is holding you in bondage, and how he is keeping you sick—is a confession of defeat. Such confessions as those simply glorify the devil. Confessions that glorify the devil are *wrong* confessions!

Remember, our confession is proclaiming a truth that we've accepted wholeheartedly or it is declaring something we know to be true and stating something we believe. Testimonies that we give in church, for example, are our confessions. And sad to say, many of them glorify the devil rather than God.

I remember some time ago, one woman got up in one of my meetings, and said, "The devil has been after me all week, bless his holy name." I know she got her praise misplaced and didn't mean to praise the devil! She meant to praise God, yet she was glorifying what the devil was doing by getting up and talking about it.

Now I want to ask you a question. When you talk about what God has done and what Jesus has done and is doing, aren't you glorifying Him? Well, by the same token then, if you talk about what the devil is doing and what he has done, you are glorifying the devil. And so many times people miss it by making the wrong confession. They lose the blessing and they are defeated, and life is a grind to them.

So a wrong confession glorifies the devil, and we don't have any business glorifying the devil. Actually, a wrong confession is an unconscious declaration that your Father God is a failure.

And as I said, many of the testimonies and confessions we hear today glorify the devil. Such confessions simply sap the very life out of you. A wrong confession destroys your faith; it holds you in bondage. But the confession of your lips that has grown out of faith in your heart will absolutely defeat the devil in every combat.

On the other hand, the confession of Satan's ability to hinder you and to keep you from success, gives the devil dominion over you. You see, *with your mouth you are either going to give God dominion over you or you are going to give Satan dominion over you!*

For example, to be saved, you had to confess the Lordship of Jesus. Romans 10:9 says, *"If thou shalt confess with thy mouth the Lord Jesus* [or, Jesus as Lord]. . . ."* That means you are to confess Him as *your* Lord. You are to confess Jesus' Lordship over you. Then He begins to have dominion over you as you give place to Him in your life.

But, you see, when you confess Satan's ability to hinder you and to keep you from success, then even though you are a Christian, you are giving Satan dominion over you. Satan is the god of the world (2 Cor. 4:4), and he will move right in to your life if you permit him to. Now it may be a permission of ignorance or an unconscious consent, but if you give Satan dominion over you, it is still consent. And naturally, when Satan has dominion over you, then you are filled with weakness and fear. Don't ever confess your fears.

Don't Confess Fear—Resist It!

"Yes," someone might say, "but what if I am afraid?"

Well, you're not really afraid because the Bible says God has given you a spirit, not of fear, but of power and of love and of a sound mind (2 Tim. 1:7).

Fear isn't something that is coming from the inside of you if you're a Christian. It's something that is coming from the outside of you, trying to get ahold of you. It is from the enemy.

2 TIMOTHY 1:7

7 For God hath not given us the spirit of fear; but of POWER, and of LOVE, and of a SOUND MIND.

You have a spirit of power—now *say* you do. And when you confess it, then what you confess begins to dominate you.

We have to recognize that God has not given us a spirit of fear. We need to learn to stand our ground against the enemy. The Bible instructs us, *"Resist the devil, and he will flee from you"* (James 4:7). That means you *can* resist the devil.

I've always practiced dealing with fear this way, and I've done it since I was a young Baptist boy: I would always just speak to fear and treat it as though it was a spirit because the Bible says God has not given us a *spirit* of fear. That means fear is an evil spirit, because fear has torment (1 John 4:18), and it certainly isn't good. If I'm tempted to be afraid, I say, "Fear, I resist you in the Name of Jesus Christ. I refuse to be afraid."

When I first started practicing that, I had a little battle, because fear tried to take advantage of me. But by practicing that through the years, the devil always runs when I start talking.

In other words, it's sort of like this: If you happen to be a person who has a hot temper, and that's your natural make-up, when you yield to that then the devil can come in. And the more you just let yourself go and just fly off the handle, the more that temper will grow and will rule you. But the more you resist that natural tendency and hold your flesh in check, the easier it will be to control your temper.

When you first start holding your temper in check, there will be a little battle to do it. But every time you win the victory, the easier it will be the next time. Practice these things. You don't just arrive at spiritual maturity overnight. You don't grow up spiritually overnight. Spiritual growth is similar to physical growth. The Bible teaches that. As we practice doing God's Word, we grow spiritually.

Don't Confess Doubt—Resist It!

The same thing is true about doubt that is true about fear. Don't confess your doubts. Don't confess your fears. I did not tell you to say you weren't doubting or that you didn't have fears if you have them. I said just don't say anything about them.

Confess the Word instead. In fact, you haven't got any business with doubt. You don't have any more business with doubt that you have with drugs. It's of the devil. Doubt is contraband goods. Doubt is just as evil as drugs or cussing. And if it is evil, we haven't got any business with it. Doubt is evil. Doesn't the Bible say that (Num. 13:32)?

You see, you haven't got any business talking doubt because it doesn't belong to you. To tell the truth about it, a lot of people think they are being honest when they confess that they are afraid or that they are doubting. But if you are saved, you are not full of doubt. You may have been *tempted* to doubt, and you may have listened to the devil and yielded to the temptation. But you can put the devil on the run by resisting him. You haven't got a heart full of doubt. If you do, you need to get saved! So quit talking negatively—that you have doubts and fears—because that's not what you have or who you are at all.

Start talking about who you are and what you are in Christ. You are a believer. You are a new creature. *Talk* that. *Believe* that. *Think* that. And if you are tempted to doubt or fear (and you can be tempted because none of us are above temptation), you can resist the devil, and he will flee from you (James 4:7).

Refuse to doubt and fear in the Name of the Lord Jesus Christ, and doubt and fear will leave you. But if you entertain doubt and fear, they'll come right in and buddy up to you, and they will rob you and blind you spiritually, and defeat you if you let them.

Doubt and fear are tormenting twins of the enemy. So if you are going to say anything, say what God says. God says, "Fear thou not." So you just simply say, "No, I'm not going to fear. I'm a child of God, and God has not given me a spirit of fear. I'm not afraid. I refuse to be afraid. I resist you, Satan, in Jesus' Name."

And don't get up and brag on how the devil tempted you to doubt. You should be just as embarrassed to get up and talk about being tempted to doubt as you would be if you were tempted to steal. It's wrong to steal and you know that. But it is also wrong to doubt. There is no use getting into a discussion about which is more evil—doubting or stealing — because if it's evil, we just don't have any business with it.

You don't have any more business talking doubt words than you do talking *curse* words. Doubt is the devil's language. Now quit talking the devil's language and start talking God's language! God is a faith God. We are faith children of a faith God. I want to show you how to put into practice what we are studying.

If you were tempted to steal or lie (and the devil does tempt people in these areas) you wouldn't get up and tell about it, would you? No, you would resist that temptation and say, "Devil, you are a liar and I'm not going to do that. I resist you." And if you did any testifying, you would just simply praise God for victory over the devil in Jesus' Name.

Well, do the same thing when you are tempted to doubt. Quit entertaining doubt. Quit talking about doubt. Quit bragging about how you've been tempted to doubt. Instead, say, "Satan, I resist you in Jesus' Name. I refuse to doubt."

You don't have to doubt unless you want to, because you are not a doubter, you are a believer. So keep on believing!

Let me say it again, your confession of Satan's ability to hinder you and to keep you from success gives Satan dominion over you. Your confession of your fear gives fear dominion over you. If you confess fear, your fears become stronger and you get more and more into bondage to the enemy. But if you will boldly confess your Father's care and protection, and confess God's Word and declare that what God says about you is true, you will rise above satanic influence every single time.

Every time you confess your doubts and fears, your weakness, and your disease, you are openly confessing that the Word of God is not true and that God has failed to make His Word good in your life. Think on that for awhile! I want you to see the place that confession holds in your life.

Don't Confess Your Sickness— Confess your Healing!

What does God's Word say? Ask yourself that question on any subject. Take healing or sickness, for example. What does God have to say about the subject of healing?

The Word declares that with Jesus' stripes, you were healed (Isa. 53:5; 1 Peter 2:24). The Bible also says, "Surely He has borne our sicknesses and carried our diseases" (Isa. 53:4). And Matthew 8:17 says, *"Himself took our infirmities, and bare our sicknesses."*

But many times, instead of confessing that Jesus has borne their diseases and put them away, people confess they still have them. You see, the reason we miss it so much of the time is, *we take the testimony of our physical senses instead of taking the testimony of the Word of God.* But when they start confessing that Jesus has done something about their sickness and disease—that He has taken them away—then healing and health will become a reality in their lives.

Healed by Hearing and Confessing the Word

Years ago I saw an example of someone being healed just by hearing the Word and by changing her confession to line up with the Word of God. In one of my meetings, a woman said to me, "Brother Hagin, I'm going to the state institution to get my sister. She isn't really bad off mentally, but she does need institutional care. When someone speaks to her, she does understand what is being said. And the doctors usually let her come home for two-week periods anytime I want to come and get her. I believe these services will help her, so I'm going to bring her to them."

And, you know, I never prayed for this woman's sister during those two weeks. But just from hearing the Word, that woman's mind was made clear, and she never went back to the hospital. The doctors gave her a clean bill of health.

You see, she had begun confessing defeat, fear, and doubt, and those things became a part of her. That's how her mind became sick in the first place. But in these services, she saw where she had missed it, and she began to make the right confessions and was healed. Even the doctors said she was healed. Before she attended those services, they had said her mind would never be right.

Because this woman's recovery was so dramatic, another woman in the church said she was going to ask her neighbor to come. Her neighbor was mentally disturbed and had been committed to the state hospital, but had not yet gone. She said neither she nor her husband was saved, but she said she was going to tell the husband what had happened to the other woman at these meetings, and see if she could bring the man's wife to the meeting.

She came with her neighbor to several morning meetings. When that week was over, that woman had been saved, healed, and filled with the Holy Ghost, and never did go to the state hospital. Five years later I preached in that same church, and the woman still attended, and her husband had gotten saved too.

The first woman who was mentally ill had been saved and filled with the Holy Ghost before she became mentally disturbed. But you know people can get sick mentally as well as they can get sick physically. And God can heal a mentally ill person as well as He can a physically ill person.

Believing God's Word for Your Own Healing

You need to understand that your will and your believing have a lot to do with your receiving healing or whatever it is you need from God. If you don't believe the Word or you don't want to be healed, then God won't push healing off on you. You have a part to play in receiving from God too. God doesn't override your will in the matter.

Let's look at it from the natural standpoint. Doctors today don't just say to people, "This is what's wrong with you. Take this medicine and you'll be healed." It doesn't automatically work that way. In fact, the doctor can't help anyone without the person's cooperation. For instance, the doctor could write someone a prescription, but if that person didn't fill the prescription and actually take the medicine, he wouldn't get well.

Well, if the natural physician can't help you without your cooperation, how is the Heavenly Physician going to help you without your full cooperation? He won't be able to.

God has certain rules and laws that He works by, and even those to whom He gives the healing ministry don't go around pushing healing off on folks. There has to be cooperation on the part of the people receiving healing. So many people have thought that if someone would just pray the prayer of faith for them, they would automatically be healed, whether they themselves believed anything or not.

But even if these people did receive healing by someone else's faith, it would not be permanent. For example, I've seen people temporarily helped, but later they lost what they had received because they didn't know how to hold on to their healing through their own faith.

If you are going to receive any permanent help, then you are going to have to act in faith yourself. You must practice God's Word for it to work for you.

As long as you hold on to the confession of weakness, sickness, and pain, you will still have weakness, sickness, and pain. You may search for some man of God to pray the prayer of faith for you, but it will be of no avail, because your unbelief will destroy the effects of his faith. It's true, however, that baby Christians can be carried for awhile by other people's faith. But the time comes when even they have to begin to exercise and develop their own faith.

That's exactly the reason people receive their healing and then lose it. They have been in a service where there was mass or corporate faith and they received healing. But when they got on their own, Satan took advantage of their unbelief and put the ailment back on them because they didn't know how to stand against him with their own faith.

Don't Confess Your Sins and Weaknesses— Confess God's Forgiveness

The believer who is always confessing his sins and his weakness is building weakness, failure, and sin into his consciousness. If we do sin, when we confess our sins, God is faithful and just to forgive us and to cleanse us from all unrighteousness (1 John 1:9). Once you make confession of your sin, don't ever refer to it again. It is not past history because past history can be remembered.

After you confess your sin, it is as though it had never been because God said, *"I, even I, am he that blotteth out thy transgressions . . . and will not remember thy sins"* (Isa. 43:25). God doesn't have any memory of your sin, so why should you? It is not good taste to remind God of your sins because He has already told you in Isaiah 43:25 that He doesn't remember that you did anything wrong.

But this is why a lot of people don't have any faith. They talk themselves right out of faith because when they pray, they bring up every sin, shortcoming, fault, mistake, and failure they can think of to accuse themselves with. And when they get finished condemning themselves, they don't have any faith at all because they are holding themselves under condemnation; they are making the wrong confession.

Confess God's Forgiveness for Your Sin

What should you confess? If you are going to confess anything, confess what God says in regard to your mistake, sin, or failure. Confess that He has forgiven you, cleansed you, and has forgotten your sin. Confess and say, "Thank God, I'm forgetting it too. I stand in God's Presence as though I had never done wrong."

And if the devil tries to bring your sin before you, say, "Yes, that's right, Mr. Devil. I did that and I was wrong. But First John 1:9 says that if I confess my sin, God is faithful and just to forgive me and to cleanse me from all unrighteousness. So God has forgiven me and I'm thanking Him for it."

At first, you may not feel a thing, but practice it for a while, because you have been going in the wrong direction for so long, it may be a little hard at first to break yourself of the habit of wrong confession. But as you practice doing the Word, you will eventually experience the victory! You see, acting on the Word is making the right confession. Acting on the Word is *believing* the right thing; it is *thinking* the right thing.

No matter how long someone prays for you, as long as you act against the Word, the Word can't work for you. But when you act in line with the Word, it will work for you.

Also, you should never confess your sins to people. You might have to ask someone to forgive you, but after you have done that, forget it. Don't confess your sins to people. If you are going to tell anyone your sin, tell the Lord, and then forget it.

These are the ways you learn to turn your faith loose: by believing right, by thinking right, and by making the right confession. Always confess in line with God's Word regardless of contradictory circumstances, and watch God's Word work for you as you learn to turn your faith loose!

Questions for Study

1. If you trust and are confident that whatever you asked for is granted, then what are you going to say?

   _____

   _____

2. What does a physical or natural mind that isn't renewed by the Word of God want to do?

   _____

   _____

3. What is a wrong confession a confession of?

   _____

   _____

4. What does our confession proclaim?

   _____

   _____

5. What will a wrong confession do to you?

   _____

   _____

6. If you are a Christian, fear isn't something that comes from the inside of you. Where does it come from?

   _____

   _____

7. What is spiritual growth similar to?

   _____

   _____

8. What will happen if you entertain doubt and fear?

   _____

   _____

9. What question should you ask yourself on any subject?

   _____

   _____

10. What are the ways you learn to turn your faith loose?

    _____

    _____

Chapter 13

Seven Steps to the Highest Kind of Faith—Part 1

We've already covered most of the points contained in this chapter. But I wanted to bring them together so that you could intelligently check up on the progress you are making in your faith walk and get ready for your exam, so to speak.

If you have read these lessons on faith and they have taken hold in your heart, the devil is going to try to contest you. But the Lord wants you to be prepared for Satan's wiles. You can be fully prepared for any situation or circumstance that may arise. That's why I want you to check up on your own life and your faith walk and keep pressing on to attain the highest kind of faith.

There are seven steps to attaining the highest kind of faith—the faith which takes God at His Word and gets results. In this lesson we will discuss the First three steps.

Step Number One: Know the Integrity of God's Word

The first step necessary to attain the highest kind of faith is to know the integrity of God's Word. You must know that God's Word is actually what it declares itself to be. The Word of God is a revelation from God to us. We should also realize that the Bible is God speaking to us now—today.

The Bible is not only a Book of the past and a Book of the future, but it is a Book of the now. This Book, the Bible, is a God-breathed, a God-indwelt, and a God-inspired message.

HEBREWS 4:12
12 For the word of God is QUICK, and powerful, and sharper than any twoedged sword, piercing even to the dividing asunder of soul and spirit, and of the joints and marrow, and is a discerner of the thoughts and intents of the heart.

Moffatt's translation reads, *"For the Logos [Word] of God is a living thing."* You see, "quick" means *alive* or *living.* And so the Word of God is a living thing. But it will only come alive to you and work in your life as you *accept* it and *act* upon it.

Therefore, the first step to attaining the highest kind of faith is to settle on the absolute integrity of God's Word. The Word of God should be of foremost importance in your life.

Sometimes folks feel that God hasn't spoken to them unless they have received a message in tongues or a prophecy, but God's Word—the Bible—is God speaking to us! And tongues and interpretations or prophecy are *not* to be put above the holy written Word of God.

The Word Comes First

The Word of God comes first! The gift of tongues, interpretation of tongues, and prophecy are inspirational vocal gifts given to us in order to inspire us in line with the written Word of God. And if someone gives an utterance that is *not* in line with the Word, then it is not the Holy Spirit in manifestation. No, it is just someone speaking out of his own thinking or speaking by a wrong spirit. We need to judge these things in the light of the Word, as we are told to do.

The Word of God is of foremost importance because it is God speaking to us. I've always maintained that attitude and just acted upon the Word in that way—as though the Lord Jesus Christ Himself were here in person speaking to me. When you settle on that fact, you have gone a long way to under-standing faith.

There is no need to try and argue about the Word. It is amazing to me how many folks will endeavor to get around certain truths in the Bible or explain them away. But you should always accept the Bible for what it says, and walk in the light of it.

Then again, it seems that some folks want the Word to say certain things, so they just sort of read certain things into the Word, whether they are in the Word or not. But we only have the right to believe what the Word says, not what we *think* it says.

When you really begin to study the Word for yourself and accept it as it is, you will wonder why in the world you believed some things the way you did. It is absolutely astounding some of the things people believe that really aren't in the Word at all. It seems we often accept what someone says about the Word instead of seeing for ourselves what the Word of God actually says.

My Decision to Believe the Word

One way I got headed in the right direction was by constantly studying the Bible as I lay bedfast on the bed of sickness. I studied in detail on the subjects of faith and healing. My church didn't teach faith and healing, but the more I studied the Word of God, the more I saw that faith and healing were true.

And regardless of church teaching, I determined I was going to walk in the light of what the Word says, because the Word of God is God speaking to us now. And I know in my own experience, when I settled on the fact that God's Word was God speaking to me *now*, about sixty percent of the faith battle was won!

In order to actually believe the Word of God, I had to go against the teaching of my own church. And not only that, I had to go against what my entire family believed.

You know, it is amazing how we become so church-minded instead of *Bible* minded; sometimes we act "churchy" instead of born again! And it is amazing how your loved ones (those who think they have your best interests at heart) can often oppose you and try to keep you from walking in the light of God's Word and many times even become a tool of Satan to hinder you.

When I was studying God's Word for myself and endeavoring to receive my healing, I realized that my family members were discouraging me instead of encouraging me, so I just quit talking to them about faith and healing. I just kept my thoughts to myself and quietly determined to just obey the Word of God for myself.

Say it out loud: "God's Word is God speaking to *me*."

Step Number Two: Know the Reality of Our Redemption in Christ

The second step necessary to attain the highest kind of faith is to know the reality of our redemption in Christ. We should understand redemption not just as a doctrine and not as a philosophy or as a creed of some kind. But we should know that *in* Christ we have actually been redeemed from the authority of Satan (Col. 1:13), for in the new birth we have been translated into the Kingdom of God's Son, the Kingdom of God. In other words, we have been placed into the very family of God.

Delivered From Satan's Kingdom

COLOSSIANS 1:12–14

12 Giving thanks unto the Father, which hath made us meet [able] **to be partakers of the inheritance of the saints in light:**

13 WHO HATH DELIVERED US FROM THE POWER OF DARKNESS, and hath translated us into the kingdom of his dear Son:

14 In whom WE HAVE REDEMPTION THROUGH HIS BLOOD, even the forgiveness of sins.

Another translation of verse 12 reads, *"which made us ABLE to be partakers of the inheritance of the saints in light"*! Thank God, we are able to be partakers of our inheritance and we can enter into our inheritance in Christ.

Now read verse 13: *"Who HATH delivered us from the POWER of darkness."* This verse does not say God is going to deliver us; it says He has already delivered us when we were born again into God's Kingdom.

The Greek word translated "power" here means *authority*. In other words, we could read that scripture, "Who has delivered us from the *authority* of darkness."

Now that word "darkness" means *everything that Satan is*—the kingdom of Satan. But in Christ we have been delivered from the power or authority of Satan's kingdom.

Notice Colossians 1:14 says, *"In whom we have redemption through his* [Jesus'] *blood."* Therefore, Satan cannot lord it over the believer, for we have been redeemed!

Let's look again at Revelation 12:11.

REVELATION 12:11

11 And they overcame him [the accuser of the brethren, Satan] **BY THE BLOOD OF THE LAMB, and BY THE WORD OF THEIR TESTIMONY.**

The American Standard Version reads, *"they overcame him because of the blood of the Lamb, and because of the word of their testimony."*

The blood of Jesus is the basis for our victory. But, you see, you have to add your testimony to that; or we could say, you have to add your *confession* to it.

You have to stand your ground against the enemy with your confession of faith in God's Word, because Satan is the god of this world and he will *try* to have authority over you. Yes, Satan will *try* to exercise his authority over you in this life. But you simply have to know that you have been delivered from the power of darkness and from the authority of Satan through the blood of Jesus Christ.

You have to know that by virtue of the new birth, you have been translated into the Kingdom of God's dear Son, Jesus Christ (Col. 1:13). In Christ you have redemption through His blood, and you can overcome the devil in every single combat, no matter what the test or trial is. Because of the Blood of the Lamb and because of the word of your testimony or your confession of faith, you are more than a conqueror! Thank God, there is power in the blood!

So as new creatures in Christ, Satan's dominion over us is ended! Jesus is the Lord and the Head of the new creature. And corporately, the Church is the Body of Christ and Christ is the Head of His Body. The whole Body of believers (that is the born again ones) is a new man in Christ. And each one of us individually is a new creature, because we are all members of that Body.

Satan has no right to rule over the Body of Christ, and he has no right to rule over us individually either. Christ is the Head of the Body. *He* is the One who is to rule and dominate His own Body, corporately and individually.

Redeemed From Sickness

I have had some people tell me that they didn't succeed in a particular venture because success isn't in line with the Word of God.

People have actually said to me, "Brother Hagin, our spirits belong to the Lord, all right, but our bodies haven't been redeemed yet. So we'll have to go right on suffering sickness and disease in the physical realm in this life. The time is coming when we won't have to suffer with sickness and disease, but that time hasn't come yet."

But I don't read that in the Bible!

1 CORINTHIANS 6:19–20

19 What? know ye not that your body is the TEMPLE OF THE HOLY GHOST which is in you, which ye have of God, and ye are not your own?

20 For ye are bought with a price: therefore glorify God in your body, and in your spirit, which are God's.

Here the Bible says not only your spirit, but your *body* is bought with a price, so glorify God in your body *and* in your spirit, which are God's.

Notice it says, *"glorify God in your body"* (1 Cor. 6:20). That means *you* are to glorify God in your body. Does God get any glory out of the devil dominating you physically with sickness and disease? Could God get any glory out of a body, which is the temple of the Holy Ghost, being deformed or afflicted by the enemy with sickness or diseases? No, certainly not!

We need to see these things clearly in the light of God's Word and then we will learn to take a stand against anything that attacks our bodies, just as quickly as we would stand against *any* of Satan's attacks.

Let's turn back to Colossians 1:12, which says, *"Giving thanks unto the Father, which hath made us meet [or able] to be partakers of the inheritance of the saints in light."*

Healing is part of our inheritance as children of God as we walk in the light. Healing is revealed to us in God's Word.

The Bible tells us that we have dominion and authority over the devil through the blood of Jesus, which includes sickness and disease (John 10:10; Matt. 8:17; 1 Peter 2:24).

As we saw in Revelation 12:11, it is revealed to us in God's Word that it is by the blood of the Lamb *and* the word of our testimony that we overcome Satan. If we are born again, we have already been delivered from the power of darkness and have already been translated into the Kingdom of God's dear Son (Col. 1:13).

Now notice this verse says, *"Giving thanks unto the Father, which hath made us meet [able] to be PARTAKERS of the inheritance"* (Col. 1:12). Thank God, I can partake of my inheritance right now! Don't relegate that to the future—when you get to Heaven. We have an inheritance *now*.

We are delivered from the authority and power of darkness *now*. We are translated into the Kingdom of God's dear Son *now*. We have deliverance and redemption from the hand of Satan *now*. We can overcome the enemy *now* by the blood of the Lamb and by the word of our testimony, or our confession. We can glorify God *now* in our bodies and in our spirits which are God's *now*.

No Trespassing—Devil, This Means You!

I like the way one retired missionary prayed for folks. I asked him once to help me in my prayer line to pray for the sick. The first person he prayed for was a woman.

He said, "Father, this woman is Your child. She belongs to you. It is not right that the devil should dominate her through sickness and disease. So we thank You, Father, because You have made provision for her deliverance. You laid her sickness and her diseases on Jesus, for it is written, '*Himself took our infirmities, and bare our sicknesses*'" (Matt. 8:17).

Then this retired missionary talked to the devil. No, he wasn't *praying* to the devil, he was *talking* to the devil; he was exercising his authority over the devil based on the Word of God.

He said, "Now, Satan, you're going to have to take your hands off this woman's body because this body is a temple of the Holy Ghost. It belongs to God and you've got no right to trespass on God's property. Now we demand that you remove yourself from God's property."

Then the retired missionary talked to the woman. He didn't *pray* to the woman, but he *talked* to her. He said, "Now, Sister, Satan has oppressed your body with sickness, but God has made provision for your deliverance. Your body is a temple of the Holy Ghost, and you are commanded to glorify God in your body and in your spirit. Can God be glorified in your body by the devil dominating it? No, therefore, you stand against this sickness with me, and together we will demand that Satan stop trespassing on God's property."

One time I saw a sign on a lawn which read, "Gentlemen *will* not, and others *must* not trespass on this property." So I put up a sign on my body, so to speak, in the spiritual realm. You cannot see it because it is in the spirit, but the devil can, and it says, "NO TRESPASSING! Devil, this means you!" I did that by faith. You can't see the sign because I did it in the spirit. And I've had that sign up for years, so Satan doesn't trespass on my body, which is God's property.

You see, you are the custodian of your own body. *You* are to glorify God in *your* body and in your spirit, which are the Lord's.

Step Number Three: Know the Reality of the New Creation

The third step necessary to attain the highest kind of faith is to know the reality of the new creation and to know the legal side of redemption. You need to know that in the mind of Justice, we were recreated in Christ Jesus.

You should also know the reality of the new birth vitally for yourself. You should know and understand that the moment you accepted Jesus Christ as your Savior and confessed Him as your Lord, you were *recreated*. That is when the *legal* act of redemption, which was wrought in Jesus' death, burial, and resurrection became a reality in your own life. In the new birth, you have in your spirit the very life and the very nature of God.

The new birth is not just an experience. It is not a religion, and it is not joining a church. It is the actual rebirth of our spirits. We are the very sons and daughters of Almighty God. He is our very own Father; we are His very own children. We know that we have passed out of Satan's dominion—spiritual death—into the realm of life through Jesus Christ.

John said, *"We know that we have passed from death unto life, because we love the brethren . . ."* (1 John 3:14). We know that we are in the family of God. We know we are children of God. We were born into the family. You cannot *join* the family; you have to be *born* into it.

What will be the effects of this knowledge of the reality of the new birth and the new creation? In the new birth, God becomes your very own Father and you are His very own child. You have as much freedom to fellowship with the Father as Jesus had in His earthly walk because God loves you even as He loved Jesus (John 17:23).

Someone might say, "I just can't believe that God loves me as much as He loved Jesus." Well, thank God, I can believe it! I believe the Word and I am thrilled about it.

COLOSSIANS 1:18

18 And he [Jesus] **is the head of the body, the church: who is the beginning, the FIRSTBORN FROM THE DEAD; that in all things he might have the preeminence.**

You see, we were born again and redeemed from spiritual death, too, but Jesus is the *firstborn* from the dead (Rev. 1:18). We are begotten of God, but Jesus was the first One who was begotten of God (Heb. 1:6; Rev. 1:5). Peter said, *"Being born again* [begotten] *not of corruptible seed, but of incorruptible, by the word of God, which liveth and abideth for ever"* (1 Peter 1:23).

Thank God, we are begotten of God. We are born of God. We are children of God. We are heirs of God. We are joint or equal heirs with Jesus Christ (Rom. 8:17).

We are not magnifying ourselves when we talk about our inheritance in Christ; we are magnifying God and what He has done for us through the Lord Jesus Christ. We did not make ourselves new creatures; *God* made us new creatures. And Jesus is the Author and the Finisher of our faith (Heb. 12:2). Thank God, we are new creatures created by God in Christ Jesus.

EPHESIANS 2:10

10 For we are his workmanship, created in Christ Jesus.

Don't Pass Judgment on God's Creation

We didn't make ourselves who we are and what we are—God did. And I tell you, you had better be careful about passing judgment on God's creation.

You know, folks have thought they were being humble by saying, "I am so unworthy." But God didn't make any unworthy new creation.

You see, if you say you are unworthy, you are not looking at things the way God does and you are not living in line with the epistles which were written to you as a member of the Body of Christ. Many folks look at others from the physical or natural standpoint. But I'm not unworthy, because I am in Christ, and you are not unworthy either!

People just thought by saying they were unworthy that they were being humble. They didn't know they were being ignorant and giving place to the devil to dominate them. You see, Ephesians 2:10 says we are God's own workmanship, and when you belittle yourself, you are actually complaining about what God has done for you in the new birth; you are belittling His work in your life. And you are speaking contrary to the Word of God.

We are God's workmanship, created in Christ Jesus. Quit looking at yourself from the natural standpoint. Keep looking at yourself in Christ, and you'll look much better! God the Father doesn't see you like anyone else sees you. He sees you in Christ.

What defeats people is that they are looking at themselves and others from the natural standpoint. You and I have no right to do that. We need to look at things the way God does, and He tells us how He sees us in His Word.

Repentance vs. Doing Penance

One minister said to me when he was having a hard time, "I guess I'm just paying for the life I lived before I got saved. You know I was awful rough." But, friends, when you are born again, you are *redeemed* from the penalty of sin. If you are going to go on paying for your wrongdoing, then you're going to go on and go to hell too! But we know that is not true if we are in Christ (2 Cor. 5:17).

Pay attention to what the Word has to say about redemption because a lot of folks are defeated because they won't take a stand against the devil. In other words, they don't take a stand against what comes against them because they think it ought to be that way—that they deserve the test or trial that has come upon them.

You see, they don't know the difference between *repentance* and *doing penance*. If you accused them of being religious and just following certain religious practices, they would deny it. And yet, that is the very thing they are doing! They are actually trying to do penance over their past life.

When you have repented, God forgives you, and He doesn't even have any knowledge that you *ever* did *anything* wrong.

ISAIAH 43:25

25 I, even I, am he that blotteth out thy transgressions for mine own sake, and will NOT REMEMBER thy sins.

So if God doesn't remember your sins, why should you? *You shouldn't.* After you get saved, if you are going to continue to reap what you sowed when you were a sinner, then you would have to go to hell when you died, because that's part of the penalty too. If you are going to have reap *any part* of the penalty, you are going to reap *all* of it. Thank God, we are redeemed not only from the *power* of sin, but also from the *penalty* of sin. Jesus took our place and suffered the penalty of sin for us.

What am I saying to you? I am saying that a lot of folks are permitting—*they* themselves are allowing—tests and trials to take place in their lives because they are not standing in their place of authority against Satan. And they are being robbed of deliverance and victory, because they think it ought to be that way. Of course tests and trials in life come to all of us, but on the other hand, that doesn't mean we have to allow Satan to run over us either! And if we are in Christ, God has promised us the victory in every circumstance (1 Cor. 15:57).

Instead of accepting the fact that they have been delivered from the results or penalty of sin, some believers let the devil dominate them and keep them sick and beaten down. But God doesn't hold your sin against you after you have asked for forgiveness. God forgives, forgets, and He cleanses us from all unrighteousness by the blood of Jesus (1 John 1:9). Now the devil doesn't have any right to dominate you.

I am glad that God has made us able to enjoy the inheritance of saints in light (2 Peter 1:4; Col. 1:12). He has made us *able* to be partakers of our inheritance. Since God has done His part, let's do our part. Let's partake of our inheritance and enjoy what rightfully belongs to us in Christ!

Questions for Study

1. Name the three steps to attaining the highest kind of faith that are listed in this chapter.
   _____
   _____

2. What is the highest kind of faith?
   _____
   _____

3. When is the only time that the Word of God will come alive to you and work in your life?
   _____
   _____

4. Why is the Word of God of foremost importance?
   _____
   _____

5. In Colossians 1:13, what does the Greek word translated "power" mean?
   _____
   _____

6. What is the basis for our victory?
   _____
   _____

7. What do you have to add to the blood of Jesus to obtain victory?
   _____
   _____

8. Who is the firstborn from the dead, the first One who was begotten of God?
   _____
   _____

9. If you say you are unworthy, what are you not doing?
   _____
   _____

10. When you are born again, you are _____ from the penalty of sin.

Chapter 14

Seven Steps to the Highest Kind of Faith—Part 2

In this lesson we are going to continue our discussion on the third step necessary to attain the highest kind of faith. Then we will go on to the fourth step.

2 CORINTHIANS 6:14–17

14 Be ye not unequally yoked together with unbelievers: FOR WHAT FELLOWSHIP HATH RIGHTEOUSNESS WITH UNRIGHTEOUSNESS? and what communion hath light with darkness?

15 And what concord hath Christ with Belial? or what part hath he that BELIEVETH with an infidel?

16 And what agreement hath the temple of God with idols? for ye are the temple of the living God; as God hath said, I will dwell in them, and walk in them; and I will be their God, and they shall be my people.

17 . . . come out from among them, and BE YE SEPARATE.

Separation From the World, Not Segregation

Many people read that passage of scripture and think it is talking about what they call *separation* from the world. This passage is talking about *separation* from the world, but not *segregation* from the world. However, some people read this passage and begin practicing segregation from the world, and they think that is separation from the world and its ways. (There is a vast difference between separation and segregation.)

These people read Second Corinthians 6:14–17, and then they think that they can't have anything to do with the world or with anyone in the world. They sometimes even think they are supposed to separate themselves from other Christians, if other Christians don't believe just like they do.

But Jesus didn't say that. He said, *"Ye are the salt of the earth . . . Ye are the light of the world"* (Matt. 5:13–14). Believers are in the world, but Jesus said they are not *of* the world (John 17:16). Believers are not to segregate themselves from the world, or how could they be the salt of the earth and the light of the world? However, on the other hand, they are to be separate from the world and not adopt the world's standards (2 Cor. 6:17); they are to be like Jesus or they couldn't be the salt of the earth, nor the light of the world either.

A man once asked me to pray for him. He seemed to have the idea that he was to be segregated from the world. He didn't understand the difference between separation and segregation. He said to me,

"I work in a certain company, and I am the only Christian in my department. Please pray that God will move me out of there."

I said, "Oh, no, why the whole department would putrefy if you were gone. You stay right there. You're the salt of the earth, so you stay right there and salt it."

We are *in* the world, but not *of* the world (John 17:12-16). Some people try to segregate themselves from the world, but we are not to do that because that is unscriptural.

Believers are Called 'Righteousness' and 'Light'

I want you to notice something else in Second Corinthians chapter 6 that God is saying to us. First, He talks about believers and unbelievers. Then He says, *". . . for what fellowship hath RIGHTEOUSNESS with UNRIGHTEOUSNESS"* (2 Cor. 6:14). The believer is called *righteousness* and the unbeliever is called *unrighteousness*.

Did you ever think of yourself as being *righteous*? Have you ever called yourself righteousness? Well, if you are a believer, the Bible says you are! When I said that one time, one woman denied it and told me that she wasn't! I told her either she or God was lying about it because God said as His child that she is righteous. By saying that she was *not* righteous, she was really disagreeing with God.

That is the reason many of God's people haven't enjoyed the blessings of God in life and are not reigning in life by Christ Jesus. Instead of believing the Bible, so many times they take sides against the Bible. But you have to side in with the Bible if you are going to enjoy the blessings and benefits of it.

Let's continue to read here in Second Corinthians.

2 CORINTHIANS 6:14–15

14 Be ye not unequally yoked together with UNBELIEVERS: for what fellowship hath RIGHTEOUSNESS with UNRIGHTEOUSNESS? and what communion hath LIGHT with DARKNESS?

15 And what concord hath Christ with Belial? or what part hath he that BELIEVETH with an infidel?

In this verse of scripture, the believer is actually called light. Notice in this scripture, Christians are called *believers* and sinners are called *unbelievers* (2 Cor. 6:14). Then the believer is called *righteousness*, and the unbeliever is called *unrighteousness* (v. 14). Then the believer is called *light*, and the unbeliever is called *darkness* (v. 14).

As a Christian I am a *believer*; because I am *in* Christ, the Bible says I am *righteousness*; and I am *light*. And if you are a Christian, you are a *believer*; you are *righteousness*; and you are *light* too!

It is strange to me that people don't mind our saying they are light, but when I call them righteousness, they are not sure that is true. When I say that, they think I am trying to start some new doctrine. But you know, if one third of Second Corinthians 6:14 is true, then the whole verse is true. I am not saying that believers are righteous in themselves, of course not! But we are righteous *in* Christ: *"For he hath made him to be sin for us, who knew no sin; that we might be made the righteousness of God in him"* (2 Cor. 5:21).

Think on that a minute and let it soak into your spirit! Hold all this in your mind, as these scriptures are just going to lead us right into steps four and five of attaining the highest kind of faith. They just dovetail right together.

Step Number Four: Know the Reality of Our Righteousness in Christ

The fourth step necessary to attain the highest kind of faith is to know the reality of our righteousness in Christ.

ROMANS 3:23–26

23 For all have sinned, and come short of the glory of God;

24 Being justified freely by his grace through the redemption that is in Christ Jesus:

25 Whom God hath set forth to be a propitiation through faith in his blood, to declare his righteousness for the remission of sins that are past, through the forbearance of God;

26 To declare, I say, at this time his RIGHTEOUSNESS: that he might be JUST, and THE JUSTIFIER of him which believeth in Jesus.

The same Greek root word that is translated "righteousness" here in Romans 3:25 and 26 is also translated "just" and "justifier" in this same verse. The margin of my Bible reads, "that he might himself be righteous" (Rom. 3:26). The words "just" and "righteous" or "righteousness" can be inter-changeable terms.

What is this verse in Romans 3:26 telling us? That God has declared His righteousness to us through Jesus. And that God Himself is righteous

and He has become my righteousness. God is the righteousness of all who have believed on Jesus (2 Cor. 5:21). This is not theory but a Bible fact.

God's Righteousness Is a Gift

Most people have thought that righteousness is some kind of a state they had to attain to by right living, but that isn't true at all.

ROMANS 5:17

17 For if by one man's offence death reigned by one; much more they which receive abundance of grace and of the GIFT OF RIGHTEOUSNESS shall reign in life by one, Jesus Christ.

Of course believers are to live right. But, actually, "righteousness" means *rightness* or *right standing*. And righteousness is a *gift*. If you can't see that, read Romans 5:17 again and let it sink in. Righteousness as a gift is something that is received now. Righteousness as a stage of spiritual development is a fruit of the born-again recreated human spirit and it takes time to grow.

Other scriptures in the Bible do talk about "the fruits of our righteousness," but they are referring to the fruit that is a product of our rightstanding with God (Phil. 1:11; 2 Cor. 9:10). Righteousness as a fruit of the born-again human spirit is a result of our being vitally connected to the Vine (John 15:1–8).

But if the word "righteousness" referred to in Romans 5:17 was a fruit of the spirit, it would have said, ". . . *and of the FRUIT of righteousness"* (Rom. 5:17). In other words, you would have to grow or develop to that place of righteousness. But it doesn't say that. It says that we receive "the *gift* of righteousness" (Rom. 5:17).

Every one of God's dear children has the same righteousness and the same standing with God because we are *in* Christ and He is our righteousness. God doesn't love one of His children more than He loves another, and He won't listen to one praying more than He will listen to another praying. When you know this, your faith will abound, and your prayers will work.

So many people struggle so long in the realm of self-condemnation and, in the process, let the enemy rob them. People who do this just know their prayers won't work and that God won't hear them. They think if they could just find a righteous man to pray, his prayers would work because James 5:16 says, *"The effectual fervent prayer of a righteous man availeth much."*

However, people who live in the realm of self-condemnation don't know that they are righteous; they think they are not righteous. They think if they could just find a righteous man to pray, *his* prayers would be heard and answered. So instead of studying the Word and finding the answer to their problems, they have sought desperately for some righteous man to pray for them. But, thank God, according to Romans 3:26, *"To declare, I say, at this time his righteousness: that he might be just* [righteous], *and the JUSTIFIER* [righteousness] *OF HIM which believeth in Jesus."*

God Is Our Righteousness

God Himself has become our righteousness. God the Father became our righteousness when He imparted to us His nature—eternal life—when we were born again in the new birth. Jesus became our righteousness the moment we took Him as our Savior and confessed Him as our Lord. He then became our Sponsor, our Lord, our Head, and our very Life.

2 CORINTHIANS 5:17–21

17 Therefore if any man be in Christ, he is a new creature: old things are passed away; behold, all things are become new.

18 And all things are of God, who hath reconciled us to himself by Jesus Christ, and hath given to us the ministry of reconciliation;

19 To wit, that God was in Christ, reconciling the world unto himself, not imputing their trespasses unto them; and hath committed unto us the word of reconciliation.

20 Now then we are ambassadors for Christ, as though God did beseech you by us: we pray you in Christ's stead, be ye reconciled to God.

21 For he hath made him to be sin for us, who knew no sin; that WE MIGHT BE MADE THE RIGHTEOUSNESS OF GOD IN HIM.

I want you to know that God did not make any unrighteous or unworthy creatures. That would be an insult to Him. No, Jesus who knew no sin was made to be sin for us that we might be made the righteousness of God in Him (2 Cor. 5:21). In Christ believers are the righteousness of God.

Now go back to Second Corinthians 6:14.

2 CORINTHIANS 6:14

14 Be ye not unequally yoked together with unbelievers: for what fellowship hath RIGHTEOUSNESS with UNRIGHTEOUSNESS? and what communion hath LIGHT with DARKNESS?

You see, you *are* righteousness! Say that out loud: "I am the righteousness of God in Christ."

My Own Search to Understand Righteousness In Christ

The first gleam of light on this verse came to me when I was on the bed of sickness. I was having the same struggles that many of you have had in order to get to the place of receiving deliverance, victory, and health. I teach on the subjects of faith and healing so that you may grasp these truths as I did and be complete overcomers.

I began to read and to study the Word, and to look up references. Among the scriptures I studied were James 5:14 and 15.

JAMES 5:14–15

14 Is any sick among you? let him call for the elders of the church; and let them pray over him, anointing him with oil in the name of the Lord:

15 And the prayer of faith shall save the sick, and the Lord shall raise him up; and if he have committed sins, they shall be forgiven him.

I began to cry because I knew my church didn't believe in healing, especially by anointing with oil. I began to cry to the Lord and say, "Lord, I can't be healed, then, because I don't know any elders to call on."

The Lord spoke to me and said, "Did you notice that it is *the prayer of faith* that heals the sick?"

I said, "Yes, I noticed that."

"Well," He said, "you can pray that prayer just as well as anyone can."

There I was, a sixteen-year-old boy who had just been born again for a few months, just a babe, spiritually speaking. But God said *I* could pray that prayer. After the Lord said that, immediately my wrong thinking defeated me. I should have listened to my heart but instead, I listened to Satan. Satan said, "Yes, but the next verse, James 5:16 says, 'The prayer of a *righteous* man avails much.' You could pray the prayer of faith if you were righteous. But you are not righteous."

"Well," someone might say, "a fellow lying on a bed of sickness couldn't do too much that's wrong." No, I know he couldn't, but he surely could *want* to. You might not be able to do a lot that's wrong, but you could still *want* to do what's wrong. You could think a lot of things that would be wrong. And I was just sure, because I was acquainted with all of my mistakes and shortcomings, that I wasn't righteous.

I knew I didn't know anyone who could come and pray for me, and I didn't understand what the Lord meant when He told me that I could pray the prayer of faith just as well as anyone could. I thought I couldn't because I wasn't righteous, and yet I could, because God said I could. It took me months to realize that I was righteous, but one day I proceeded to read a little further in James chapter 5. You know, it pays to read the whole context of a scripture and not just take a verse out of its setting.

Elijah, An Example of a Righteous Man

In reading further, I read that James gave Elias or Elijah as an example of a righteous man praying.

JAMES 5:17–18

17 Elias was a man subject to like passions as we are, and he prayed earnestly that it might not rain: and it rained not on the earth by the space of three years and six months.

18 And he prayed again, and the heaven gave rain, and the earth brought forth her fruit.

I read that to begin with, but it didn't register with me because I wasn't familiar with this man Elijah. But in the process of time, I read a little bit about Elijah, and I said, "Well, there's something wrong here, because if I remember correctly, James gives this man as an example of a righteous man praying. And Elijah is surely not my idea of a righteous man. I know he had his good moments, but most of us have had our good moments too. However, Elijah had his bad moments too.

For example, although the hand of the Lord came upon Elijah at one time, enabling him to outrun the king's chariot (1 Kings 18:44–46), when Elijah later found out that Jezebel wanted to take off his head, he started running away in fear. Finally, Elijah became exhausted and hid under a juniper tree and begged the Lord to let him die. I thought, "Well, Elijah is just about as inconsistent as I have been!"

Elijah didn't really want to die. He was just talking to God in a desperate state. After all, if he had really wanted to die, why didn't he just stay where he was? Jezebel would have been glad to accommodate him!

No, Elijah didn't want to die any more than you would if you said in a desperate state that you wished you were dead. For a man to be so inconsistent and double-minded in his talking, was just not my idea of a righteous man. You see, many times we have our own ideas instead of taking God's Word for what it says.

Then not only was Elijah wrong in his thinking but he was wrong spiritually speaking, too, because he said, "Lord, after all, I'm the only one who is living right" (1 Kings 19:10). He didn't put it in those exact words, but when you analyze it, that is what he said.

We hear people talk like that today too: "Practically everyone's backslidden but me. Just me and my little bunch are right with the Lord, and no one else has anything in God."

Well, God had to correct Elijah. God said, "No, you're all wrong about it, Elijah. I've got 7,000 reserved to Myself who have not bowed their knees to Baal."

In other words, God was saying, "Elijah, you're not the only pea in the pod; you're not the only pebble on the beach." Elijah had become discouraged, and what he said to the Lord was just his own despairing words coming from his discouraged spirit. But a fellow acting that way was not my idea of a righteous man. And I thought, "How in the world could James ever give him as an example of a righteous man praying? In my opinion, he isn't any more righteous than I am."

Then I remembered that James had said that Elijah was a man, or a mere human, as we are. James 5:17 says, *"Elias was a man subject to like passions as we are,"* and yet God still called Elijah righteous. When we read about Elijah, we see him not only subject to like passions as we are, but we see him *giving in* to those passions too. Yet the Bible says he was righteous. I asked myself how God could call that fellow righteous. But then the light began to come to me.

Then I read in Psalm 32:1 and 2, where it says, *"Blessed is he whose transgression is forgiven, whose sin is covered. Blessed is the man unto whom the Lord imputeth not iniquity."*

Under the Old Covenant the blood of innocent animals covered the people's sins. That's why the Bible says, *"Blessed is the man unto whom the Lord imputeth not iniquity"* (Ps. 32:2). God did not impute iniquity to His covenant people living under the Old Testament even though they had done wrong. He covered their sins and forgave them and He imputed righteousness unto them.

In His sight He said they were righteous. He counted them as righteous because their sins had been atoned for or covered. Maybe man looked upon them and said they weren't righteous, but God said they were. That's why God could say, "When I see the blood I'll pass over you" (Exod. 12:13).

The Blood of Jesus Cleanses Us From Sin

Then I saw that the Word said that under the New Covenant we have a better covenant established upon better promises (Heb. 8:6). The blood of Jesus Christ doesn't *cover* our sins; it *cleanses* us from our sins.

The last part of Rev. 1:5 says, *"Unto him that loved us, and WASHED us from our sins in his own blood."* I saw then that because I was born again, all of my sins were remitted in the sight of God. All of my past life no longer existed. I saw that I had become a new creature in Christ Jesus and I knew that God didn't make an unrighteous new creature.

But the devil saw I was getting the truth and that I was going to be able to pray the prayer of faith, so he said to me, "Well, now, that's all true, all right. But what about *since* you were born again? It hasn't been very long ago that you lost your temper and got mad and knocked the tray off the bed. And that is no way for a righteous person to act."

You see, the devil got me looking right back at the natural again, and he put the light out on God's Word for me. But then as I read further in the Bible, I finally got into First John 1:9, which says, *"If we confess our sins, he is faithful and just to forgive us our sins, and to CLEANSE us from all unrighteousness."* The Bible isn't talking to sinners here, it is talking to *believers.*

Then I saw it. I had become the righteousness of God in Christ when I was born again. Now if I sinned since becoming a new creature in Christ, and of course I had, I was simply to confess my sins, and God would forgive me of my sins and cleanse me from all unrighteousness. And when I'm cleansed from unrighteousness, then I'm in fellowship with God again.

Thank God, I saw that truth. I had already decided that if I ever got to be righteous, I'd be a whiz when it came to praying the prayer of faith according to James 5:15 and 16. But when I saw the truth of God's Word about the believer's righteousness, then I said, "Thank God, my prayers will work! God hears me! And He will hear me just as quickly as He will hear anyone else."

I wrote beside that scripture in James, "I am a righteous man." That's not bragging on me, Kenneth E. Hagin, that's bragging on who I am *in Christ.* That's bragging on God and what He has wrought for me in Christ's redemptive work at Calvary.

Then I knew that I had my own faith and that I could pray my own prayer and God would hear me.

I knew my prayers would work. I have a standing at the throne of God, and it is just as good a standing as Jesus Himself, for Jesus *is* my right standing.

2 CORINTHIANS 5:21

21 For he hath made him to be sin for us, who knew no sin; that we might be made THE RIGHTEOUSNESS OF GOD IN HIM.

Thank God for this great revelation.

Thank God we are who God says we are. We have what God says we have. And we can do what God says we can do.

That means we can stand in God's Presence without any sense of guilt, condemnation, or inferiority. That means the prayer problem is settled. Our righteousness in Christ settles it. And these are the scriptures that settled it for me on the bed of sickness. The prayer problem is settled. We no longer need to go into God's Presence tongue-tied because of condemnation. We don't need to be fear-filled because of ignorance.

Jesus said, *"And ye shall know the truth, and the truth shall make you free"* (John 8:32). What sets me free? The truth. What will set you free? The very truth of God's Word that I am giving you. Of course, if you aren't going to accept the truth, then you can't be set free, because it is the truth that sets you free.

Friends, we know what we are in Christ. We know that in the new birth God made us who we are. *We* didn't make ourselves God's righteousness in Christ. Jesus did that for us through His death, burial, and resurrection.

Since we know we are in Christ, it is not a problem of whether or not we *feel* righteous. It is not even a problem of faith; it is a problem of knowing our rights and privileges in Christ—that we are the righteousness of God in Christ and that we can come boldly before our Heavenly Father without a sense of guilt or condemnation.

That's why in the final sense, going into God's Presence does not require faith any more than it requires faith for Jesus to go into the Presence of the Father. Jesus did not stop and examine Himself and say, "Have I got enough faith to go into the Presence of the Father God and pray?" Jesus was righteous, and thank God, we are too because we are *in* Him.

Therefore, you can enter into God's Presence without fear and in complete faith that your Heavenly Father hears your prayers, just as He heard Jesus' prayers when Jesus was upon the earth.

Questions for Study

1. Some people try to segregate themselves from the world, but we're not to do that. Why?

   _____

   _____

2. What is one reason why many of God's people haven't enjoyed the blessings of God in life and are not reigning in life by Christ Jesus?

   _____

   _____

3. Name the fourth step to attaining the highest kind of faith.

   _____

   _____

4. What is Romans 3:26 telling us?

   _____

   _____

5. What is the difference between righteousness as a gift and righteousness as a stage of spiritual development?

   _____

   _____

6. When did Jesus become our righteousness?

   _____

   _____

7. According to James 5:16, whose prayer avails much?

   _____

   _____

8. What does James 5:17 say about the prophet Elijah?

   _____

   _____

9. 2 Corinthians 5:21 means we can stand in God's Presence without any sense of _____ _____ or _____.

10. According to John 8:32, what will set you free?

    _____

    _____

Chapter 15

Seven Steps to the Highest Kind of Faith—Part 3

We are continuing our teaching on the several steps necessary to attaining to the highest kind of faith.

Step Number Five: Know the Reality of the Indwelling Presence of the Holy Spirit

The fifth step in this series of lessons is to know the reality of the indwelling Presence of the Holy Spirit. First John 4:4 says, *"greater is he that is in you, than he that is in the world."* Of all the mighty truths connected with redemption, this is the apex: God Himself, after He recreated us and made us new creatures and made us His own, is actually making our bodies His home!

When you are born again, it is more than an experience. The Holy Ghost, the Third Person of the Godhead, a divine Personality, comes to live *in* you. In fact, the Bible even goes so far as to say that God Himself is living in you.

2 CORINTHIANS 6:16

16 . . . for ye are the temple of the living God; as God hath said, I will dwell IN them, and walk IN them; and I will be their God, and they shall be my people.

God no longer dwells in the man-made Holy of Holies. Through the new birth, our bodies have become His temple.

1 CORINTHIANS 6:19–20

19 What? know ye not that YOUR BODY IS THE TEMPLE of the Holy Ghost which is IN you, which ye have of God, and ye are not your own?
20 For ye are bought with a price: therefore glorify God in your body, and in your spirit, which are God's.

We need to become "God-inside minded." In other words, we need to just simply take God at His Word. We need to believe and act like the Bible is true when it says, *"greater is he that is IN you, than he that is in the world"* (1 John 4:4)! "He that is in the world" is the god of this world, Satan (2 Cor. 4:4). But, thank God, He who is in us, the Holy Spirit, the third Person of the Godhead, is greater than he who is in the world!

The Greater One Lives in Us

Thank God, God indwells us as believers, through the Person of the Holy Spirit, today too. Because of the indwelling Presence of the Holy Spirit, it should be a common practice in the Church today for believers to say in every crisis of life, "I am more than a conqueror." However, the truth is, making positive confessions based on our rights and privileges in Christ is almost an unknown practice in the church world today.

The Christian's continual confession should be, "I am a victor. The Creator dwells in me; the Greater One lives in me. The Person and power of the Holy Ghost dwells in me. Praise God, He can put me over. He can make me a success. I cannot fail because of Him."

Many people think when you say those things that you are bragging on yourself. That's not bragging on you; it is bragging on the *Greater One who is in you.* Bragging on the Greater One in you will put Him to work for you.

The Power Source Within

You must remember that the Book of First John and the other epistles were letters written to the churches—to believers. Actually, they were written to folks who are not just born again, but were Spirit filled too. It was the exception back then for believers not to have received the Holy Ghost with the supernatural sign and evidence of speaking in other tongues.

But you know, when faced with tests and trials, sometimes even people who have been filled with the Holy Ghost and have received the enduement of power from on High will sometimes run around like a chicken with its head cut off, trying to find someone who can help them. They don't always realize that they have received the Powerhouse, the Holy Spirit, who is living inside of them.

So many times, they will just run to someone to find comfort, shed a few tears, quote a few scriptures, and call that praying. Then they wonder why the victory doesn't come. But all the time they were trying to find someone to help them, the Greater One was on the inside of them, trying to help them and give them their answers.

Many times, people don't realize what they received and *who* they received when they received the Holy Ghost. Too many times those who have been filled with the Holy Ghost just think they too, have simply received a blessing or had some kind of an experience. They miss entirely what the Word of God teaches about being filled with the Holy Spirit. They were filled with the Holy Spirit and thought it was just some kind of an experience or a blessing.

Later when tests and trials come, they believe if they could just feel the way they did when they were first filled with the Holy Spirit, they could be victorious. Well, we shouldn't be looking back to that experience in order to obtain the victory we need today. You don't need to try to have the same kind of "experience" you did when you first received Him; just learn to tap into His indwelling Presence and power today!

This has never been taught as it should have been taught. How many of us have been taught to trust the God who is *in* us? I'm not talking to sinners, I'm talking to Spirit-filled and born again ones. How many of us have been taught that you have in you, ready for use, all the power you'll ever need to put you over in life? No, we've been taught practically everything else but that vital truth.

The way some people talk, they had some kind of an experience back when they were baptized in the Holy Ghost and spoke with tongues, but they've been left destitute ever since then. They might say, "We need the power, and if we could just get the power, we would be all right. But we don't have the power. We're still seeking it."

Actually, the potential of all the divine Power there is dwells in us. If we'll begin to believe what the Bible says and begin to confess what God's Word says, then He will rise up in us and give illumination to our minds and direction to our spirits and health to our bodies, and He will help us in every aspect of life. We can be conscious of His indwelling Presence and power every moment.

I preached at a camp meeting in the mountains of California in 1954. Then I went back the next year to preach and a woman there said to me, "You know, last year when I was here, I received the baptism of the Holy Ghost. It was wonderful up here on the mountaintop of God's blessings. But I went back home, and it wasn't long before I got back into the valley because of the cares of life. And I've been in the valley all winter. All year I have been looking forward to getting back up here to receive another blessing."

This dear woman didn't know that the same Holy Ghost she had received last year was in her all the time and was just as real at her home in her everyday life as He was up there in those services in the mountains.

Other times when people don't feel like they did when they first received the Holy Ghost, they think, "Well, He's gone now. I've lost Him." But Jesus said, *"I will pray the Father, and he shall give you another Comforter, that he may abide with you FOR EVER"* (John 14:16). God didn't send the Holy Spirit, the Comforter, just as a guest to spend a few days with us. No, praise God, Jesus said that the Holy Spirit would abide with us forever. God intended for the Holy Spirit to come and *dwell* in us!

Believers Are the Body of Christ

2 CORINTHIANS 6:14–16

14 Be ye not unequally yoked together with unbelievers: for what fellowship hath righteousness with unrighteousness? and what communion hath light with darkness?

15 And what concord hath CHRIST with Belial? or what part hath he that believeth with an infidel?

16 And what agreement hath the temple of God with idols? for ye are the temple of the living God; as God hath said, I will dwell in them, and walk in them; and I will be their God, and they shall be my people.

What are these verses saying? They are saying that we as believers are *righteousness;* we are *light;* and we are the Body of *Christ.* Jesus said, *"I am the vine, ye are the branches"* (John 15:5).

You don't look at a tree and say the branches on that tree aren't a part of the tree because they *are.* The tree and the branches are *one.* We as believers are the Body of Christ. We are the fruit-bearing part of Christ because the branches of a tree are what bear fruit. The Bible talks about us bearing fruits of righteousness.

As we said in chapter 14, righteousness, meaning rightstanding with God, is a *gift* and it is to be received immediately when you accepted Jesus as your Savior (Rom. 5:17). Righteousness as a stage of spiritual development is a *fruit* of the born-again recreated human spirit and it takes time to grow.

PHILIPPIANS 1:11

11 Being filled with the FRUITS OF RIGHTEOUSNESS, which are by Jesus Christ, unto the glory and praise of God.

2 CORINTHIANS 9:10

10 Now he that ministereth seed to the sower both minister bread for your food, and multiply your seed sown, and increase THE FRUITS OF YOUR RIGHTEOUSNESS.

Someone asked, "What are *fruits of righteousness?"* The fruits of our righteousness are the products of abiding vitally connected with the Vine (John 15:1–8). Some think fruits of righteousness mean being good, or just living a good life. And when they think of being good, they think of doing good works, such as giving to the poor.

Those things are well and good, but, actually, the fruits of righteousness are doing the works of Jesus. We are to cast out devils and heal the sick and do the same works Jesus did when He was here on the earth (Mark 16:15–20; John 14:12), because we *are* the Body of Christ. Fruits of righteousness are also produced as a result of being a doer of the Word (James 1:22), and conforming to God's will in every area.

But the point I am making is that Jesus is the Head of His Church and the Church is His Body (Col. 1:18). We are the Body of Christ. As I said in the last lesson, your head doesn't go by one name and your body by another. No, you and your body are one body.

Notice also it says, *"And what agreement hath the temple of God with idols? for YE ARE THE TEMPLE OF THE LIVING GOD"* (2 Cor. 6:16). We are the temple of God. God indwells us, not only as the Body of Christ, but God indwells each of us individually. Let's look at the *Amplified Bible, Classic Edition* of this verse.

2 CORINTHIANS 6:16 (AMPC)

16 What agreement [can there be between] a temple of God and idols? For we are the temple of the living God; even as God said, I will dwell in and with and among them and will walk in and with and among them, and I will be their God and they shall be My people.

We are the temple of the living God, both individually and collectively!

We Have the Holy of Holies Within Us

1 CORINTHIANS 3:16 (AMPC)

16 Do you not discern and understand that you [the whole church at Corinth] are God's temple (His sanctuary), and that God's Spirit has His permanent dwelling in you—to be at home in you [collectively as a church and also individually]?

I like that expression "to be at home *in* you." God is actually making our bodies His home. No longer does God dwell in a man-made Holy of Holies. In the Old Testament, the Presence of God was kept shut up in the Holy of Holies. God's people had to go to the Holy of Holies where the Presence of God was located in the Ark of the Covenant.

You remember the woman at the well of Samaria said to Jesus, *"The Jews say you have to worship God in Jerusalem, but our forefathers worshipped God in this mountain"* (John 4:20). Let's look at Jesus' reply.

JOHN 4:21, 23–24

21 Jesus saith unto her, Woman, believe me, the hour cometh, when ye shall NEITHER in this mountain, NOR yet at Jerusalem, worship the Father. . . .

23 But the hour cometh, and now is, when the true worshippers shall worship the Father in spirit and in truth: for the Father seeketh such to worship him.

24 God is a Spirit: and they that worship him must worship him in spirit and in truth.

Jesus was indicating that the time would come when man would no longer be confined to worship God in a designated *place* such as Jerusalem for the Jews, or Mt. Gerizim where the Samaritans worshipped God. The day was coming when man would worship God in his heart or spirit where God would make His abode with man (Jer. 31:33; John 14:16–17, 23; Heb. 8:8–13).

You see in the Old Testament, it was required that every Jewish male present himself at least once a year in Jerusalem before the Lord. Each man had to go to where the Presence of God was kept shut up in the Holy of Holies. But no one dared to approach the Holy Presence of God for himself. Only the high priest could go into the Holy of Holies on behalf of the people, and then he only did so with great precaution.

If anyone else intruded into that holy place, he fell dead (Num. 3:10). Some actually did fall dead for wrongfully intruding into that holy place.

Just before Jesus gave up the Ghost and died on the cross, He said, "It is finished" (John 19:30). Jesus was not talking about the New Covenant being finished or ratified, or the plan of redemption being finished because it wasn't finished just because Jesus died. Jesus had to be raised from the dead and to ascend into Heaven for the plan of redemption to be completed.

But on the cross, when Jesus said, "It is finished," Jesus was referring to the fact that the *Old Covenant* was finished. What does it mean, the Old Covenant was finished? If you'll read in Matthew 27, you'll find out what happened.

MATTHEW 27:50–51

50 Jesus, when he had cried again with a loud voice, yielded up the ghost.

51 And, behold, the veil of the temple was rent in twain from the top to the bottom; and the earth did quake, and the rocks rent.

On the cross, when Jesus "cried with a loud voice" (Matt. 27:50), and said, "It is finished," the curtain that separated the Holy of Holies was rent in twain or torn in two from top to bottom.

Jewish historians tell us that the curtain was forty feet wide, twenty feet high, and four inches thick. The Bible doesn't say the curtain was rent in twain from *bottom* to *top*. The Bible says the curtain was rent in twain from *top* to *bottom* (Matt. 27:51). The Presence of God moved out of that man-made Holy of Holies, and God has never dwelt in a man-made Holy of Holies anymore.

A Better Covenant

Thank God, the holy divine Presence of the Holy Spirit indwells us as believers! That Presence lives in me and in you.

We have carried many truths from the Old Testament over into the New Testament, and have really failed to understand the full truth concerning our redemption and the reality of the indwelling Presence of the Holy Spirit.

Many people, for instance, mix the truths of the Old Covenant with the truths of our rights and privileges in Christ in the New Covenant.

For example, if you are mixing cement and you don't get the mixture right, it won't work; the cement will crumble. That is what many people have done spiritually speaking. They have carried truths over from the Old Testament into the New Testament and have not understood their proper relationship with God in the light of the New Covenant.

They haven't gotten the mixture right. That's sometimes the reason the circumstances of their lives seem to crumble around them; they've really missed what God is saying to them under the New Covenant and are still trying to live under the provisions of the Old Covenant. But under the New Covenant, we have a better covenant based on better promises (Heb. 8:6). God actually dwells in us under the New Covenant! Our bodies are God's temple or house.

God Dwells in People—Not in Buildings

One example of believers trying to live under the provisions of the Old Covenant is believers calling the church building the "house of God."

Most church dedication services I've ever attended were centered around the idea that the building they were dedicating was the house of God. The ministers usually read about the dedication of Solomon's Temple in the Old Testament; however, this leaves the impression that the church building is a house of God just as Solomon's Temple was a house of God. But nothing could be further from the truth!

Under the New Covenant God dwells in people—not buildings. If people aren't careful, they will put too much significance on a place—on buildings and on other material things.

For example, I know of a beautiful church in one state, and chiseled across the front of the building at the top, is a scripture from the Old Testament about the church being a temple of God. I get provoked every time I drive by that church. I think, "Dear God, they've got a lie right on the front of the church building, and people go there and think it's a holy place."

If we say any church building is the house of God in the sense that God dwells there, we're wrong. In the New Testament, God *does not* dwell in any buildings made with human hands.

On the other hand, if we mean that a church building is the house of God because it is dedicated to the Lord and used for worship, that's all right. But you must be careful that you don't get out of line with the Word of God in this area because it is so easy to become taken up with material things in the sense realm—the natural realm which you can see—and miss the spiritual reality.

I was holding a meeting in 1957 in San Diego, California, and one night, some women from England were present in the service. We had a time of praise and worship, and we sang a few choruses and clapped our hands to keep time to the music as we do in Full Gospel circles. After the service was over, these women said to the pastor's wife, "Oh, my, this is the house of God! People shouldn't be clapping their hands in the house of God." The women were almost talking in a whisper.

Some people think you should sit in church like you had a poker for a backbone and like you had been pickled in vinegar! The Bible doesn't say anything about the saints being pickled; but it does say they are to be preserved! Some people think you should sit in church like you were at a funeral, because the church building is so holy. They call that reverencing God. But if you are a Christian, your *body* is the house of God, not the building where you attend church.

Full gospel folks need to realize that *we* are God's temple—not some church building! At the last church I pastored down in the east Texas oil fields, we had monthly fellowship meetings and had services all day and then had dinner on the grounds. These meetings were held at different churches in the area. I remember we went to one church fellowship meeting, and it rained that day. This was a small church and they didn't have a Sunday school annex, so one of the officials said, "Let's just turn these benches in the church around and eat inside the church."

Some of the folks said, "Oh, look at those folks eating in the church! Don't they know that's the house of God?" And these folks got angry and went home. They didn't know that the church building wasn't the house of God at all! Your *body* is the house of God.

When John Wesley and his brother came over to the United States as missionaries to the Native Americans in Georgia, they weren't successful in their attempt to convert them. While traveling back to their home by boat, the Wesleys learned some deeper truths about God from a group that was present on the boat.

When John Wesley returned to England, he was preaching some of these truths, and the church leaders put him out of the church right in the middle of his sermon. Wesley wanted to finish that sermon, so he stood on his father's tombstone in the churchyard and preached. In England in those days, the dead were buried in the churchyards.

As Wesley stood on his father's tombstone outside and preached, some of the people came outside and listened. Surprised, Wesley reportedly said, "To my astonishment, God met us out there. Up till then we didn't know God would meet us anywhere except in that building. But God met us out there in the open air."

Later, John Wesley and John Whitfield became the first, what we call, "field preachers." They hadn't known God would meet them anywhere else but inside the church building. They had attached great significance to the building. But they learned that one can sit and listen in reverence to a service outside in a tent or in an open-air crusade just as well as he can in a church building.

Certainly, people should be taught to be reverent to God while a service is going on or while the Spirit of God is manifesting Himself to minister to people. But if we are not careful, we can attach too much significance to natural places and things and miss the Person of Jesus, whom we are actually worshipping. And we can miss the reality of our own bodies being the temple of the Holy Spirit.

I was holding a meeting in Texas in 1951. After the meeting was over, I went down to east Texas to preach. A man came up to me and said, "I hear you just left such and such a place."

And I answered, "Yes."

He said, "What kind of church does the pastor have there?"

I asked, "What do you mean?"

He said, "How many does he run in Sunday school?" So I told him.

Then he said, "What kind of a revival did you have?"

I said, "Well, the old-timers said it was the best revival they'd ever had. (The church had been in existence for more than forty years.) They said it was the greatest revival in the history of the church."

"How did your crowds run?" the man asked.

I said, "We filled the building up and had to borrow one hundred folding chairs from one of the local business places. We set the chairs down in the aisles and then we moved the altar bench out and used that space to seat people."

He said, "You moved the altar out?"

"Yes," I said, "we took the altar bench out."

"Well," the man said, "I thought you got people saved."

I said, "Yes, there were about one hundred people who responded to the call for salvation."

He said, "How in the world did you ever get anyone saved without an altar bench?"

"Well," I said, "I never heard of an altar bench saving anyone yet! I thought Jesus was the One who saves, not the altar bench!"

There is nothing holy about a piece of furniture. You can make an altar anywhere, isn't that true? I know of people who got saved out in the cotton fields picking cotton. They got saved going down those rows of cotton dragging a cotton sack! They made an "altar" out there on their knees between those rows. I also know of folks who have been saved and who have received the Holy Ghost out behind a barn.

Don't Place Too Much Significance On Natural Things

You see, if we're not careful, we attach too much significance to natural things and miss the real import of the message of God.

I pastored a church one time when I was just twenty-one years old, where some of the people had had the Holy Ghost for twenty-three years. They had an altar bench in that church that had never been varnished or painted for those twenty-three years. I wanted to sand it down and take the paint off and varnish it, but some of the church members objected.

One of the members said, "If you'll look there at the end of that altar bench, you can see my tear stains at the place where I got saved twenty years ago."

I said, "But the altar didn't save you, and your tears didn't have a thing in the world to do with your getting saved. If tears could save people, nearly everyone would be saved, wouldn't they?"

He said, "But I got the baptism of the Holy Ghost there. God met me right there, and since then, I always get right there in that spot to pray."

I said, "Yes, and it probably makes you mad as the devil if anyone else gets in your place too! You probably get so angry you won't even pray. You probably just go and sit down and get depressed and put on a long face over it." Then I said to him, "God is not confined to that little space at the end of that altar bench!"

No, there is nothing holy about a church building or an altar bench, for they are natural things. But the Bible *does* say our bodies are holy, for they are the temple of the Holy Spirit.

1 CORINTHIANS 3:16–17

16 Know ye not that YE ARE THE TEMPLE OF GOD, and that the Spirit of God dwelleth in you?

17 If any man defile the temple of God, him shall God destroy; FOR THE TEMPLE OF GOD IS HOLY, WHICH TEMPLE YE ARE.

The Greater One in Us, Can Make Impossibilities—Possibilities

God is actually making our bodies His home, His dwelling place. Now there are very few people, who are conscious of God *in* them. Very few of us are conscious of God living in our bodies. We couldn't be conscious of His living in our bodies and talk as we talk.

What do I mean when I say that? Well, when a need arises, most of us are always quick to say, "No, I can't do that." Why? Because we are trusting in our own sufficiency, and we know we don't have the ability.

But if we know *He* is in us, we know *He* has the ability. Since *He* is in us, we can stop saying, "I can't," and begin saying, "I can because I am trusting in Him." We say, "I can because greater is He who is in me than he who is in the world."

I don't care what impossibilities we may each be facing, we can confidently say, "The Greater One will put me over. He'll make me a success. The Greater One indwells me." That kind of believing and that kind of talking is faith talking, and it will put God to work for you!

The Holy Spirit Is a Gentleman

The sad thing is, the Greater One is in believers, but many believers have ignored Him. They might think that if the Holy Spirit is going to move on their behalf, He is just going to come in and take over and run their lives for them without them doing anything. But He won't.

Let me say it like this. The Holy Ghost is a Gentleman. He is not going to come in you and just take you over and run your life on His own. You can't find any Scripture to back that up.

Devils, demons, and evil spirits will do that. They will try to make people do things they don't want to do and will try to force them into doing certain things. But throughout the Bible, we see that the Holy Ghost leads, guides, prompts, urges, or gives us a gentle push. But devils and evil spirits drive people and use force and control.

The Holy Spirit Is Our Helper

Some Christians ask, "Why doesn't the Holy Spirit do this?" And "Why doesn't He do that?" But the Holy Spirit is a Gentleman. He won't do anything until you put Him to work for you. And the Holy Spirit works in line with God's Words spoken through your lips.

You see, the Holy Spirit is sent to be your Helper (John 16:7 AMPC). He's not sent to do the job, but to *help you* do the job. The Holy Spirit is in us. God is in us. And He is our Helper.

HEBREWS 13:5–6

5 . . . for he hath said, I will never leave thee, nor forsake thee.

6 So that we may boldly say, THE LORD IS MY HELPER, and I will not fear what man shall do unto me.

EPHESIANS 3:16–17 (AMPC)

16 May He grant you out of the rich treasury of His glory to be strengthened and reinforced with mighty power in the inner man by the (Holy) Spirit [Himself]—indwelling your innermost being and personality.

17 May Christ through your faith [actually] dwell—settle down, abide, make His permanent home—in your hearts! May you be rooted deep in love and founded securely on love.

How does the Holy Spirit permanently make His home in your heart? Through your faith.

Notice Paul was writing to those who were already born again and filled with the Holy Ghost. He wrote, "May Christ through your faith [actually] dwell—settle down, abide, make His permanent home—in your hearts!(Eph. 3:17). That's what folks haven't allowed Him to do and that's what He wants to do—make His permanent home in our hearts. How does He do that? Through our faith! That is exactly where we are failing in our faith walk.

We haven't let Christ make His permanent home in our hearts through our faith in His Word.

The Holy Spirit Works Through Us As We Act in Faith

People are looking on the outside of themselves for God to do something, so they sing, "Come by here, Lord, come by here." What they are really saying is, "He is not here, but if we could only get Him to come by, He might do something for us." We sing, "Reach out and touch the Lord as He goes by," but, actually, that idea is based on sense knowledge; it's all based on what we can *see* on the outside in the physical realm.

Someone said, "Didn't that woman with the issue of blood reach out and touch Jesus?" Yes, but Jesus was there physically on the earth then. Jesus is not here on the earth in the physical now. He is *in* us through the Holy Spirit (John 14:16–17). I don't have to reach out and touch Him because He is *in* me. You see, we've missed the truth of the indwelling Presence of the Holy Spirit and that has hindered our faith.

In the natural, in the physical, we struggle and strain, trying to reach God. In other words, we're trying to get Jesus to "come by here." There is the song that goes something like this: "Just to have a touch, Lord, from You." Well, what do I want with *touches* when I've got *Him* on the inside of me in my spirit?

Really, all of those types of songs are primarily written from the physical standpoint or from the standpoint of the sense realm, not from a spiritual standpoint at all. I say that kindly, but it is true.

Thank God, God is *in* me and He is *in* you if you are born again. But the fact that God is in you is not going to do you any good unless you know it, believe it, and act upon it. As I said, the Holy Ghost will not just rise up and take over in your life. But when you know the Holy Spirit, the Greater One, is in you, you can act upon God's Word intelligently, and He will work through you.

I believe "greater is He who is in me than he who is in the world," don't you? Is He in you? If you'll just put Him to work and trust Him, the Word will work and the Holy Spirit will move in your life just like the Bible says because the Bible is true.

Trust the God who is in you. He is in there. Learn to become God-inside minded. As you do, God will rise up in you and give illumination to your mind, and He will direct your spirit. You can even look death in the face and laugh because God is in you and you know that He is.

The Lord once said to me, "Now you know why I said that all things are possible to him that believes." The scripture declares that with God all things are possible (Matt. 19:26; Mark 9:23). All things that are possible with God are possible to him that believes because the believer has God, the God with whom all things are possible, dwelling *in* him.

Now put God and His Word to work for you, for He will surely rise up in you and give illumination to your mind, direction to your spirit, and health to your body. Yes, He will manifest Himself through you even to others and through your hands as you lay them upon others; for the Lord your God, He it is who does dwell in you.

I have said in these lessons that there are seven steps to attaining to the highest kind of faith. Is your faith being helped? Is your faith being built up? Are you being strengthened? This is what God's Word will do for you. God's Word will build faith.

So constantly say to yourself, quietly if you are with others, or out loud if you are by yourself, "Greater is He Who is in me than he who is in the world. The Greater One is in me. I am depending on Him. He will live big in me. He will put me over. He will make me a success. He is in me. The Master of all of creation is in me. God is making His home in my body."

Your poor old natural mind, if it is not educated in the Word, doesn't want to accept that. But at the same time your head is giving you trouble, if you will look to your spirit, your spirit will rejoice in it! Your confession of faith will send a thrill through your spirit.

When others say they don't know what they are going to do, you will say, "I may be in the same situation, naturally speaking, but the Greater One is in me! He is in me, and I'm trusting Him Who indwells me. He will put me over."

Meditate on truth such as that and feed your spirit on the Word of God. Think on the Holy Spirit's indwelling Presence, and see how real the Greater One will become to you!

Questions for Study

1. Name the fifth step to the highest kind of faith.

   _____

   _____

2. What happens when you are born again?

   _____

   _____

3. What are the fruits of righteousness?

   _____

   _____

4. What was Jesus indicating by His answer to the Samaritan woman in John 4:21, 23–24?

   _____

   _____

5. On the cross, what was Jesus referring to when He said, "It is finished"?

   _____

   _____

6. Under the New Covenant, where does God dwell?

   _____

   _____

7. What will happen if we attach too much significance to natural things?

   _____

   _____

8. When does the Holy Spirit permanently make His home in your heart?

   _____

   _____

9. The fact that God is in you is not going to do you any good unless you _____ it, and _____ upon it.

10. What will happen as you learn to become God-inside minded?

    _____

    _____

Chapter 16

Seven Steps to the Highest Kind of Faith—Part 4

Let us continue where we left off in chapter 15 on the seven steps necessary to attain the highest kind of faith. We were discussing step five which is to know the reality of the indwelling Holy Spirit. I said that believers need to be God-inside minded. We need to be assured and always be aware that *"greater is He who is in us than he who is in the world"* (1 John 4:4).

Then we can go out and face life's problems with the sense of being a conqueror. We can know that we are fortified from within with God's strength, and that no matter what comes, the Greater One is in us.

If we know that the Greater One is in us, we will not be moved by tests and trials. We won't be perturbed about anything that happens because we know the Greater One is in us and that He will put us over in every circumstance as we lean on Him.

As I said before, it is an almost unknown practice in the church today for Christians to say in every crisis of life, "I am more than a conqueror. I am a victor because the Creator dwells in me. He can put me over. He can make me a success. I cannot fail." And yet this should be the confession and the belief of every believer. As for me personally, I am continually making these faith confessions based on God's Word.

The Holy Spirit: Our Intercessor and Guide

As the Holy Spirit dwells within believers, He fulfills two other important roles. He is our Intercessor and our Guide (John 16:13; Rom. 8:26). And the believer who also has experienced the infilling of the Holy Spirit has the added benefit of being able to pray out the perfect will of God in any situation by praying with other tongues (Rom. 8:26–27; 1 Cor. 14:2).

For example, many times in the past concerning my own children, I have said to the Lord, "Well, I just don't know for what to pray as I ought."

Certainly, I know to pray for God to bless my children and to keep them. I remind the Father God and I remind myself of God's Word. And I remind the Holy Spirit in me that He is in there to help me. Paul said, *"For if I pray in an unknown tongue, my spirit* [by the Holy Spirit within me] *prayeth"* (1 Cor. 14:14). So I just tell the Holy Spirit that I am expecting Him to help me. And then I immediately lift my voice (*I* do it) and start praying in tongues.

Many times when I've prayed that way, the Holy Spirit has given me wisdom and has shown me what would happen concerning certain situations (John 16:13), and the answer has *always* come just as God said it would.

It isn't necessary to see the answer right then when you pray because the Bible says when you pray in the Spirit, your understanding is unfruitful (1 Cor. 14:14). And the Bible also says you are to believe you have received your answer when you pray (Mark 11:24). But sometimes God will let you know exactly the answer and what is to come. Actually Paul said in First Corinthians 14:13, *"Wherefore let him that speaketh in an unknown tongue pray that he may interpret."*

Paul was not referring to the fact that you might be an interpreter in the church. He was talking about your own personal praying, so that sometimes as the Holy Spirit wills, you can interpret what you prayed in tongues. When you interpret what you are praying in tongues, you will know in your own language what you prayed for. *This gift belongs to every Spirit-filled believer*, because Paul plainly stated, *"Let him that speaketh in an unknown tongue pray that he may interpret"* (1 Cor. 14:13).

Actually, what that scripture is saying in First Corinthians 14:13 is just as much an instruction as any other instruction in the Bible. That scripture belongs to you just as much as any other verse of scripture belongs to you. The Holy Spirit *wants* to show you what you have prayed about when it is important and necessary to have such knowledge. At times, when you do not receive the interpretation, you can rest in the knowledge that you have prayed according to God's perfect will.

Now let's tie together these verses in First Corinthians 14 just as they are recorded in the Bible, so we are not taking one or two verses out of context.

1 CORINTHIANS 14:13–15

13 Wherefore let him that speaketh in an unknown tongue pray that he may interpret.

14 For if I pray in an unknown tongue, my spirit prayeth, but my understanding is unfruitful.

15 What is it then? I will pray with the spirit, and I will pray with the understanding also: I will sing with the spirit, and I will sing with the understanding also.

Now what are these verses saying to you? They are simply saying this: When you pray in an unknown tongue, your spirit by the Holy Spirit prays. When you pray in the Spirit, your understanding is unfruitful. You need to pray that you may also interpret so your understanding may be fruitful; then you can understand what you are praying about.

I prayed in tongues and interpreted my prayers in my own personal devotions for a long time before I ever interpreted a message given in tongues in public. The way I have learned nearly everything I know about the things of God was by praying it out in tongues and then praying the interpretation out in English.

Sometimes by praying in tongues the Lord has led me to certain portions of the Bible. The Holy Ghost is our Teacher (John 14:26 AMPC). He would take me through several chapters of the Bible that way, as I prayed in tongues and then prayed out the interpretation of what the Holy Spirit was teaching me. Then I began to see things in the Word that I never saw before.

Praying in the Spirit in this manner and interpreting what is prayed in tongues doesn't belong just to me. It belongs to every Spirit-filled believer. Because of the ability to pray in tongues and to be conscious and aware of the indwelling Presence of the Spirit of truth, there is nothing that happens in our family but what I know about it, sometimes as many as two years ahead of time.

Nine times out of ten that is the way it comes to me—by praying and interpreting what I pray. It doesn't come through any spiritual gifts or gifts of the Holy Spirit which may operate in my ministry as a prophet. It comes by simply praying in tongues and interpreting what I prayed.

The Holy Spirit Will Show Us Things to Come

You see, the Holy Spirit knows the future, for the Word says, *"he [the Holy Spirit] will shew you things to come"* (John 16:13). And you must remember that this blessing isn't promised just to a preacher or just to a few believers. *The Holy Ghost will show the believer things to come.*

I am convinced that if Spirit-filled people would learn to listen to the Holy Spirit, nothing would ever happen in their lives to confound them. No accident or tragedy or anything would ever slip up on them. In other words, they would know ahead of time about what was going to happen, and they could avert many things by responding to the Holy Spirit.

Praying in Tongues Helps Make the Spiritual Realm More Distinct

But you see, spiritual things are not as distinct to us as they ought to be because we are walking too much in the natural and that is where praying in tongues helps us.

1 CORINTHIANS 14:14
14 For if I pray in an unknown tongue, my spirit prayeth.

When you are praying in tongues, the spirit is active, but not the mind and not the body. When you are speaking with tongues, the tongues are coming out of your spirit. So, you see, your spirit is active, and your spirit is in contact with God. Your spirit can begin to pick up things from God.

I don't know about you, but I appreciate the gift of the Holy Spirit and the ability to pray in other tongues. Besides the new birth, being baptized in the Holy Ghost and being able to pray in tongues is the greatest blessing that has ever happened to me in my life. Being filled with the Holy Ghost with the evidence of speaking in tongues and then praying in tongues is the greatest single blessing in my life besides the new birth.

I received the baptism of the Holy Spirit with the evidence of speaking in other tongues in 1937. Five years later in 1942, while I was pastoring a church in east Texas, I had prayed in the manner about which I've been telling you, and by so doing I received some revelations from the Word of God.

No one had told me that it was possible to receive revelations from the Word of God by praying in tongues and meditating on the Word. At first, I would accept it, and then I would draw back from it. I wasn't as knowledgeable in the Word as I should have been, and I wasn't sure if I was being scriptural, even though I was deriving great blessings from praying in the Spirit.

In those days, it always took me at least an hour of praying in other tongues to get my mind quiet. This is another reason I appreciate praying in tongues. At first when you begin to pray in tongues, your mind will continue to be active, but if you pray long enough, your mind will become quiet.

After practicing this method of praying in tongues all of these years, I can get my mind quiet and get right into the Spirit. Then as I get over into the Spirit by yielding to the Holy Ghost, I can begin to operate in the spiritual realm.

Your Emotions Have Nothing to Do With Speaking in Tongues

I remember how the devil would keep trying to torment me about praying in other tongues. At first I didn't recognize that it was Satan. And then my own natural mind, which was not as thoroughly educated in the Word as it should have been, would side in with the devil and say, "You're wasting your time."

Finally, I recognized that those thoughts were coming from the enemy, and so I would say, "Well, I'm going to get down here and pray for an hour in tongues." (You see, many people think they have to feel some kind of an ecstasy or emotion in order to believe they are being effective in their praying. But feelings don't have a thing in the world to do with praying in the Spirit.)

So I just got down on my knees and deliberately started praying in tongues. Paul said, *"I thank my God, I speak with tongues"* (1 Cor. 14:18). You don't have to work yourself up emotionally or feel like you are up on cloud nine or anything else to pray in tongues or be effective in tongues. That is unnecessary. If folks do get emotional when they are praying in tongues, it is probably just something *they* are doing, not something the *Holy Ghost* is doing.

It is a strange thing what some Christians feel they must do in a service when they are about to give what we call a message in tongues. They think they should pitch their voice high and speak in some kind of falsetto voice, but that is unnecessary. When you give a message in tongues, just speak out like you ordinarily do. Many of us want to do something to try to make others believe that the power of God is really on us. But we know the Holy Ghost is *in* us all the time, so just hook up with Him and flow with Him.

One time when I was in Beaumont, Texas, there was a woman in one particular meeting who wanted everyone to know that the Holy Ghost was really using her, and you talk about yelling! That woman could *scream* in tongues! It was not very edifying. If you happened to be sitting in front of her, you would nearly jump out of your seat when she would begin to scream. I told her she didn't have to do that. I told her she could just talk as she normally talked at any other time.

If you scream when you give out a message in tongues, that's just you doing it; it is not the Holy Ghost. We are supposed to do that which edifies folks.

So when the devil tried to tell me, "You're just wasting your time talking in tongues," I just started deliberately, purposely, talking in tongues. And I prayed an hour in tongues there in my office. Then I got up and sat down in the chair, and something said to me (I knew this time it was the devil because anything that discourages a person is of the devil), "Well, you've wasted an hour now. You could have been out visiting folks."

So I said, "Just for that, Mr. Devil, I am going to get down and pray another hour in tongues." So I got down and prayed another hour in tongues. Then I got up and sat down in my chair.

Make Your Flesh Submit!

You see, you have to make your flesh do some things, because the flesh and your unrenewed mind will try to fight you (Rom. 8:7). The flesh doesn't know what you're doing when you are in the spirit realm, and the flesh doesn't want to pray in other tongues. The flesh can't enter into the spirit realm.

Also, if your mind or your understanding has not been renewed with the Word of God, your mind will try to keep being active and will not want to meditate on the Word of God and the things of God. After all, your mind doesn't know what you are saying in tongues and since the mind has been used to running things, it doesn't want to get into the Spirit. Everything about you physically and mentally will cry out, "This isn't right, I don't want to do this!" because the flesh and the mind do not want to pray in other tongues. But the Word of God says it is right.

Anyway, after I prayed the second time for an hour in other tongues, the devil said, "Well, now you've wasted two hours."

So I said, "Just for that, I'm going to get down and pray another hour." So I got down and prayed my third hour.

And I got up and sat down in my chair.

The devil said to me again, "Now you've wasted three hours today. You could have been studying and getting your sermons for Sunday. You could have been out visiting people. You could have been doing something worthwhile." You see, the devil wanted me to operate strictly in the sense realm, in the natural realm.

I said, "I'll tell you what I'm going to do, Mr. Devil. I'm going to get down here and I'm going to pray two hours in tongues instead of one, and if I get back up here and sit down and you bother me with doubt and unbelief again, I'm going to start doubling my prayer time. Next time it'll be four hours, and then the next time, it'll be eight hours."

That day after praying for five hours and forty-five minutes, I broke into a realm in the Spirit that I had never been in before, and it was a changing point in my ministry. But it took that length of time to break something down within me and also to break through in the spiritual realm.

During that five hours and forty-five minutes I prayed in a half dozen different tongues, not just one. I began to pray in one of these tongues and then I began to interpret what I had prayed. I wrote it down and dated it and I still have it. Not only that, but I shared what I learned, and other preachers there in east Texas can tell you that I preached it three years before it ever happened.

As I was praying for those five hours and forty-five minutes, God gave me the interpretation of what I was praying about. We were in World War II at that time, and God said, "At the end of World War II there shall come a revival of divine healing to America."

I proclaimed this truth the first Monday of September of 1943. So, you see, I preached it several years before the war was over in 1945. And the revival did come. But that is what I was praying about several years before.

Friends, the Church is not progressing as it should because one person alone cannot carry this kind of prayer, but *all* of us need to participate in praying out the plan of God for our lives and for God's will to be done in the earth. This really solves the prayer problem.

And by practicing praying in tongues, now I can get my mind quiet as fast as you could snap your fingers, and step right over into the spiritual realm where I can begin to speak out of my spirit. And the Holy Ghost is in me to help me pray (Rom. 8:26).

Step Number Six:
Know the Reality of Our Fellowship With the Father

We covered five of the seven steps necessary to obtain the highest kind of faith. Now let's discuss the sixth step. Step number six is to know the reality of our fellowship with the Father God. The very heart reason for redemption is fellowship.

1 CORINTHIANS 1:9
9 God is faithful, by whom ye were called UNTO THE FELLOWSHIP OF HIS SON JESUS CHRIST OUR LORD.

Notice, you were called unto *fellowship* with God's Son, Jesus Christ.

1 JOHN 1:3–4, 7
3 That which we have seen and heard declare we unto you, that ye also may have fellowship with us: and truly our fellowship is with the Father, and with his Son Jesus Christ.
4 And these things write we unto you, that your joy may be full. . . .
7 But if we walk in the light, as he is in the light, we have fellowship one with another, and the blood of Jesus Christ his Son cleanseth us from all sin.

The highest honor that the Father has ever conferred upon us is to be "joint-fellowshippers" with Himself, with His Son, and with the Holy Spirit in carrying out His dream for the redemption of the human race. But *relationship* without *fellowship* is an insipid thing. It is like the marriage relationship without love or fellowship.

Fellowship is the very mother of faith. And fellowship is the parent of joy. It is the source of victory. And God has called us individually into fellowship with His Son. If you have fellowship with God and you are walking in the light as He is in the light, then prayer becomes one of the sweetest and one of the greatest assets to which we have become heirs in Christ.

Prayer Should Be a Rest, Not a Struggle

You can listen to some people talk, and they will tell you they are fighting and struggling and trying to believe God's Word. But if they are struggling to believe, then their praying is all wrong and so is their believing. I hear people talk about what praying takes out of them.

Now I'm neither complaining, nor am I bragging about it, but that day I prayed five hours and forty-five minutes in tongues, as well as other times spent even longer in prayer, and it has never been a problem or a struggle for me to pray. It has always been a joy and has never taken anything out of me to pray. *Prayer always puts something in me!* The trouble is, instead of letting the Holy Ghost help them, too many people are praying in their own energy, and they wear out.

I'll tell you exactly what many do when it comes to praying. They do just like a couple of minister friends of mine did. One of them was holding a tent meeting for the other. The evangelist would turn the amplifier up so loud on the speakers that it was running people off instead of bringing them in. One day the pastor asked him what made him want those speakers so loud.

He said, "Well, I'll tell you. When I turn it up loud it gives me a feeling that I'm getting my message across to the people."

And the pastor said to him, "*You* don't have to get your message across, anyhow; you ought to be depending on the *Holy Ghost* to do that for you, not the microphone or the speaker."

You see, so many times folks are depending on something natural to put them over in life. For example, when this evangelist could sound really loud over the speakers, that gave him the feeling and the sense that he was really getting his message across. People wear themselves out because they are trying to carry the load themselves without God's help. There is such a thing as resting in the Lord. In Isaiah 28, Isaiah prophesied that speaking in tongues is the rest wherewith the weary shall rest (Isa. 28:11–12). It ought to refresh people to pray in tongues.

Step Number Seven: Know the Authority in the Name of Jesus

Step number seven to obtaining the highest kind of faith is to know the authority in the Name of Jesus. We should know that authority as a reality in our own lives.

The authority you have in the Name of Jesus is just as though some wealthy man gave you the power to use his name in an unlimited capacity. What effect would it have if he gave you a legal document? What if he said to use this legal document in order to supply every one of your needs? What if you could do anything you wanted to do in that man's name!

Well, God has given us the power of attorney to use the Name of Jesus. This means we have power in that Name over Satanic forces. Jesus said, "*In my name . . . they shall lay hands on the sick, and they shall recover*" (Mark 16:17–18). Jesus said, "*whatsoever ye shall ask of the Father in my name, he may give it you*" (John 15:16).

We have authority to use that Name. The Name of Jesus carries authority on this earth. It is not a matter of faith, but it is a matter of knowing your legal rights in Christ and taking your rightful place as a son or daughter. It is a matter of taking your place in carrying out God's will in the earth. Getting *us* to cooperate with God is the biggest problem!

We Have the Power of Attorney in Jesus' Name

A Full Gospel minister told me about his brother who went out as a missionary to Africa for the Assemblies of God back in the Depression Days. He went by boat. This missionary brother had a piece of property his wife had inherited which a certain company wanted to buy to use as a plant site. The company bought it before the brother went to Africa, though they hadn't completed the transaction. A few days before this missionary sailed, he went to his brother's house and asked him to sign legal papers for him in the missionary's stead, since he would be gone to Africa.

The missionary brother had it arranged so that his brother, this Full Gospel minister, would have the power of attorney to complete the transaction. The missionary told his brother to take part of the money from the sale of the property and build a house for their parents. But the brother said, "I can't do that." The missionary brother assured him that he could sign the papers and it would be legal.

The minister said his missionary brother went on to Africa and the day came for the lawyers to come to finish the legal transaction on the sale of the property. He still didn't believe the power of attorney would work, but he went ahead and signed his brother's name and the lawyers gave him the check for the property.

The minister then deposited the check in his brother's account and went home and told his wife he still didn't think it would work. He said that he was on pins and needles for several days just wondering what would happen. But the transaction went through and the minister was able to build the house for their parents as they had planned.

This minister explained that it wasn't his *faith* that made everything work out all right, because he wasn't even sure it would work! It worked because it was *legally right*.

What I am trying to show you is that using the power of attorney—Jesus' Name—is not a matter of *faith*. It is a matter of knowing what belongs to you and just doing what the Word says. You only need to exercise the authority in that Name!

If you don't use the authority vested in the Name of Jesus, the authority that is already legally yours in the Name won't work for you. If you can just understand that the Name of Jesus belongs to you, and you start using that Name, you'll find that it does work, because it is in the Word. And God's Word works all the the time.

Questions for Study

1. What should be the confession and belief of every believer?

   _____

   _____

2. What two roles does the Holy Spirit fulfill as He dwells within believers?

   _____

   _____

3. What added benefit does the believer who has experienced the infilling of the Holy Spirit have?

   _____

   _____

4. Why aren't spiritual things as distinct to us as they ought to be?

   _____

   _____

5. What do feelings have to do with praying in the Spirit?

   _____

   _____

6. How should you speak when giving a message in tongues?

   _____

   _____

7. Name step number six and seven to attaining the highest kind of faith.

   _____

   _____

8. What is the believer's power of attorney?

   _____

   _____

9. Using the power of attorney is not a matter of faith. What is it a matter of?

   _____

   _____

10. What will happen if you don't use the authority vested in the Name of Jesus?

    _____

    _____

Chapter 17

Six Big Hindrances to Faith

FIGHT THE GOOD FIGHT OF FAITH, lay hold on eternal life, whereunto thou art also called, and hast professed a good profession before many witnesses.

— 1 Timothy 6:12

Fight the Good Fight of Faith

I want you to notice particularly the first clause of this verse, *"Fight the good fight of faith."* The only fight the believer is called upon to fight is the fight of faith. Sometimes I hear folks say that they are going to fight the devil. But I don't know why they would want to do that because they wouldn't be a match for him anyway. Besides that, Jesus has already defeated the devil for us. Jesus was our Substitute when He defeated Satan, death, hell, and the grave in His redemptive work!

Then again I hear folks say, "I'm going to fight sin." Well, I'm not. No, I'm going to preach *the cure* for sin. There is no use fighting sin. I have a cure for it! Jesus is the cure. He put away sin by the sacrifice of Himself (Heb. 9:26).

No, the only fight the believer is called upon to fight is the good fight of faith. And there *is* a fight to faith, for this text says, *"FIGHT the good fight of faith"* (1 Tim. 6:12).

If there is a fight to faith, then there must be enemies or hindrances to faith. If there weren't any enemies or hindrances to faith, there wouldn't be any fight to it. So we are going to talk about the six big hindrances to faith.

Lack of Faith Comes From Lack of Knowledge of God's Word

ROMANS 10:17
17 So then faith cometh by hearing, and hearing by the word of God.

Many people confess their lack of faith when actually they don't lack faith at all. They are only failing to *release* their faith. A lack of faith is really not their problem. In other words, they have faith; they just aren't exercising it or releasing it.

The real reason for lack of faith is a lack of knowledge of God's Word, for *"faith cometh by hearing, and hearing by the word of God"* (Rom. 10:17). Someone said to me, "Yes, that is my problem. I don't know much about the Word, but I need faith." But you can't get faith any other way except through the Word!

Someone else said, "I'm praying God will give me faith." Well, you are wasting your time. You might as well be twiddling your thumbs, saying, "Twinkle, twinkle, little star," because it would do just about as much good as it would by praying for faith.

But if you'll take time to feed upon the Word of God yourself, and listen to the many ministry gifts that God has set in the church, such as the ministry gift of the teacher, then faith and life will come to your spirit because Jesus said, *"The words that I speak unto you, they are spirit, and they are life"* (John 6:63). You can receive revelation knowledge through reading and meditating upon the Word and through hearing the Word being preached.

A lack of knowledge will hinder us and hold us in bondage because we cannot act upon God's Word beyond actual knowledge of God's Word. Faith will grow with an understanding of the Word. If your faith is not growing, then your understanding of the Word is not growing. A lack of knowledge of what God's Word says, a lack of knowledge of our redemption, and a lack of knowledge of our redemptive rights in Christ Jesus are often the reasons for unbelief.

Hindrance Number One: Lack of Understanding Regarding the New Creation

Let me show you six big hindrances to faith. The first hindrance to faith is a lack of understanding of what it means to be a new creature in Christ, or a lack of understanding of what the new creation means.

2 CORINTHIANS 5:17
17 Therefore if any man be in Christ, he is a new creature: old things are passed away; behold, all things are become new.

A lack of understanding of what the new creation is and what it means to be a new creature can hinder the believer's faith life. Many believers do not know that they are new creatures. They think God just forgave them of their sins.

But it wouldn't help the sinner a bit in the world if all the sinner received was the forgiveness of sins. He would still go to hell, for he would still be a child of the devil. No, the sinner has to be born again. He has to become a new creature in Christ Jesus. He has to receive a new nature—God's nature (2 Peter 1:4).

Therefore, we as believers are not just forgiven sinners. We are not poor, staggering, sinning, barely-getting-along church members. We are not living down at the end of the block on Barely-Getting-Along Street next to Grumble Alley! That's not who we are.

We are new creatures, created by God in Christ Jesus, with the very life and nature of God in our spirits (2 Cor. 5:17). We are children of God, sons of God, and heirs of God—joint-heirs with Jesus Christ (Rom. 8:17).

Many people do not know they have eternal life. They think of themselves only as being saved from sin. But John says in his first epistle, *"These things have I written unto you that believe on the name of the Son of God; that ye may know that ye have ETERNAL life"* (1 John 5:13). When you know what you have and who you are in Christ, it makes all the difference in the world.

I Knew I Was a New Creation

I remember a scripture I first read while on the bed of sickness. I read it, and it never left me. The scripture I'm talking about is Second Corinthians 5:17, which says, *"Therefore if any man be in Christ, he is a new creature."*

I was just a youth, fifteen years of age, when I was saved on the bed of sickness. I remained in a bedridden condition until I was about seventeen years of age when I was healed by the power of God.

After I was healed for the next several years, possibly three or four, I wasn't around Full Gospel people. I was a denominational Christian and I fellowshipped with those who were members of my particular denomination. But I'll tell you, I lived just as good a life then as I ever have.

I went back to high school and I never had the problems mingling with the world that many other young people had. I believe the difference was I told everyone I was a new creature in Christ Jesus.

I was just a young Baptist boy, but it didn't bother me what people said about me. I wasn't afraid of being criticized or talked about. In fact, criticism never bothered me a bit in the world. I just testified to my schoolmates on the school grounds, to the teachers, to the principal, to the school superintendent, and to everyone I came in contact with that I was a new creature in Christ.

In fact, the first time I walked to town after I was healed, I ran into a friend of mine, who had been a good pal of mine before I had become bedfast. He came to visit me one time after I became bedfast, and I never did see him anymore.

After I was healed, I ran into him and when he saw me, he made over me as though he was so thrilled to see me. He and I sat down on the running board of a car and began to talk. He began to talk about things we had done before I had become bedfast and had gotten saved, and I just sat there with a mask-like look on my face as though I didn't know what he was talking about. I did remember, however, what he was talking about, but I wasn't that same person anymore.

At one point, my friend looked at me and said, "What's the matter with you?"

I said, "Not a thing."

He said, "You act as if you don't even know what I'm talking about." He pointed down to a building not too far away and laughed about something that had happened one night.

You see, there are two things that I could always do. One, I could always tame any kind of a wild animal. Two, I could always open any kind of a lock. I suppose it was just a natural ability, but locks always intrigued me. (I'm telling you this so you'll know what my friend was talking about.)

I had opened doors to some locked buildings when I was about thirteen, but I wouldn't go inside. The other boys would go in and get candy. Of course, I would help them eat the candy after they got it!

That is what this boy was talking about. This night he was referring to, the boys had gotten some candy and I was responsible for opening up the store. He was laughing about it and I just sat there. I said to him, "The boy who was with you that night is dead."

He said, "You didn't die! I see you sitting right there."

I told him I wasn't talking about physical death. I told him he was looking at the outside and I told him about the new man on the inside. I told him the man on the inside, the real Kenneth Hagin, had become a new creature in Christ Jesus. I quoted Second Corinthians 5:17 to him. I told him he was looking at the same body, the same outward house I lived in, but the man who was responsible for that stealing had become a new creature and hadn't stolen anything since, and was not about to!

This boy knew what a liar I had been in the past, and I told him that the new creature I was now had not been telling lies, and that I didn't plan on ever telling any lies again. I told him I was a new creature in Christ Jesus and had been born again.

I remember he got off the running board of the car and looked at me as though he thought I was a nut. I sat there just laughing and he finally walked around the corner and turned around and peeked at me. He thought there was something wrong with me. But there was nothing wrong with me! I had become a new creature in Christ.

Hindrance Number Two:
Lack of Understanding of Our Place in Christ

The second hindrance to faith is a lack of understanding of our place in Christ and of Christ's place in our lives. I suggest to Christians everywhere that we need to do some definite study along certain lines. I always suggest to folks that they go through the New Testament, particularly the epistles which were written to them, and write down entire phrases that tell them who they are in Christ and what they have in Christ; because what we write down, we seem to remember better.

You will find expressions in the epistles such as, "in Christ," "in whom," and "in Him." Expressions such as these occur 133 or 134 times in the New Testament. The reason I say 133 or 134 is because I use a couple of phrases that don't say these exact words "in Christ," "in whom," or "in Him," but they infer it.

For instance, I use First John 4:4 that says, *"greater is he that is in you, than he that is in the world."* The other one I use like this is Colossians 1:13, which says, *"Who hath delivered us from the power of darkness, and hath translated us into the kingdom of his dear Son."* "Who" refers to God, the Father. If you'll go through the New Testament and confess, "This is who I am. This is what I have," you'll find life will be different for you.

I was preaching in one church and I suggested going through the New Testament and finding the "in Him" scriptures as I usually do almost everywhere I minister.

The pastor of this church was telling me about a woman in his church who was a graduate of a Full Gospel Bible school and who later went to a Baptist seminary and received a degree or two in Christian education.

This woman was the Christian education director in this pastor's church, and worked free of charge except for expenses, as she did a lot of visiting. This pastor said she was one of the most outstanding Christian workers he had ever known.

About a month later when I was preaching a revival there, this woman came to me and told me that she had written out twenty-five of these "in Him," "in Christ," and "in whom" scriptures and had begun to confess them.

This woman told me all about her education, but she said that since she had begun writing out these scriptures and confessing them, she had become an entirely different person. She found that she didn't ever worry anymore and that she thought and acted differently. She said she felt like a new person! She said at times she couldn't help but say, "Is this really me?"

This woman told me, "I know you can't be born again *again*, but it does seem like I've been born again *again*."

I told her that she was just now beginning to walk in the light of what she had possessed as a believer all along. It is really sad that a person can be a Christian for so long and not really walk in the light of what he has. If he doesn't have an understanding of what he has in Christ and who Christ is in his life, his faith will be hindered. Getting this understanding cured this woman of her worry habit. And it allowed her to walk in the fullness of her rights and privileges in Christ.

Hindrance Number Three:
Lack of Understanding Regarding Our Righteousness

The third hindrance to faith is a lack of understanding of righteousness—what it is and what it gives to the believer. A lack of understanding of righteousness holds more people in bondage than anything else.

We talked in chapter 14 about my own search to understand righteousness in Christ. I never shall forget when I lay bedfast on the bed of sickness years ago, I began to read the scriptures and to receive light on the subjects of healing and faith. I came to James 5:16 which says, *"The effectual fervent prayer of a righteous man availeth much."* I looked at that verse of scripture and I thought, "Oh, my, if I were only righteous—if I could ever get to be righteous—God would hear my prayers."

One day I happened to be reading that passage of scripture a little more closely and noticed that God said Elijah was subject to like passions as we are (James 5:17), and yet God gave Elijah as an example of a righteous man! Something registered in me and I thought if this man could be called a righteous man, I could be righteous, too, because I was like him.

Elijah had his high moments and his low moments. I thought to myself, "How could God call a person like that righteous, when Elijah was so inconsistent?" But then I read in Psalm 32, where it says, *"Blessed is he whose transgression is forgiven, whose sin is covered. Blessed is the man unto whom the Lord imputeth not iniquity"* (Ps. 32:1–2).

God imputed righteousness to those in the Old Testament whose sins had been covered by the blood of bulls and goats. Then I found in Second Corinthians 5:21, where it says, *"For he hath made him to be sin for us, who knew no sin; that we might be made the righteousness of God in him."* I saw then that in the New Testament the blood of Jesus cleanseth us from all sin and that by the new birth we become a righteous new creature.

God did not make any unrighteous new creature. We are created by God in Christ Jesus. He made us righteous new creatures in Christ. We are sons and daughters of God and stand before God as though we had never sinned. We can stand in His Presence without any sense of embarrassment, guilt, or condemnation. We don't have to be tongue-tied in the Presence of our Heavenly Father because of fear. We can come into His Presence because we belong there.

When we were born again, our sins were remitted because our past life stopped existing. God said that He would not remember our transgressions (Isa. 43:25). Since God doesn't remember them, why should we?

Someone may say he has sinned since he was born again and that he is so weak in areas, but I have good news for him. First John 1:9 says, *"If we confess our sins, he is faithful and just to forgive us our sins, and to cleanse us from all unrighteousness."*

When a believer sins he feels guilty, and he has a sense of unrighteousness. He feels embarrassed and spiritually inferior to come into God's Presence. But God does two things for the believer who may have sinned. First, when the believer confesses his sins, the Lord forgives him.

Second, the Bible says that God also *cleanses* us from *all* unrighteousness. "Unrighteousness" is the word *righteousness* with the prefix "un" on the front of it. And "unrighteousness" simply means *not righteous* or *non-righteous*. And according to First John 1:9 the believer is cleansed from non-righteousness; therefore, he is made righteous again because the blood of Jesus actually *cleanses* us from all sin!

I've found many times that when I get folks to see this, they automatically get healed. Many times the reason folks aren't able to receive healing is that they have been under condemnation and have thought God was mad at them. They failed to understand that they are the righteousness of God in Christ (2 Cor. 5:21).

As God's Righteousness Receive the Bountiful Fullness of God

Smith Wigglesworth told of a time in England when an Episcopal minister, who was eighty years of age, asked Wigglesworth if he would come and pray for him because he wanted to receive the Holy Ghost. Wigglesworth went to him and they read the scriptures and began to pray.

Wigglesworth said that he had never heard a more beautiful prayer than the one he heard that man pray. But Wigglesworth told the man that God is not interested in beautiful prayers; God is interested in faith. As they were praying, the elderly gentleman said, "God make me holy."

That elderly gentleman thought that before he could receive the Holy Ghost he had to be made holy. Wigglesworth then told the man to get up off his knees, and Wigglesworth explained to the man that he *was* holy already because he was a believer, and that the blood of Jesus had cleansed him from all sin.

Just as Wigglesworth said this to him, the elderly man began to speak in tongues. He didn't have to do anything else in addition to being born again in order to be filled with the Spirit. When we know that we are the righteousness of God in Christ, then we step out of the narrow place of failure and weakness in which we have lived into the boundless fullness of God.

Hindrance Number Four:
Lack of Understanding Regarding Our Right to Use the Name of Jesus

The fourth hindrance to faith is a lack of understanding of our privilege and right to use the Name of the Lord Jesus Christ. This lack of understanding will hold us in bondage and will give us a sense of weakness. But when we know what that Name will do, we can take our rightful position of authority over Satan and enjoy victory.

Most believers understand that the Name of Jesus can be used in prayer because of what Jesus said in John 16:23 and 24.

JOHN 16:23–24

23 Whatsoever ye shall ask the Father IN MY NAME, he will give it you.

24 Hitherto have ye asked nothing IN MY NAME: ask, and ye shall receive, that your joy may be full.

I also suggest that the Name of Jesus can be used everywhere that the Word indicates it can. Jesus Himself said that in the verses I just quoted in John 16:23–24.

Jesus also said something else about the use of His Name in Mark chapter 16.

MARK 16:15–18

15 Go ye into all the world, and preach the gospel to every creature.

16 He that believeth and is baptized shall be saved; but he that believeth not shall be damned.

17 And these signs shall follow them that believe; IN MY NAME shall they cast out devils; they shall speak with new tongues;

18 They shall take up serpents; and if they drink any deadly thing, it shall not hurt them; they shall lay hands on the sick, and they shall recover.

These signs follow those who believe the gospel. These signs aren't just for the Early Church or just for the apostles. These signs are not just for preachers, but they are for *believers*. *Believers* can cast out devils in Jesus' Name.

Also, I don't believe Jesus is just referring in Mark 16:17 to casting devils out of someone who is demon possessed. I believe He is referring to the fact that *every believer* has authority over demons and evil spirits in the Name of Jesus.

And verse 18 says that in Jesus' Name believers will speak with new tongues. In His Name believers shall lay hands on the sick, and they shall recover.

Believers can lay hands on the sick, and in the Name of Jesus, the sick shall become well.

The Bible says another way to receive healing is to call for the elders of the church (James 5:14–15). But what if you are off somewhere where you can't get in contact with the elders? You see, you need to learn to appropriate healing for yourself, for it legally belongs to you in your redemption.

I am thoroughly convinced that we ought to leave the pastor free to take care of the spiritual babies in a church who don't know how to act on the Word for themselves. But the older Christians should learn to appropriate healing for themselves. If you can't appropriate healing for yourself, then by all means, send for help.

I believe we should learn to use the Name of Jesus. We should know that His Name has authority and power on the earth today and that His Name belongs to us.

Hindrance Number Five:
Lack of Understanding About Acting on the Word

The fifth hindrance to faith is a lack of understanding about acting upon the Word. We should stop trying *to make* God's Word work and start *acting* on the Word. The Bible says, *"Trust in the Lord with all thine heart; and lean not unto thine own understanding"* (Prov. 3:5). All that is necessary for you to do in any situation is to ask, "What has God said?" or "What does God's Word have to say about this?" If we know that the Word is true and if we act as though it is true, it becomes a reality in our lives.

Many times people come to me and ask why they don't get their healing. They say they know all the scriptures I've quoted. They begin to quote to me Matthew 8:17, which says, *"Himself took our infirmities, and bare our sicknesses."* Another scripture they quote is First Peter 2:24, which says, *"Who his own self bare our sins in his own body on the tree, that we, being dead to sins, should live unto righteousness: by whose stripes ye were healed."*

Act Like the Word Is True!

And I always say to those people, "Have you ever acted like those verses of scripture were true?" That sometimes startles them.

But let me share with you the testimony of A.B. Simpson who just acted like the Word is true, and he received his healing. I read his testimony years ago in a Christian magazine. At the age of forty-six, Dr. A.B. Simpson, who was a Presbyterian minister at the time and later founded the Christian Missionary Alliance, was told he was dying of a heart condition and was given only about six months to live.

Dr. Simpson said he had heard many testimonies of healing even in his own church. He took a short leave of absence and went up to his farm where he could spend a lot of time studying the Word of God.

At the end of two weeks, Dr. Simpson took a piece of paper and a pencil and wrote, "After searching the Word of God for two weeks, I am convinced the Bible teaches that divine healing is for us today. And I, this day, accept Jesus Christ as my Healer and declare that I am now healed from heart trouble and that I am well. And I promise God to use this new-found strength and life and energy entirely for His purpose and to further the gospel. I promise God I will share this truth of healing with others and will help them."

After that time, Simpson went to a luncheon where he was to be the speaker. All that came to him to speak about was the one word out of Matthew 8:17, "Himself." So Dr. Simpson opened his Bible and read the entire verse and told the audience he wanted to focus his attention on that word "Himself." Then he gave them his testimony about how he had been searching the Bible and had come to the conclusion that Jesus was still the Healer today.

After the luncheon, he was invited to go mountain climbing by the men to whom he had spoken. The thought immediately came to him that he wouldn't be able to because of his heart condition. But then he remembered he had declared his healing, so he accepted the invitation and went. Up to this point, he had not really seen or felt his healing, but had just accepted it and had declared it by faith.

All the way up the mountain, every time he got his mind off the Word of God, he would begin to feel the symptoms of his heart condition. But he overcame these feelings because as he claimed the Word again for his healing, all the symptoms would go away. He fought this battle all the way up the mountain. But when he got up the mountain, he walked about victorious without any symptoms!

Dr. Simpson was seventy years old when I read his testimony in this magazine article, and he said he'd never had any more symptoms whatsoever after that mountain-climbing experience.

P.C. Nelson said that more people lose their healing over a counterattack than anything else.

For an example, an assistant chaplain boy during the Korean War said the United States took one mountain over there in battle fourteen different times and each time lost it. Actually, they lost it thirteen times and the fourteenth time, they kept it.

It's the same way with faith. Real faith holds on to the blessings of God. Real faith is the child of the knowledge of the Word. Dr. Simpson acted on the Word and got real faith from it. Instead of trying to believe, he just acted upon the Word. He acted like the Word is true.

Hindrance Number Six: Lack of Understanding About Holding Fast to Our Confession of Faith

The sixth hindrance to faith is a lack of understanding that we are to hold fast to our confession of faith. In Hebrews 10:23 it says, *"Let us hold fast our profession [confession]."* Our faith keeps pace with our confession.

HEBREWS 10:23
23 Let us HOLD FAST the PROFESSION [confession] OF OUR FAITH without wavering; (for he is faithful that promised;).

ROMANS 10:10
10 For with the HEART man believeth unto righteousness; and with the mouth CONFESSION is made unto salvation.

MARK 11:23
23 That whosoever shall SAY unto this mountain, Be thou removed, and be thou cast into the sea; and shall not doubt in his HEART, but shall believe that those things which he SAITH shall come to pass; he shall have whatsoever he SAITH.

When I was preaching in St. Louis once, a young Full Gospel minister who was serving as youth director of the church there, said to me, "Brother Hagin, I'm thirty-two and the doctors have said it is impossible for my wife and me to have any children. Will you talk with me and my wife and pray with us?"

I told them I would. So we talked and his wife said she would begin to confess that they would have a child. She said that she would begin to say that they *would* have a child, instead of saying they would *like* to have one.

After twelve months, I received a letter that said they had a bouncing baby girl! All they needed to do was to act upon the Word.

Faith is measured by our confession. Our usefulness in the Lord is measured by our confession. Sooner or later, we become what we confess.

There is a confession of our hearts and a confession of our lips and when these two harmonize, we become mighty in our prayer life.

The reason so many are defeated is that they have a negative confession. They talk of their weaknesses and failures and invariably they go down to the level of their confession.

There is a scriptural law that I discovered from the lips of Jesus in Mark 11:23: *"he shall have whatsoever he saith."*

The scriptural law is this: *Our confessions rule us.* In other words, you are what you say.

We see an example of a confession of faith which resulted in healing in Mark chapter 5.

MARK 5:28, 34

28 For she SAID, If I may touch but his clothes, I SHALL BE WHOLE. . . .

34 And he [Jesus] **said unto her, "Daughter, THY FAITH hath made thee WHOLE; go in peace, and be whole of thy plague.**

What she said was her faith speaking. And it came to pass!

We have discussed six big hindrances to our faith. By recognizing these six hindrances to our faith and by renewing our minds with the Word of God, we will cause our faith to grow and increase. Every believer can see the promises of God come to pass in his life if he will take time to meditate on who he is in Christ and what he has in Christ and act like God's Word is true!

Questions for Study

1. Name the six big hindrances to faith listed in this chapter.

   _____

   _____

2. What is the only fight a believer is called upon to fight?

   _____

   _____

3. Where does a lack of faith come from?

   _____

   _____

4. What two things does God do for the believer who may have sinned?

   _____

   _____

5. Why are believers already holy?

   _____

   _____

6. What action will we take when we know that we are the righteousness of God in Christ?

   _____

   _____

7. Who are the signs listed in Mark 16:17,18 supposed to follow?

   _____

   _____

8. What is faith measured by?

   _____

   _____

9. Which two confessions have to harmonize before we become mighty in our prayer life?

   _____

   _____

10. How can every believer see the promises of God come to pass in his or her life?

    _____

    _____

Chapter 18

The God-Kind of Faith

In this chapter we will study the God-kind of faith. The God-kind of faith is the same faith that believes and speaks (2 Cor. 4:13). Jesus demonstrates this kind of faith, for example, in Mark 11:12–14, 20–24.

MARK 11:12–14, 20–24

12 And on the morrow, when they were come from Bethany, he [Jesus] was hungry:

13 And seeing a fig tree afar off having leaves, he came, if haply he might find anything thereon: and when he came to it, he found nothing but leaves; for the time of figs was not yet.

14 And Jesus answered and said unto it, No man eat fruit of thee hereafter for ever. And his disciples heard it. . . .

20 And in the morning, as they passed by, they saw the fig tree dried up from the roots.

21 And Peter calling to remembrance saith unto him, Master, behold, the fig tree which thou cursedst is withered away.

22 And Jesus answering saith unto them, HAVE FAITH IN GOD.

23 For verily I say unto you, That whosoever shall SAY unto this mountain, Be thou removed, and be thou cast into the sea; and shall not doubt in his heart, but shall believe that those things which he SAITH shall come to pass; he shall have whatsoever he SAITH.

24 Therefore I say unto you, What things soever ye desire, when ye pray, believe that ye receive them, and ye shall have them.

Have Faith in God

Now let us focus our attention on the statement,

"Have faith in God" (Mark 11:22). In several Bible versions the margin of that verse reads, "Have the faith of God." Or, as some Greek scholars tell us this verse says, "Have the God-kind of faith." In the cursing of the fig tree, Jesus demonstrated that He had the God-kind of faith because what He said came to pass.

The Bible says Jesus saw the fig tree from far away, and He saw that it had leaves. Jesus went to the tree to see if there were figs on the tree because the time for figs had not yet come.

"Well," someone said, "why was He looking for figs if it wasn't yet time for them?" Because in that country, those trees that had leaves usually also had figs.

Jesus spoke to the tree and said unto it, *"No man eat fruit of thee hereafter for ever"* (Mark 11:14). Then the next day when Jesus and the disciples passed by the fig tree, they saw it had dried up from the roots.

MARK 11:21

21 And Peter . . . saith unto him, Master, behold, the fig tree which thou cursedst is withered away.

Peter's response to the withered fig tree brought that startling and amazing statement from the lips of Jesus, *"Have faith in God"* (Mark 11:22), or "Have the God-kind of faith."

MARK 11:23–24

23 For verily I say unto you, That whosoever shall say unto this mountain, Be thou removed, and be thou cast into the sea; and shall not doubt in his heart, but shall believe that those things which he saith shall come to pass; he shall have whatsoever he saith.

24 Therefore I say unto you, What things soever ye desire, when ye pray, believe that ye receive them, and ye shall have them.

In verses 23 and 24, Jesus defines and describes for us the God-kind of faith He spoke about in verse 22.

The God-kind of faith is the kind of faith whereby a man believes in his heart and says with his mouth what he believes in his heart, and it comes to pass.

Jesus demonstrated that He had that kind of faith, for He believed that what He said would come to pass. He said to the tree, *"No man eat fruit of thee hereafter for ever"* (Mark 11:14). That is the same kind of faith that spoke this world into existence.

HEBREWS 11:3

3 Through faith we understand that the worlds were framed by the word of God, so that things which are seen were not made of things which do appear.

How did God make the world? God believed that what He said would come to pass. He said, *"Let there be light"* (Gen. 1:3), and light *became.* God spoke into existence the vegetable kingdom (Gen. 1:11–12). He spoke into existence the animal kingdom (Gen. 1:20–25).

God spoke into existence the heavens as well as the earth; He spoke into existence the moon, the sun, the stars, and the universe (Gen. 1:1, 8–9, 14–18). God just said it, and it was so, because He believed it would be so. That's the God-kind of faith. God believed what He said would come to pass and it did.

Jesus demonstrated He had that kind of faith, and then He said to the disciples that *they* had that same kind of faith. It is the kind of faith whereby a person believes something in his heart, and says with his mouth what he believes in his heart, and it comes to pass.

Don't Pray for Faith— Exercise the Faith You Already Have

Someone said, "I want that kind of faith. I'm praying that God will give me that kind of faith."

Well, you're wasting your time praying if you're praying for faith, because faith doesn't come by praying. In fact, if you are a believer, you already have that kind of faith. Every believer has a measure of the God-kind of faith (Rom. 12:3). The believer must now exercise the measure of faith he already possesses.

ROMANS 12:3

3 For I say, through the grace given unto me, to every man that is among you, not to think of himself more highly than he ought to think; but to think soberly, according as God hath dealt to EVERY MAN THE MEASURE OF FAITH.

That is not referring to every person in the world. Every person in the world doesn't have the God-kind of faith. We know this because in writing to the Church in Thessalonica, Paul says, "all men have not faith" (2 Thess. 3:2). So every man in the world does not have this faith. But every believer does!

Romans 12:3 says, "to every man THAT IS AMONG YOU. . . ." That is not talking about every man in the world, but about believers.

Paul did not write this letter to sinners in the world. He addressed this letter, the Book of Romans, "To all that be in Rome, beloved of God, called to be SAINTS" (Rom. 1:7). Paul said, *"I say . . . to every man that is among you, not to think of himself more highly than he ought to think; but to think soberly, according as God hath dealt to every man the measure of faith"* (Rom. 12:3).

Every believer—every child of God, every Christian—does have a measure of the God-kind of faith. Let me prove this to you further.

Faith Is a Gift of God

EPHESIANS 2:8

8 For by grace are ye saved through FAITH; and that not of yourselves: it is THE GIFT OF GOD.

The faith by which you are saved is not of yourself. Paul is *not* talking about grace because everyone knows that grace is not of yourself. Paul is saying that the faith by which you are saved is not of yourselves. In other words, it is not a natural human faith. It is a faith given to the sinners by God.

Well, how did God give the sinner faith to be saved? Romans 10:17 says, *"So then faith cometh by hearing, and hearing by the word of God."* Then notice these expressions, "So then faith cometh" and "according as God hath dealt" (Rom. 10:17; 12:3). And notice again Ephesians 2:8: *"ye [are] saved through faith; and that not of yourselves: it is the gift of God."*

Paul says that this faith to be saved is *given*; it's *dealt*; it *cometh*. It cometh by hearing the gospel preached.

ROMANS 10:8

8 But what saith it? The word is nigh thee, even in thy mouth, and in thy heart: that is, the WORD OF FAITH, which we PREACH.

This Bible, this message of God, is called the word of faith. Why is it called the word of faith? Because the Bible contains *words* that are spirit and life (John 6:63) which cause faith *to come* into even the heart of the unsaved. The Word of God causes the same kind of faith to be dealt to our hearts that God used to speak the universe into existence. Faith *is given* or imparted to us through the Word. Hearing the Word brings faith.

Read Romans 10:8 again, *"But what saith it? The word is nigh thee, even in thy mouth, and in thy heart."* Notice that this verse agrees exactly with what Jesus said in Mark 11:23: *"whosoever shall say . . . and shall not doubt in his heart. . . ."*

Do you see the idea of believing with the heart and saying with your mouth what you believe in your heart? Jesus believed it and He said it. God believed it and He said it. The earth came into existence.

God Gives Faith to the Sinner to Be Saved

ROMANS 10:9–10

9 That if thou shalt CONFESS WITH THY MOUTH the Lord Jesus, and shalt BELIEVE IN THINE

HEART that God hath raised him from the dead, thou shalt be saved.

10 For WITH THE HEART MAN BELIEVETH unto righteousness; and WITH THE MOUTH CONFESSION IS MADE UNTO salvation.

We can see that a measure of faith is dealt to the sinner through hearing the Word. Then the sinner uses that faith to be saved. The sinner uses that faith to bring the reality of salvation into his own life.

When did God save you? You may say, "Oh, on such and such a day." Well, you're mistaken because God saved you when Jesus died for you and rose from the dead nearly two thousand years ago. It only became a reality to you—in your life—when you believed it and confessed it.

Every man and woman in this world has a legal right to salvation because Jesus died for the whole world, not just for you and me. That is the reason I like the statement Brother T. L. Osborn makes, "No man has a right to hear the gospel twice until every man has heard it once."

Every person has a right to hear the gospel because salvation was bought and paid for, for everyone in the world, not just for you and me. When the truth of the Word is preached to the sinner, it causes faith to come. When he believes and confesses the truth—that Jesus is his Lord—he creates the reality of it in his own life by his faith.

ROMANS 10:13–14, 17

13 For whosoever shall call upon the name of the Lord shall be saved.

14 How then shall they call on him in whom they have not believed? and how shall they believe in him of whom they have not heard? and how shall they hear without a preacher? . . .

17 So then faith cometh by hearing, and hearing by the word of God.

Faith Comes by Hearing God's Word

The same thing is true of anything that you receive from God. The God-kind of faith comes by hearing God's Word. You know, God doesn't have any other kind of faith except the God-kind. That is the only kind He has! This God-kind of faith comes by hearing, and the hearing by the Word of God.

In other words, God gives the God-kind of faith, or causes it to come into the hearts of those who hear the Word of God. No wonder Jesus said, "Take heed what you hear" (Mark 4:24). You cannot let the Word go in one ear and out the other because it won't do you any good that way. Faith won't come. You can act as though the Word of God were a fairy tale or something of little importance and faith will not come into your heart.

But when you accept the Word of God reverently and sincerely, and act upon it, faith comes into your heart. Too many times, we have the idea about preaching that my son did when he was five years old. He said, "Mother, all of those tales Daddy tells when he's preaching—are they really so or is he just preaching?" The truths revealed in the Word of God are so rich, I sometimes believe people think we are just "preaching" or telling tales!

Exercise the Faith You Have to Be Healed

A woman came to see me once who was a Full Gospel Christian. A Methodist woman had just been healed of an incurable condition in one of my meetings and had been made perfectly whole. This Full Gospel woman had tears in her eyes and asked me if I would tell her something. She said, "How come God would heal that Methodist woman and she doesn't even have the baptism in the Holy Ghost yet? She hasn't even spoken in tongues, but He won't heal me?"

I answered her, "It's not a matter of His healing you. God has done all He is ever going to do about healing you. Two thousand years ago He laid your sickness on Jesus and Jesus bore sin, sickness, and disease for you. With His stripes you were healed way back then. But you won't accept it, and you won't believe it. You're trying to get God to do what He has already done for you.

"If you will come to the place where you *willingly* and *gladly* praise God for what He has already done in your redemption in Christ, and you will believe it, and confess it, then the manifestation will come. For the Bible says it's with the heart that man believes and with the mouth that confession is made *unto* the promise of God" (Rom. 10:10).

"If you are a Christian," I told this woman, "you have enough faith to be healed. You're just not using the faith you already have. You're not turning your faith loose. You don't need any more faith. Just learn to exercise the faith you already have. After all, you've already believed God for the biggest thing of all—your salvation. The new birth is the biggest thing that can happen to you. It is the greatest miracle that can ever happen in a person's life. The new birth is much better than being healed from some disease."

I continued, "You've already believed for God's biggest blessing. Now all you have to do is use that same measure of faith that you already have and just turn it loose. Jesus told us how to turn our faith loose or how to exercise it. He said to say with your mouth what you believe in your heart (Mark 11:23–24). If you believe the Bible, then you already believe that Jesus has taken your infirmities and has borne your sicknesses. If you believe the Bible, you believe He did that nearly two thousand years ago."

1 PETER 2:24

24 Who his own self bare our sins in his own body on the tree . . . by whose stripes YE WERE HEALED.

This scripture tells us that Jesus already bore our sicknesses and diseases for us. Therefore, if you say that God is going to heal you *sometime,* you are not in line with the Bible, which says, *"ye WERE healed"* (1 Peter 2:24), because "were" is past tense.

If you say, "I believe I'll be healed *sometime,*" you are turning your faith loose according to man's tradition and not according to the Word. But real faith—Bible faith—is present tense. Saying you hope you'll get healed is *future tense.*

You have a measure of the God-kind of faith, so use what you already have *now.*

Believers Have the Same Spirit of Faith

2 CORINTHIANS 4:13

13 We having the SAME SPIRIT OF FAITH, according as it is written, I BELIEVED, and therefore have I SPOKEN; we also BELIEVE, and therefore SPEAK.

Paul was writing to the Church in Corinth—

to believers. But what belonged to the Church in Corinth belongs to the Church in your town today. And Paul said, *"We HAVING the same spirit of faith"* (2 Cor. 4:13).

Not one single time in the Bible did Paul or any of the other apostles ever write to encourage people to believe or to have faith. The need to encourage believers to *believe* or to have faith is a result of the Word of God having lost its reality to us.

But we are believers! You don't write to your children when they are away from home and say to them, "Be sure and keep breathing." They're going to naturally breathe as long as they are alive. In the same sense, you don't have to encourage believers to believe, because that's what they are—believers.

Years ago I was holding a meeting in Clovis, New Mexico. One night after the service, a dear woman came forward whose husband was a state senator of New Mexico and also president of the largest bank in Clovis. She asked me to pray for her so she would have more faith. I told her I wouldn't do it, because you don't get faith by praying for it. I asked her if she was a believer and she said yes.

Then I told her, "Well, who ever heard of a believer who doesn't believe?" I did pray for her healing for high blood pressure. I also told her about receiving the baptism in the Holy Spirit with the evidence of speaking in other tongues, and she received the Holy Spirit. Afterwards, she said that she could have had this experience years ago, but no one had ever told her about it.

Don't Let Your Words Become Your Prison

Friends, if you're defeated in life, you've defeated yourself with the words of your own mouth. For Jesus said, *"whosoever shall say . . . and shall not doubt in his heart, but shall believe that those things which he saith shall come to pass; he shall have whatsoever he saith"* (Mark 11:23).

One writer put it this way, "You said you could not, and the moment you said it, you were whipped. You said you did not have faith, and doubt rose up like a giant and bound you."

You are imprisoned with your own words. You talk failure and failure holds you in bondage.

PROVERBS 6:2

2   Thou art snared with the words of thy mouth, thou art taken with the words of thy mouth.

The margin of my Bible reads, "Thou art taken captive with the words of thy mouth."

Mighty few of us realize that our words dominate us. A young man once said that he was never whipped until he confessed he was whipped. Many people say they always speak their minds. That isn't a bad practice if you have the mind of Christ! We as believers are to have the mind of Christ (1 Cor. 2:16).

But when you have a mind that is dominated by the devil, few people care to hear what's on your mind! If you have a mind dominated by doubt and unbelief, you have a mind dominated by the devil. If you have a mind dominated by fear and negativity, you have a mind dominated by the devil.

Never talk failure. Defeat and failure do not belong to the child of God. God never made a failure. God made us new creatures. We are born not of the will of the flesh or of the will of men but of the will of God (John 1:13). We are created by God in Christ Jesus.

Failures are man-made. Failures are made by wrong believing and wrong thinking. First John 4:4 says, "greater is he that is in you, than he that is in the world."

Learn to trust the Greater One Who is in you. He Who is in you is mightier than any force or power that is in the world. God created the universe with words. Words filled with faith are the most powerful influence in all the world.

Confess What You Believe

As I said previously, P.C. Nelson once said, "More people lose their healing over a counterattack than any other thing." I almost lost my own healing that way. After I was healed, people would ask me if my heart was better. I would answer that it wasn't because I didn't always feel good, and my heartbeat was still irregular and beating sporadically. As soon as I would say I didn't feel good, I would begin feeling even worse.

One day as I lay on the bed, I began to analyze my situation and to ask myself where I was failing in faith.

I realized what I was doing. I was confessing my sickness instead of my health! So I immediately started saying I was well when people asked me how I felt. And that is exactly what came to pass—I was healed!

I prayed about healing because I desired it. I believed with my heart and confessed with my lips that I was healed by Jesus' stripes (1 Peter 2:24; Mark 11:23–24). I told people I was fine and that I was healed. People would look at me strangely sometimes, but when I made the right confession, I found that my symptoms lessened and eventually left.

When people would ask me if I needed a ride because of my condition, I wouldn't accept a ride; I would say that I would rather walk. I would just automatically tell everyone I was fine. Many would tell me that healing wasn't for people now in these days, but I just told them that was from the devil. The Bible says that the devil is a liar.

Think about it for a moment. The "whosoever" in Mark 11:23 means "me" just as much as the "whosoever" in John 3:16 does.

JOHN 3:16

16 For God so loved the world, that he gave his only begotten Son, that WHOSOEVER believeth in him should not perish, but have everlasting life.

MARK 11:23

23 For verily I say unto you, That WHOSOEVER shall say unto this mountain, Be thou removed, and be thou cast into the sea; and shall not doubt in his heart, but shall believe that those things which he saith shall come to pass; he shall have whatsoever he saith.

If any *whosoever* can believe and be saved, then any *whosoever* can have what he speaks that is in line with God's Word.

The key to overcoming sickness and overcoming problems in life is *believing* with the heart and *confessing* with the mouth. I knew I had the faith to be healed because just a measure of the God-kind of faith will do it. So I knew it wasn't a problem of not having enough faith. But I didn't know how to turn my faith loose by confessing with my mouth what my heart believed.

The Power of Our Words

Our lips can make us millionaires or keep us paupers. Our lips can make us victors or keep us captives. The woman with the issue of blood in Mark chapter 5 spoke her faith and her faith made her a victor. Jesus told the woman with the issue of blood that it was her faith spoken out of her lips that had made her whole (Mark 5:34).

Your lips can keep you sick. You can fill your words with faith or you can fill your words with love that will melt the coldest heart. You can fill your words with love that will help the discouraged and brokenhearted. You can fill your words with faith that will stir Heaven. Or you can fill your words with hatred and poison. You can make your words breathe out the very atmosphere of Heaven. But your faith will never register above the words of your lips.

Let Negative Thoughts Die Unborn

Thoughts may come and they may try to persist in staying. But if you refuse to put those thoughts into words, they die unborn.

One time a man asked me to pray that the devil would never put any more evil thoughts in his mind. I told him if I could do that, I would pray that for myself. I told him that we are on the devil's territory in the sense that we live in the flesh and Satan is the god of this world (2 Cor. 4:4). As the god of this world, Satan operates in the mental or sense realm—in the realm of the flesh.

Therefore, you can't help it if the devil brings thoughts to your mind. You've heard the saying, "You can't keep the birds from flying over your head, but you can keep them from building a nest in your hair"! So you can refuse to think Satan's thoughts. You can also refuse to put evil thoughts into action. The best thing to do is to laugh at the devil because he is a liar. Cultivate the habit of thinking big things according to the Word.

Faith's Confessions Create Realities

Learn to use words that will react upon your own spirit. *Faith's confessions create realities*. Realization follows your confession. Confession precedes possession. Remember, *"with the mouth confession is made unto . . ."* (Rom. 10:10).

There are two things to notice about the God-kind of faith: First, a man believes in his heart. Second, he believes in his words. It won't be enough just to believe something in your heart. To get God to work for you, you have to believe in your words and your words have to speak the faith that is in your heart.

MARK 11:23

23 whosoever shall say . . . and shall not doubt in his heart, but shall believe that those things which he saith shall come to pass; he shall have whatsoever he saith.

This scripture contains the inevitable law of faith. You must believe in your heart and you must believe in your words. The God-kind of faith results in believing in your heart and speaking with your mouth. The Word of God must be on your lips. The Word of God in your heart and on your lips gives you power over disease, demons, and evil circumstances and causes you to walk in victory in Christ in every area of your life.

Questions for Study

1. What is the God-kind of faith as defined in this chapter?

   _____

   _____

2. How did Jesus demonstrate that He had the God-kind of faith?

   _____

   _____

3. How did God make the world?

   _____

   _____

4. Why are you wasting your time if you are praying for faith?

   _____

   _____

5. In Ephesians 2:8, what does Paul say is given to the sinners by God?

   _____

   _____

6. How does God give the sinner faith to be saved?

   _____

   _____

7. Why is the Bible called the word of faith?

   _____

   _____

8. What are the most powerful influence in all the world?

   _____

   _____

9. Which scripture contains the inevitable law of faith?

   _____

   _____

10. What will give you power over disease, demons, and evil circumstances and cause you to walk in victory in every area of your life?

    _____

    _____

Chapter 19

Confession Brings Possession

For verily I say unto you, That whosoever shall SAY unto this mountain, Be thou removed, and be thou cast into the sea; and SHALL NOT DOUBT IN HIS HEART, but shall believe that those things which he SAITH shall come to pass; he shall have whatsoever he SAITH.

Therefore I say unto you, What things soever ye desire, when ye pray, believe that ye receive them, and ye shall have them.

— Mark 11:23–24

These are my two favorite verses of scripture in the Bible. I guess the reason they are my favorite is that these two verses brought me off the bed of sickness many years ago. Faith is fed by feeding on God's Word.

Feed and Exercise Your Faith

Many people wonder why they are not growing in faith. Many times it is because they are not feeding on God's Word. Faith will grow by feeding it and exercising it. We feed our faith by reading and meditating on the Word, and by hearing the Word of God being preached.

We *exercise* faith by being doers of the Word, and not hearers only. James said, *"But be ye doers of the word, and not hearers only"* (James 1:22). Being doers of the Word means that we *act on the Word.*

Simply reading and meditating upon the Word will not build faith. Reading and meditating on the Word will feed your faith and build a capacity for faith, but faith must also be a part of our daily speech. In other words, the Word that you feed on has to be exercised daily. It has to become a part of your daily speech. That word has to become a part of your daily conduct and actions.

As faith grows, Satan's dominion over us wanes. Circumstances become less formidable and fear is destroyed. Nearly everyone longs for the day when he can be rid of fear; people can have so many fears. For years as a minister, I was bound with certain fears. But it has been so long since I've had those fears, that now it seems like I never had any at all. Fear does not need to dominate us in life because we have been redeemed from fear. Fear can become a thing of the past.

As your faith grows, you begin to possess your rights in Christ. You begin to take ahold of what belongs to you in Christ. You begin to *take* the things that you only *hoped* for before. You hoped for money before, but now by faith you have it.

If you are sick, you need to confess, "By His stripes I am healed!" But you can't confess that and confess that you're still sick at the same time! If you say you are still sick, then you are perhaps agreeing that the Word is still true, but you haven't acted upon it and received it for yourself in your own life.

If you say, "By His stripes I am healed, and, therefore, I'm not sick," then you are acting upon the Word. You can reach that place of walking in divine health by acting upon God's Word.

Exercising My Own Faith

When I was a Baptist preacher, I hadn't ever heard of anything such as Full Gospel churches, and I didn't know that anyone else believed in divine healing except me. As a young Baptist boy preacher, when any kind of a symptom attacked my body, I would stop that very minute and start laughing out loud.

Then I'd say "Satan, don't you know that you can't put that on me? The Word of God says that I'm healed. The Bible says that Jesus took my infirmities and bore my sicknesses (Matt. 8:17), and I declare that I am well." I would stand against sickness just like I'd stand against the temptations of sin.

We need to take a stand against that which doesn't belong to us. When those physical symptoms would come, I would praise God and then I would just go on and forget about the symptoms, praising God continually.

I remembered reading in James where it says, *"count it all joy when ye fall into divers temptations"* (James 1:2). I knew that "temptation" here meant *tests* or *trials*. So I started counting it all joy when I would go through a test or a trial, when symptoms would try to attack my body. I would start praising God with all diligence and fervor, and sometimes as I was doing this, all the symptoms would leave my body.

After I received the Holy Ghost, sometimes symptoms would try to attack the bodies of my children. I would get mad at the devil when this happened. I would immediately start praising God for the opportunity to act upon His Word and to experience His saving power. Nine times out of ten, my children would get their healing before I ever got up from praying and praising God that way.

One time my little girl was sick and had a fever, and I was kneeling by the bedside praying for her. There I was thanking God in the midst of that test for the privilege of believing His Word, because He said, *"count it all joy when ye fall into divers temptations"* (James 1:2).

I was joyous about the integrity of God's Word—that healing belongs to us in our redemption. While I was rejoicing about the Word, I felt my daughter's forehead, and suddenly it was cool again. I didn't even get to pray about it! As I said, this would happen nine times out of ten. My children would always get their healing as I praised God for healing and for His Word.

That was my faith in action. I was acting upon the Word because I had read that the Bible says, *"count it all joy when ye fall into divers temptations"* (James 1:2). And the fact that my daughter was sick was a test and a trial. I would rather have been sick than to have one of my children be sick. But it is wonderful to just be able to look up and say, "Father, I thank Thee that I am what you say I am. You say that I am healed and, thank God, I am healed. You say my children are healed by Jesus' stripes, and they are healed!"

We *Have* Because We *Believe*

Believing and confessing is possessing. The Bible says in effect, "He that believes *has*" (John 3:36). A person has his petition because he believes it and confesses that the Word of God is so.

Faith grows in the atmosphere of the confession of the Word of God. I'm not talking about the confession of sin. Certainly, if we have done wrong, we confess it, and God forgives us. But I'm talking about the confession of who we are in Christ and what we have in Christ. It is the confession of our lips that's grown out of the faith in our hearts that puts us over that mountain or that hindrance that seems to stand between us and victory.

I once thought I was doing too much teaching along this line, but the Lord spoke to me some time ago and told me that He wanted me to do even more teaching along the lines of faith and confession. He said that the Church was sadly lacking in teaching in this area.

Believe *and* Say

MARK 11:23

23 For verily I say unto you, That whosoever shall SAY unto this mountain, Be thou removed, and be thou cast into the sea; and shall not doubt in his heart, but shall BELIEVE that those things which he SAITH shall come to pass; he shall have whatsoever he SAITH.

I hadn't noticed it before, but the Lord once pointed out to me that Mark 11:23 mentions the word, "believing" one time and some form of the word, "say" three times. He whispered to my heart that I was going to have to do three times as much preaching about the *saying* part of that verse as I was about the *believing* part. The Lord told me that Christians are failing primarily in the *saying* part and not in the believing part.

You see, it doesn't work just to believe the Word. No, you have to say the Word, too, in order for it to work for you.

ROMANS 10:8

8 But what saith it? The word is nigh thee, EVEN IN THY MOUTH, and IN THY HEART: that is, the word of faith, which we preach.

This verse says, *"The word is nigh thee, even in thy mouth."* This word of faith must not only be believed in your heart, but it also has to be confessed with your mouth.

Too many times, even though we are believers, this word of faith, the gospel, is not in our mouths. We are talking something else besides the word of faith. What we have to do is correct ourselves and speak in line with the Word. To tell you the real truth about it, what I confess, I possess. And that is all I will ever possess.

Believe God's Word, Confess It, Then Possess It

If you want to wait and possess your petition first, and then confess it, you're wrong. You've got the cart before the horse. You'll never get what you desire from God that way. You have to believe the promises in God's Word are true *for you*, confess them for yourself; *then* you possess them. That is as true with salvation as it is with all the promises of God.

ROMANS 10:9–10

9 That if thou shalt CONFESS WITH THY MOUTH the Lord Jesus, and shalt BELIEVE IN THINE HEART that God hath raised him from the dead, thou shalt be saved.

10 For WITH THE HEART MAN BELIEVETH unto righteousness; and WITH THE MOUTH CONFESSION IS MADE UNTO salvation.

Christianity is called "The Great Confession." The law of that great confession is that I confess I have obtained the promises of God's Word before I consciously possess them in the natural realm.

That is exactly the way I received healing for my paralyzed body and incurable blood disease. That is exactly the way I received healing for a deformed heart. I saw the truth in God's Word and I confessed that I received my healing before it ever manifested in my body. I confessed I had my healing before I consciously possessed it in the natural realm. When I confessed that my heart was well, I was still in bed and my heart didn't seem any better—it didn't *feel* healed.

Also, the minute I confessed the promises in God's Word regarding healing, the devil challenged me. But, thank God, I had discovered the law of faith, which says, *"I BELIEVED, and therefore have I SPOKEN"* (2 Cor. 4:13).

The devil told me that I wasn't healed because I didn't look healed or feel healed. I told him that I was healed because the Bible says I'm healed and because I believe the Bible. I told him that by faith I had my healing; if I was lying, then Jesus Christ also lied in His Word because He said that by His stripes I AM healed! Within ten minutes, I was out of that bed and standing on my feet! The devil had tried to call me a liar, but we know that the Word of God is true.

With your lips you confess salvation. The confession of the lips for your salvation comes *before* God acts upon your spirit and recreates it. When you were born again, you had the witness of the Spirit of God in your heart that you had become a child of God; but you didn't have the witness first and then confess it. You confessed your salvation first and *then* your confession created the reality of it in your heart. Then God acted upon your spirit and recreated it.

Salvation, the Holy Spirit, and Healing: Confession First, Then Possession

A few years ago I was holding a meeting in Texas. We had some advertising material and it had been passed out all over town. In the material was part of a sermon I had preached about the laying on of hands and receiving the Holy Ghost.

One night there was a very distinguished-looking woman in the line as we were praying for the sick and for those who wanted to receive the Holy Ghost. When I came to her, she told me that she had come to receive the Holy Ghost. She said that someone had left one of our pamphlets at her house. She said that she wanted me to lay my hands on her and pray for her to receive the Holy Ghost.

But then she added that maybe she ought to get saved first because if she had ever been born again, she didn't know it! She also needed healing. She had come for the Holy Ghost but she needed all three—salvation, the Holy Ghost, and healing.

I instructed her to pray a prayer after me from her heart: "Heavenly Father, I come to You in the Name of Jesus Christ. You said in Your Word, *'Him that cometh to me I will in no wise cast out'* (John 6:37). You said, *'whosoever shall call upon the name of the Lord shall be saved'* (Rom. 10:13).

"I am calling upon Your Name. I want You to save me now. You said, *'if thou shalt confess with thy mouth the Lord Jesus, and shalt believe in thine heart that God hath raised him from the dead, thou shalt be saved'* (Rom. 10:9).

"I believe that Jesus Christ is the Son of God. I believe that He died for my sins according to the Scriptures. I believe that He is raised from the dead for my justification. With my mouth, I confess Him as my Savior, and I confess now that I am saved."

When she finished praying this prayer, she said that something had happened on the inside of her. I told her that by confessing Jesus Christ as her Savior, she had confessed eternal life and eternal life had been given to her. Her spirit had been recreated. You see, she confessed that she had it first; then she received her salvation. Then within a few minutes she also received the Holy Ghost and her healing. She received all three gifts within ten minutes' time.

The confession of the lips for salvation comes before God acts upon our spirits and recreates them. The minute I acknowledge Jesus as my Lord, I have eternal life. I confess that I have salvation before God acts and recreates me. The same law prevails when it comes to receiving the Holy Ghost or any-thing God promises in His Word. I believe it and con-fess it first, and then I receive it.

Receiving the Holy Spirit by Faith

When I began to fellowship with Full Gospel folks, I found that I knew more about faith than they did. They knew more about the Holy Spirit and gifts of the Holy Spirit, but I knew more about faith. We make a sad mistake sometimes to think that we know everything and that we can't learn from anyone else. I went to my Full Gospel pastor's house in order to receive the Holy Spirit, but he told me to wait and seek for the Holy Spirit in the service that night. But I told him it wouldn't take me long to receive.

Then my pastor wanted to show me the procedure for waiting and seeking. But I knew it wasn't scrip-tural to wait or tarry to receive a gift from God—the Precious Holy Spirit.

So I knelt by a chair in the pastor's living room and I lifted my hands and said, "Heavenly Father, I came here to receive the Holy Ghost. According to your Word in Acts 2:38, the Holy Ghost is a Gift.

"Father, Your Word says, *'Repent, and be bap-tized every one of you in the name of Jesus Christ for the remission of sins, and ye shall receive the gift of the Holy Ghost.'* The next verse says, *'For the prom-ise is unto you, and to your children, and to all that are afar off, even as many as the Lord our God shall call'* (Acts 2:39). That includes me.

"Father, I know the Holy Ghost is a Gift in the same way eternal life—receiving Jesus—is a Gift. I received the Lord Jesus Christ and healing by faith and now I receive the Holy Ghost by faith. I thank You that now, Heavenly Father, I am filled with the Holy Ghost and He has come to live within me."

That settled it for me. Then I said to the Lord, "Your Word says in Acts 2:4, *'And they were all filled with the Holy Ghost, and began to speak with other tongues, as the Spirit gave them utterance.'*"

I want you to notice here in Acts 2:4 that they didn't start speaking in tongues until *after* they were filled with the Holy Ghost. That's the reason people struggle so: They do not want to believe they have the Holy Spirit until they start speaking in tongues.

But you've got to receive the Holy Spirit and believe and confess that He has come to infill you *before* He gives you utterance in tongues. It is only as you open your mouth to speak in faith that the Holy Spirit will give you utterance to speak in tongues as the immediate evidence that you *have* received Him.

The Holy Spirit Urges—Never Forces

I've heard people say some foolish things along this line. For instance, one fellow said that the Holy Spirit makes people talk in tongues. It never says in the Bible anywhere that the Holy Ghost made anyone do anything. However, demons do drive peo-ple and try to make people do things. But the Holy Ghost leads and gently guides. He gives you a gentle urging or prompting. In Acts 2:4 it says, *"the Spirit GAVE them utterance."*

There's a vast difference in receiving something someone gives to you and in being forced to take something against your will. For example, when I was nine years old, I went to live with my grandpar-ents on my mother's side of the family. My aunt was still living at home. And for some reason or another, my aunt always thought that if she needed to take any medicine, I did too. Whatever she took, I had to take. She *made* me take it.

She was one of those people who believed you had to take a laxative every night, so I had to too. She'd take Black Draught, as we call it, the old-fashioned kind. I tell you, I took it, but I sure didn't *receive* it! She made me take it! That may be a crude illus-tration, but I think you get the point.

Confession Before Possession: Receiving the Holy Spirit

In the Acts of the Apostles it says that the believers at Ephesus received the Holy Ghost; they weren't forced into it. They weren't made to receive Him. The Holy Ghost is a Gift. (You need only to be saved first in order to receive Him.) You receive the gift of the Holy Spirit; then you confess you've received the Gift; and then you speak in tongues.

Notice you confess first before you speak in tongues. In my own case, I confessed that the Holy Spirit had infilled me, and then I said I expected Him to give me utterance in other tongues. I said that I would speak out what He gave me.

About that time, down on the inside of me there were words forming that I didn't understand. They just seemed to be going around and around inside of me. They just seemed to come up until they got up to my throat, and then I just started speaking those words out. I shut my mind off and just started speaking. I also sang three songs in tongues. I went to the church that night speaking in tongues.

The same thing was true concerning salvation. The same law of faith that applies to receive salvation worked in receiving the Holy Ghost. I've dealt with thousands of people, helping them receive the Holy Spirit in this way. If they will listen to what the Word says and let me help them, I can even get the chronic cases of folks who have been seeking and tarrying for the Holy Spirit for years filled.

One man I dealt with had been seeking the baptism of the Holy Ghost for fifty years. He had been a college professor. He told me that he and his wife had gone through the Azusa Street revival in 1906. His wife had received the Holy Spirit but he never had.

It was in 1956 when I talked to him, fifty years after the Azusa Street revival! He did receive immediately as we laid hands on him and ministered to him. What had hindered him for fifty years was that he thought he should confess he had received the Holy Ghost after he was already speaking in tongues.

But the law of faith says that you believe and confess whatever you desire from God is yours, and then it comes into being.

Confession Before Possession: Healing

The same thing is true in regard to healing. I confess that by His stripes I am healed when the disease is still in my body.

ISAIAH 53:4–5

4 **Surely he hath borne our griefs** [sickness]**, and carried our sorrows** [disease]**: yet we did esteem him stricken, smitten of God, and afflicted.**

5 **But he was wounded for our transgressions, he was bruised for our iniquities: the chastisement of our peace was upon him; and with his stripes we are healed.**

Make the confession that by His stripes you are healed. The disease and its symptoms may not leave your body at once, but as you hold fast to your confession, those symptoms will leave (Heb. 4:14). We are to hold fast to our profession or confession because we know that what God has said in His Word, He is able also to perform (Rom. 4:21).

ROMANS 4:17-21

17 **(As it is written, I have made thee a father of many nations,) before him whom he believed, even God, who quickeneth the dead, and calleth those things which be not as though they were.**

18 **Who against hope believed in hope, that he** [Abraham] **might become the father of many nations, according to that which was spoken, So shall thy seed be.**

19 **And being not weak in faith, he considered not his own body now dead, when he was about an hundred years old, neither yet the deadness of Sarah's womb:**

20 **He staggered not at the promise of God through unbelief; but was strong in faith, giving glory to God;**

21 **And being fully persuaded that, what he had promised, he was able also to perform.**

I know, too, that what God has said in His Word, He is able to make good in *my* life. I know that I'm healed because God said I am healed (Matt. 8:17; 1 Peter 2:24). It makes no difference to me what the symptoms are in my body. I laugh at them because of what the Word says.

I was holding a meeting for Brother Goodwin years ago. On three different nights of the meeting, I had alarming symptoms in my body. This third night, I just couldn't get to sleep. The devil kept telling me that I wasn't going to get my healing this time. I didn't want to disturb anyone, so I pulled the blanket up over my head and started laughing. I didn't feel like laughing, but I did it anyway. I made myself laugh. I went, "Ha, ha, ha, ha." I just kept going on like that.

The devil kept telling me that I wasn't going to get my healing, but I just kept laughing at him. Finally, Satan asked me what I was laughing about. I told him I was laughing at him. He kept asking me over and over again what I was laughing at, and I kept telling him that I was laughing at him.

Satan told me I wasn't going to get my healing, but I told him that the truth is, I didn't have to get my healing because Jesus had *already gotten it for me!* First Peter 2:24 says, *"by whose stripes ye were healed."* I told the devil that if I was healed by Jesus' stripes then, then I am healed now.

When I said this and continued to stand my ground, the devil scurried around and got his belongings and got out of there! He packed up and left! So no matter what the symptoms may be, I laugh at the devil. I command the author of disease to leave my body, in the Name of Jesus. I am a victor. I've learned the law of faith: Confession of the promises of God comes before possession of the promises. We must learn this law if we are going to be successful.

I boldly *declare* and *confess* God's Word, then and only then do I possess the promised blessing or benefit. I make my lips do the work. I give the Word its place. I take sides with the Word. If I side in with the disease and pain, there is no healing for me. But I repudiate the disease and the sickness with my words, which are an expression of my faith in God's Word. My confession gives me possession.

Faith is governed by our confession. If I say that I have been prayed for and I am *waiting* for God to heal me, then I am not in faith and I have repudiated my healing. Instead, my confession should be this: "The Word declares that I am healed. Based on God's Word, I thank the Father for my healing now, not when I *see* my healing. And I praise Him I am healed because according to His Word it is a fact."

Thanking God for the Answer

PHILIPPIANS 4:6–7

6 Be careful for nothing; but in every thing by PRAYER and SUPPLICATION WITH THANKSGIVING let your requests be made known unto God.

7 And the peace of God, which passeth all understanding, shall keep your hearts and minds through Christ Jesus.

The thanksgiving comes after the asking. I've asked God for my petition, and now I have it by faith. Therefore, I thank the Father for the answer. I'm not worrying or fretting any longer because I have the answer. I'm not going to get the money I need; I already have it. It is just as real as if it were in my pocket.

Also, I have my healing because I have God's Word on it, and my heart is filled with perfect confidence because His Word is true. Your confession of God's Word solves the problem. When you teach this way, those who are unlearned in the scriptures don't understand what you've said and they may try to come against you. But if you will stand by the Word, the Word will stand by you.

One man told me he thought that what I was preaching was like Christian Science. No, it isn't. There is as much difference between faith principles and Christian Science as there is between daylight and dark. Over in the realm of the science religions, they use some of the same scriptures we use, and they make confessions. However, they make their confessions based upon their will and ability to make their confessions work. They think their mind is God.

But we are making confessions based upon God's Word and upon His ability to bring His Word to pass in our lives. Theirs is a mental confession. Ours is a spiritual or heart confession.

Confession Is the Expression of What We Believe

Think of it this way: As humans, we are constantly affirming something. Sometimes our affirmations are disastrous. In other words, the effects of your own words upon your life have the power to defeat you. For example, if you continually say you can't do something because you don't have the strength, you will begin to feel your strength actually diminishing. You are left weak and full of indecision and doubt. Your efficiency is gone.

An affirmation or a confession is the expression of what we believe, whether good or bad. Some people say that their children are disobedient. No one ever heard me say that because my children were obedient, and I confessed that they were obedient. The confession of my faith created the reality of it.

Some people continually confess the wrong thing. They confess their doubt and failure. They little realize that their negative confession robs them of their ability and efficiency. They little realize that their confession can change the solid, straight road of life into a boggy, clogged mire.

The confession of weakness will bind you and hold you in captivity. Talk poverty and you will have plenty of it. Confess your want or lack of money all of the time and you will always have lack. These principles of confessing work because they are in the Word.

Some years ago I took the pastorate of a Full Gospel church temporarily while the pastor was gone on a leave of absence. He had a daily radio program. Tuesday night in church the offering went toward the radio program. During my meeting, every Tuesday night they would take from thirty-five minutes to an hour raising the money for the radio program because they were behind. That's too long to take up an offering. I told myself that we would get the money without pulling for it.

The first Tuesday night after the pastor left, they spent some time taking the offering and then I asked them to try it my way. I told them to just mention the offering and then pass the plate. We had a man who was called the radio minister. All he did was answer the mail. For three months while I was there, we just passed the plate and announced that it was a radio offering.

Finally at the end of the three months, the radio minister told me that the money through the mail had doubled. He said that usually the offerings decreased during the summer. But this time they had been able to pay all the bills and everything they owed and didn't owe anyone a cent!

You see, they had quit confessing lack. When you say you don't have the money, you are confessing lack. We confessed plenty and we had plenty.

The Bible says, *"For whosoever hath, to him shall be given, and he shall have more abundance: but whosoever hath not, from him shall be taken away even that he hath"* (Matt. 13:12).

Your confession is the expression of your faith. Confessions of lack and sickness shut God out of your life and let Satan in. Confessions of disease and sickness give sickness dominion over you. They honor Satan and rob God of His glory. So don't confess your doubts. Confess God's Word, and God's Word will work for you.

Questions for Study

1. What two things will cause your faith to grow?

   _____

   _____

2. How do you <u>feed</u> your faith?

   _____

   _____

3. How do you <u>exercise</u> your faith?

   _____

   _____

4. What does God's Word have to become a part of?

   _____

   _____

5. What do you have to do with the promises in God's Word before you possess them?

   _____

   _____

6. What is Christianity sometimes called?

   _____

   _____

7. What comes before God acts upon a man's spirit and recreates it.

   _____

   _____

8. In Acts 2:4, when did they start speaking in tongues?

   _____

   _____

9. When does thanksgiving take place?

   _____

   _____

10. What is an affirmation or a confession?

    _____

    _____

Chapter 20

Actions That Correspond With Faith

In this chapter we will study faith and its corresponding actions. Faith *acts*. When you are in faith, there will always be some action you can take to demonstrate your faith. That may be simply confessing with your mouth, "Thank You, Father. I believe I have received my petition *now* when I pray" (Mark 11:24). But *faith always has corresponding actions.*

JAMES 2:14–22

14 What doth it profit, my brethren, though a man say he hath faith, and have not works? can faith save him?

15 If a brother or sister be naked, and destitute of daily food,

16 And one of you say unto them, Depart in peace, be ye warmed and filled; notwithstanding ye give them not those things which are needful to the body; what doth it profit?

17 Even so FAITH, IF IT HATH NOT WORKS, IS DEAD, being alone.

18 Yea, a man may say, Thou hast faith, and I have works: shew me thy faith without thy works, and I WILL SHEW THEE MY FAITH BY MY WORKS.

19 Thou believest that there is one God; thou doest well: the devils also believe, and tremble.

20 But wilt thou know, O vain man, that FAITH WITHOUT WORKS IS DEAD?

21 Was not Abraham our father justified by works, when he had offered Isaac his son upon the altar?

22 Seest thou how faith wrought with his works, and by works was faith made perfect?

Weymouth's translation reads, *"What good is it, my brethren, if a man professes to have faith, and yet his actions do not correspond?"* (James 2:14). Verse 22 says, "You notice that his faith was cooperating with his actions, and by his actions his faith was perfected."

That is a little clearer to us. Some read this passage of scripture and think it is talking about having faith for salvation. But these scriptures were written to people who were already saved. James was writing to people who were believers. He says, *"What doth it profit, my BRETHREN . . ."* (James 2:14). James was writing to Christian brethren, and he pointed out that faith without corresponding actions won't work for you, even though you are a believer.

Confession Plus Wrong Actions Equals Faith Failures

One of the greatest mistakes many believers make is to confess their faith in the Word of God, and at the same time contradict their confession by wrong actions.

For example, we may say that we are trusting God to provide finances, but at the same time we are worrying and fretting about how we are going to pay our bills. There is no corresponding action there. One minute we confess that the Word of God is true, and the very next moment we repudiate everything we say by wrong actions.

Your actions must correspond with your believing if you are going to receive from God.

James 1:22 says, *"But be ye doers of the word, and not hearers only, deceiving your own selves."* Or as the margin reads, ". . . deluding your own selves." We have many self-deluded people. They blame their faith failures on the devil or on someone else when really they have deluded themselves. They are not acting on the Word or being a doer of the Word. The actions of a doer of the Word coincide with his confession.

MATTHEW 7:24–27

24 Therefore whosoever heareth these sayings of mine, and doeth them, I will liken him unto a wise man, which built his house upon a rock:

25 And the rain descended, and the floods came, and the winds blew, and beat upon that house; and it fell not: for it was founded upon a rock.

26 And every one that heareth these sayings of mine, and doeth them not, shall be likened unto a foolish man, which built his house upon the sand:

27 And the rain descended, and the floods came, and the winds blew, and beat upon that house; and it fell: and great was the fall of it.

Doers of the Word Withstand Life's Storms

Most people miss what Jesus is saying here. He is talking about how different people react to the storms of life. When the storms of life come to many, they fall or buckle spiritually under the pressure of the storms. Their problem is that they are not doers of the Word. They are not practicing the instruction of the Word; the Word has not been built into their spirits.

In Matthew 7:24–27, the same storm and wind came upon both of these houses—the one built on rock and the one built on sand. The reason the house built on sand was destroyed is that it wasn't built on the foundation of God's Word. One was destroyed and one wasn't because the wise builder was a doer of the Word and the foolish one wasn't.

It isn't the storms of life that defeat us. If the storms of life defeated us, we would all be defeated because the storms of life come to all of us. Some people face the same storms that others face and yet they are not defeated, while others who face the storms are destroyed. Those who are not defeated, act on God's Word. The defeated ones may be thoroughly saved, yet they do not have corresponding actions to go along with their faith. And they have not taken time to build their faith on the solid foundation of God's Word.

When the test of sickness comes, for example, some are laid low while other folks stand their ground; they refuse to give in and accept sickness or disease. The storms of life come to us all. It may be sickness, financial difficulty, or some other test or trial. The winds of adversity blow and the floods come, but he who is a doer of the Word can hold fast to his confession of faith, for he knows that God cannot fail!

Talkers vs. *Doers* of the Word

So many who profess Christ and who declare that they believe the Word of God from Genesis to Revelation are not *doers* of the Word. They are *talkers* about the Word, but they are not doers of the Word. There is a big difference.

Talkers of the Word mentally assent that the Word of God is true. But the Word doesn't do them any good or profit them because they are not making the blessings and the benefits of God's Word their own by faith. *Faith receives the promised blessing!* Faith appropriates what God has already promised in His Word.

The way you make God's Word your own is to act upon it. You do what it says. The Bible says, *"Trust in the Lord with all thine heart; and lean not unto thine own understanding"* (Prov. 3:5). The only way to trust in the Lord is to trust in His Word. You cannot trust in the Lord without trusting His Word.

God and His Word are one, just as you and your word are one. If your word is no good, then you are no good. If God's Word isn't any good, then He isn't any good. But, thank God, *His Word is good*, and He watches over His Word to perform it!

JEREMIAH 1:12
12 Then said the Lord unto me, Thou hast well seen: for I will hasten my word to perform it.

The margin reads, "I watch over my word to perform it." If you don't accept the Word and believe and confess it, God doesn't have anything to make good in your life. But He wants to make His Word good in your life. God wants you to have what His Word promises. But if you don't act upon His Word, then He doesn't have anything to make good in your life.

When I trust in the Word with all my heart and stop leaning upon human reasoning and stop looking to people for deliverance, then I have actions that correspond with my faith. My actions are then in perfect fellowship with my confession of faith.

It has taken some of us a long time to learn this. And it will take others even longer because they have been walking in the wrong pathway and in the sense realm, and their minds are so cluttered up with human reasoning. It takes those people awhile to renew their minds with the Word of God so they will have actions that correspond with their confession of faith.

Talking Doubt and Failure Brings Defeat

Until there are corresponding actions, there will be continual failure in your life. You can confess and say that God is the strength of your life because the Bible says He is, and you believe the Bible. But if at the same time you confess that God is your strength, you go on talking about your weaknesses and your inabilities and lack of faith, you will be defeated because there is no corresponding action there. You are resorting to human methods instead of trusting the Lord. Trusting in the Lord is trusting in His Word.

Talking doubt, failure, and weakness brings confusion to your spirit. It brings weakness and failure into your life. There is just one thing for you to do and that is to turn to God's Word. You need to act upon His Word.

Learning to Approach God on His Terms— According to His Word

Many years ago on the bed of sickness, before I saw these truths in God's Word, I didn't know I could be healed. For a while I went through a mental state where I really blamed God.

I said to the Lord, "Lord, You know that You have been better to others than You have been to me. For instance, there's Owen with whom I started first grade (he lived within a block of our house). I'm saved now but when I was a sinner, I was never as mean as he is. And he has never been sick, while I've been sick all of my life afflicted with a heart condition."

Then I said to the Lord, "And I never have been able to run and play and do things that other boys do. Here at fifteen years of age, I have become totally bedfast. Owen is not any older than I am. I know exactly where he is. He's probably standing downtown in front of the drugstore and his pockets are probably full of money. He has good clothes and good health."

I continued, "Lord, I have no money and don't have good health. Owen probably got his money gambling or fleecing people. Here I am going to die and I have nothing, while he's going to live, and he has everything. I was never as mean as he is! It just doesn't seem right!" Oh, I felt so sorry for myself!

My grandmother tried to pacify me by sympathizing with me. That wasn't the right thing to do, because it just made it worse. I felt that much more sorry for myself. I cried all the harder and got more peeved at God.

Then I would say, "Lord, there's another boy who lives behind us. He is big and muscular and stout. He is the kind of fellow who takes the other guy's girlfriends away from them (this boy looked so masculine).

"Here I am, incapacitated and my heart doesn't beat right. This boy even has an automobile! It has the latest of everything in it. He got that because he is a burglar—he doesn't work. The authorities just haven't caught up with him yet. I was never as mean as he is, either, Lord. It looks like You have been better to him than You have been to me. And I have to die."

I felt so sorry for myself. And I cried all the more. Grandmother and Mother would take turns sympathizing with me. I laid there half dead, and I wouldn't even talk to God. I wouldn't even speak to Him!

Finally, at about 6 o'clock one evening, Mother came in again, and I asked her if it would help any if I just *wanted* to get well. She told me wanting to get well was about half the battle. I told her that I had half of it won then because I surely wanted to get well.

Then I decided to do something about the other half of the battle, and I knew that was between me and God. I decided I had better get on speaking terms with Him. I began to pray, but He wouldn't hear me. In other words, I didn't make that connection, because I wasn't approaching Him on His terms—according to His Word. First, I had to repent.

Then I began to see what else was wrong. I had promised the Lord some months before after being saved, that I wouldn't doubt anything I read in His Word. I picked up the Bible and started reading the New Testament. I had told Him that I would put what I read into practice and would be a doer of the Word.

I began with Matthew and read up to Matthew chapter 6. I got to the end of chapter 6 and stumbled because I'd promised God that I would never doubt anything I read in His Word. But when I came to Matthew 6:25–34, I saw that I would have to stop worrying.

MATTHEW 6:25–34

25 Therefore I say unto you, Take no thought for your life, what ye shall eat, or what ye shall drink; nor yet for your body, what ye shall put on. Is not the life more than meat, and the body than raiment?

26 Behold the fowls of the air: for they sow not, neither do they reap, nor gather into barns; yet your heavenly Father feedeth them. Are ye not much better than they?

27 Which of you by taking thought can add one cubit unto his stature?

28 And why take ye thought for raiment? Consider the lilies of the field, how they grow; they toil not, neither do they spin:

29 And yet I say unto you, That even Solomon in all his glory was not arrayed like one of these.

30 Wherefore, if God so clothe the grass of the field, which to day is, and to morrow is cast into the oven, shall he not much more clothe you, O ye of little faith?

31 Therefore take no thought, saying, What shall we eat? or, What shall we drink? or, Wherewithal shall we be clothed?

32 (For after all these things do the Gentiles seek:) for your heavenly Father knoweth that ye have need of all these things.

33 But seek ye first the kingdom of God, and his righteousness; and all these things shall be added unto you.

34 Take therefore no thought for the morrow: for the morrow shall take thought for the things of itself. Sufficient unto the day is the evil thereof.

Another translation of Matthew 6:34 reads, "Be not anxious about tomorrow." A little footnote in one Bible I was reading said, "Don't worry or fret about tomorrow." The footnote referred me to Philippians 4:6, which says, "Be careful for nothing. . . ." The AMPC reads, "Do not fret or have any anxiety about anything."

As I read these verses, I realized God was telling me not to worry! He was telling me not to be anxious or to fret. I had promised to practice what I read, but there I was dying and complaining and worrying myself practically to death!

My grandmother and mother were world-champion worriers, and they had unconsciously taught me to worry. I don't think there has ever been a person who worried more than I did, even when I was a child.

Giving Up the Worry Habit

Did you know that it is a sin to worry and that worry will also hinder your faith? God doesn't want us to worry. He wants us to be free from worry. He doesn't want us bound by any kind of a habit.

Worry was the *hardest sin* I ever gave up. Did you know that it is a sin to disobey God's Word? To worry is to disobey the Word. Worry is a much worse habit than the tobacco habit. Tobacco will just *half kill* you but worry *will completely kill* you!

A fellow who uses tobacco is just half alive while he lives. He can't taste anything because he has that terrible taste of tobacco in his mouth and his sense of taste is dull. And he can't smell anything because he stinks so bad himself! If he *could* smell, he would quit using that nasty tobacco! A tobacco user really doesn't enjoy life to its fullest because he goes through life about half dead. Doctors themselves admit that. *But doctors will also tell you that worry will kill you too.*

A doctor came out to my house one time when I was bedfast and talked about forty-five minutes to me. He asked me if any of the other doctors on my case had ever told me just what was wrong with me, and I told him no, they hadn't. He said that he

believed in telling people exactly what was wrong with them and that he was going to tell me.

He took out a prescription pad and on it he wrote seven medical terms. This was in 1933. He said that at that time there were seven serious organic heart troubles known to medical science and that out of these seven, I had two of them.

This doctor went on to tell me that I was born that way. He said I had a deformed heart and that I was also deformed throughout my entire chest area. My blood was pale and watery. He said my white corpuscles were destroying the red ones faster than the red ones could be rebuilt. My body had been almost completely paralyzed. I could use my arms a little bit.

This doctor said there was nothing that could be done for me and that I should stay ready to go. He told me not to worry about anything and not to get angry or excited in any way. He said if, for example, anything exciting happened out on the street, I wasn't to look out my window to see what was happening, because I might get too excited and die.

This doctor went on to say that worry could kill a person. I suppose he could detect that my mother and grandmother were worriers, and that I was worrying because I didn't know exactly what was wrong with me. When he left, after telling me not to worry, God started dealing with me about my sin of worrying. I began to get under conviction about it.

I tell people now that I'd just as soon cuss as worry. Both are sins and we ought not to do either. About 6 in the evening I finally told the Lord that I wouldn't worry anymore. I told Him that I would practice what I read in His Word.

All the scriptures I had been reading in the New Testament up to Matthew chapter 6 had been light to me. But after I had the revelation about worrying in Matthew 6, but didn't obey it, God's Word had become dark again. God's Word must be acted upon!

God's Word is dark to many people because they are not walking in the light of what they already have. But if you go back and start walking in the light, God's Word will become light to you.

The very minute I went back to Matthew 6 and repented of worrying and started walking in the light, then the rest of the Word became light to me once again.

It had taken me three months or more to get out of Matthew chapter 6. I had tried to continue reading, but couldn't get anything out of it until I repented and began doing what I promised God I would do—to read His word and obey everything I read in it. God expects obedience from His children. Obedience is the principle by which God works on behalf of His children.

So I promised the Lord that I would never worry anymore. I said that I would never be discouraged anymore, nor would I have the blues. Every bit of that comes from the devil. Many years have come and gone and I've never worried anymore. Worry is the greatest temptation you'll ever face.

Also, I've never been discouraged and I've never felt sorry for myself. I've been disappointed in a few people, but never have I allowed them to discourage me one moment. God said not to fret or have any anxiety about anything. God said for us to be doers of the Word. We need to have corresponding actions to our faith.

It took me a long time to get my wife out of the worrying habit. She has quit worrying now. But when we were first married, she didn't know worry was a sin. For example, one time when our two children were small, she got angry with me over something. The children were just babies, and we were going into the parsonage. She was holding one child and I was holding the other one. All of a sudden she said, "I don't think you'd worry if the children and I just fell dead instantly."

I said, "Certainly, I wouldn't. I'd be a fool to start worrying then. What good would it do to start worrying after you were already dead?"

You see, worrying then wouldn't bring my family back! Worrying is foolish; worrying never accomplishes anything productive. Jesus said that in Matthew 6:27.

After I told my wife this, I think it made her madder than ever, but she finally saw the light of God's Word on this subject. When we are not doers of the Word, then we are deluding ourselves. James said, *"But be ye doers of the word, and not hearers only, deceiving* [or deluding] *your own selves"* (James 1:22).

1 PETER 5:7

7 **Casting all your care upon him; for he careth for you.**

1 PETER 5:7 (AMPC)

7 **Casting the whole of your care—ALL your anxieties, ALL your worries, ALL your concerns, ONCE AND FOR ALL—on Him; for He cares for you affectionately, and cares about you watchfully.**

God's Word enlightens our spirits and our minds!

Casting Our Cares Upon God

I accepted the pastorate of a church in 1939, which no one else would take. It was a church with a reputation for having trouble. I was the first pastor the congregation ever supported.

During the time I was the pastor there, I would go to fellowship meetings from time to time with other pastors. These other pastors would ask me how everything was going at my church, which was known to be a troublesome church, and I would always say that things couldn't be better. I would tell them that I didn't have a care in the world.

They would just scratch their heads and wonder about it, because they knew the church had always had a lot of problems. They knew that I had the hardest church in the district to pastor. Some people said that I didn't have enough sense to worry! But, thank God, I had *too much* sense to worry. It's those who don't have very much sense who worry. I'm talking about Bible sense.

And if *you* have Bible sense, you won't worry either. You will do what the Word says to do. It seems to me that people would be glad to get out from underneath the burdensome load of worry. It seems that they would be thrilled to know they don't have to carry that load. The Bible says, *"Casting ALL your care upon him"* (1 Peter 5:7).

You may be praying about your problems, but you'll be defeated if you continue to carry your burdens. Then God can't do anything for you because you are in a place where you can't reach Him since you are not obeying His Word; you're not coming to Him on His terms according to His Word.

When you worry, you are kind of out there in "No Man's Land." You're halfway between God and the devil. God can't reach you, but the devil can enter into your innermost counsel, into your thought life, and keep you confused. God is not the author of confusion, but of peace (1 Cor. 14:33).

Anyway, I knew as well as anyone that the church had troubles, but I refused to worry about it. I also knew something had to be said to the people in my church, but I didn't know what to say. So I decided that I was going to preach the Word and treat everyone right and just turn the problems over to the Lord. This was my only care and my responsibility—to preach the Word and to walk in love and practice what I preached.

So this is what I endeavored to do. As a result, for eighteen months, we had a constant revival in that church! Every Sunday in our regular services people were saved and filled with the Holy Ghost. It just makes a difference when you put God to work by obeying Him and quit trying to carry the load yourself.

I admit that there were problems in the church. The church was twenty-three years old and I was only twenty-one! The church had been there long enough so that different families had intermarried in the church and many of the people were related, so there were kinfolk problems. Family problems in a church are problems you just can't become involved in and still be successful.

There were times when I would get up to preach, and in the natural, I would just feel like blasting the whole bunch of them and telling them what I thought. But when I felt that way, I would always turn over to Revelation and preach about Heaven, or else I would preach on love.

Later after I left that church, I was at a camp meeting where I saw a minister who was pastoring that same church. He told me that as far as he was able to ascertain, I was the only one who had been able to make a success in pastoring that church. He said he was at a place where he was almost ready to leave the church himself. Sunday school was down and finances were down. He said everyone was fussing, and he asked me for my secret of success.

I told him for the next six weeks to preach on love one Sunday morning and on Heaven the next. I told him if he could get the people heavenly minded and full of love it would solve their problems.

Later this pastor stopped by to see me and told me that within six weeks' time the church had come out of the problems it was having! The Sunday school attendance was higher than it had ever been. The same people who had had problems were straightened out and were doing splendidly. He said that things couldn't be better. He stayed there as pastor for some time and when he left, they begged him to come back.

It became such a good church in time that there were forty preachers applying for the pastorate of that church. What really made the difference was the Lord. The success of that church was really attributed to the fact that the pastor cast his cares upon the Lord and was faithful to preach God's Word.

Acting as Though We've Received Our Answer

My wife had been a Methodist girl, and she didn't understand about divine healing. When we were first married, sometimes if she happened to be sick on a Wednesday, she would stay home from prayer meeting and I would go by myself. When I returned home, she would ask me if I had asked them to pray for her, and I would always say no. She just couldn't understand that.

But I told her that she and I had prayed before I went to church, and if we prayed again that would be undoing what we had already prayed for. Praying the second time wouldn't be putting corresponding actions to our faith.

Many believe that if you solicit enough people to pray, prayer will work. But that is *not* scriptural. I told her that we had already claimed her healing, and I was just acting as though we had already received the answer.

The Spirit of God said through me once in prophecy: "Now give heed unto that which is spoken. The natural man and the natural mind would say, 'I don't understand it.' You don't have to understand it, says the Lord. But you *do* have to act upon My Word, and whether you understand it or not, if you'll just believe it and act upon it, then the Word will become real to you, and you shall walk with Me."

God is a faith God. If you walk in Him, then you have to walk by faith. Regardless of the circumstances and the evil influences of the world around us, let us turn every problem over to His care. Learn to put God to work for you. He wants to go to work for you. He wants to work on your behalf. But as long as you hold on to your problems and cares and try to solve them yourself, He can't help you. It's wonderful to be able to turn our troubles over to Him.

The Language of the Senses vs. The Language of Faith

Your worst enemy is the flesh. The flesh and natural human reasoning will try to limit you to your own ability.

You look at the circumstances, the influences, the problems, the cares; the tests, the storms, and the winds of adversities, and you say that you can't be an overcomer. The language of doubt, the flesh, the senses, and the devil is, "I can't. I haven't the ability or the opportunity or the strength. I have been limited and deprived in life."

But the language of faith says, "I can do all things through Christ who strengthens me" (Phil. 4:13). Paul wrote that to one of the churches.

Some might say, "But Paul was an apostle." Just because Paul was an apostle doesn't mean he had more strength than you do. Being an apostle didn't give him any extra strength. Preachers don't necessarily have any more to draw from than others do. They just have a ministry and an anointing to fulfill that ministry. But ministers have to face the same storms of life that each lay member does.

Paul said, *"I can do all things through Christ which strengtheneth me"* (Phil. 4:13). Paul didn't say he could do all things because he was an apostle. He said he could do all things "through Christ." You are "in Christ" just as much as Paul was.

Second Corinthians 5:17 says, *"Therefore if any man be in Christ, he is a new creature: old things are passed away; behold, all things are become new."* If you have been born again, you are a new creature in Christ too. Christ didn't belong to Paul any more than He belongs to you.

The language of faith says, "I can do all things through Christ. My Heavenly Father strengthens me. I cannot be conquered and I cannot be defeated."

You can do all things through Christ, just as much as Paul could. I'm speaking from a spiritual standpoint. If a test or trial comes against you, it can't whip you, because there aren't enough natural forces in all the world to conquer the Greater One who dwells in you.

1 JOHN 4:4

4 . . . greater is he that is in you, than he that is in the world.

This verse declares that you are fortified from within. I've learned how to put the Greater One to work *for* me. I've learned how to put Him to work *in* me. Not only am I born of God and made a partaker of His love, but I have dwelling in me the Spirit of Him who raised Jesus from the dead.

Therefore, *I have God's wisdom, strength, and ability in me.* I am learning how to let that wisdom govern my intellect. I am letting the Greater One Who dwells within govern my mind and speak through my lips. I am daring to think God's thoughts after Him. I am daring to say in the presence of all my enemies of faith, *"God is my Ability."*

PSALM 23:4–5

4 Yea, though I walk through the valley of the shadow of death, I will fear no evil: for thou art with me; thy rod and thy staff they comfort me.

5 Thou preparest a table before me in the presence of mine enemies: thou anointest my head with oil; my cup runneth over.

PSALM 27:1

1 The Lord is my light and my salvation; whom shall I fear? the Lord is the strength of my life; of whom shall I be afraid?

1 JOHN 4:4

4 Ye are of God, little children, and have overcome them: because greater is he that is in you, than he that is in the world.

Psalm 23 is for us. You need to make these confessions daily:

> God prepares a table before me in the presence of my enemies. Thank God, the Lord is my Ability.

> He is the strength of my life; of whom shall I be afraid? Greater is He who is in me than he who is in the world.

> In Christ, God has made me greater than my enemies.

> God has made me to put my heel on the neck of weakness, fear, and inability. I stand and declare that whosoever believes on Christ shall not be put to shame (Rom. 10:11).

> I cannot be put to shame. The strength of God is mine and in Christ I am greater than my enemies.

I am not trusting in my own strength because the Bible never said a word about my being strong in myself. Paul wrote to the Church at Ephesus and said, *"Finally, my brethren, be strong in the Lord, and in the power of HIS MIGHT"* (Eph. 6:10). God is your strength and your ability! So many people have the wrong idea about this. They are struggling, trying to put themselves over in life.

Wrapping Ourselves in the Promises of God

For example, there is a song which says, "If I can just make it in," referring to Heaven. Some people get up in church to testify, but end up telling everyone to pray for them. They want people to pray that they'll be able to hold out till the end.

But God doesn't want you to make it into Heaven by just barely holding out till the end! He wants you to swing free, wrapped in His promises, and let Him help you. He wants to be your ability and your strength. So wrap yourselves in the promises of God and swing free!

In 1933 in San Diego, California, a group of Navy men were trying to moor a dirigible, the U.S.S. Akron, which the government had built. As the ground crew were attempting to moor the dirigible mast, the thing suddenly shot up into the air. Three men reportedly hung on and went up with the aircraft. Two of the three soon fell to their deaths.

But there was one who just kept hanging on as the aircraft rose higher and higher, until he appeared as just a speck in the sky. People were screaming below because they knew he could fall to his death any minute. But for two hours, he continued hanging on.

Afterwards, they were able to pull the dirigible downward and rescue the man who had been hanging on to the rope. An ambulance was waiting to take the man to the hospital, but he said he was fine. People were asking this young man how he had held on for so long when the other two men plunged to their deaths.

He told them that he had used the rope to make a rigging for himself, so he didn't have to hold on to the rope; and the rope held him. He had just been swinging free, enjoying the scenery, while all the people below were screaming and carrying on, thinking he was going to die at any moment.

Most Christians are like those two men who fell. They are trying to hold on and hold out until they *give* out. Some fall when all they need to do is wrap themselves in the promises of God and swing free! They can be enjoying the scenery while they put God's Word to work for them.

When I was a young Baptist boy, I heard a story about a man who was walking down a railroad track with a pack on his back, when he came to a section gang; these men were repairing the railroad. He thought the foreman was going to tell him to get off the railroad track, so he showed him a train ticket he had. But the foreman told him that the ticket only gave him a right to ride the train on that track; it didn't give him the right to *walk* on the track.

Many people are like that man. They are on the right track, but they ought to be riding instead of walking. Besides that, they ought to check in their baggage because they don't even have to be carrying it! The Bible says, *"Casting ALL your care upon him; for he careth for you"* (1 Peter 5:7). The cares of life are excess baggage you are *not* supposed to be carrying!

The strength of God is mine. The ability of God is mine. That's faith speaking. That's corresponding action. That's acting upon God's Word. If you will begin to make confessions in line with God's Word, God's Word will work for you!

Questions for Study

1. What does faith always have?

   _____

   _____

2. What is one of the greatest mistakes many believers make in the area of faith?

   _____

   _____

3. What must your actions correspond with?

   _____

   _____

4. Why was the house that was built on sand destroyed?

   _____

   _____

5. Why was one house destroyed and the other one wasn't?

   _____

   _____

6. Why doesn't the Word of God profit mere talkers of the Word?

   _____

   _____

7. What does talking doubt and failure bring?

   _____

   _____

8. How should you learn to approach God?

   _____

   _____

9. Why is worry a sin?

   _____

   _____

10. What should you do with the cares of this life and the excess baggage you aren't supposed to be carrying?

    _____

    _____

Chapter 21

How to Write Your Own Ticket With God

I was conducting a revival meeting many years ago in the First Assembly of God Church in Phoenix, Arizona. The meeting was held during the latter part of November and the first part of December in 1953. I was staying in the home of some friends who attended that church.

After an evening service, we were fellowshipping at their home with some other church folks. Just about the time they were ready to serve the refreshments, I had an urge by the Spirit of God to pray. It just seemed unusually pressing, like it was an urgent matter—more so than usual.

These were all Full Gospel people, so I felt free to tell my host that I had to pray and that I had to pray right then. He asked that everyone present pray also. So everyone stopped what they were doing and we went to prayer. My knees had hardly touched the floor when I was in the Spirit.

Do you know what it means to be "in the Spirit"? John was in the Spirit on the Lord's day (Rev. 1:10). Then we read in Acts 18:9 that the Lord spoke to Paul in the night in a vision. In the vision, the Lord told Paul, *"Be not afraid, but speak, and hold not thy peace."*

ACTS 23:11

11 And the night following the Lord stood by him, and said, Be of good cheer, Paul: for as thou hast testified of me in Jerusalem, so must thou bear witness also at Rome.

ACTS 22:17–18

17 And it came to pass, that, when I was come again to Jerusalem, even while I prayed in the temple, I WAS IN A TRANCE;

18 And saw him saying unto me, Make haste, and get thee quickly out of Jerusalem: for they will not receive thy testimony concerning me.

These are scriptural illustrations of being "in the Spirit." Since ministers had experiences like that in the days of the Early Church, we ought to have those same kinds of experiences now because we have the same Holy Ghost.

As I knelt to pray in the home of those Full Gospel people, by the time my knees touched the floor, I was praying in tongues, and I was in the Spirit. Or as Paul said in Acts 22:17, I was in a trance.

When you are in the Spirit, it doesn't mean you don't know what you are doing. It just means that your physical senses are suspended; you are more in *the spirit realm* than you are in the natural realm. You are more conscious of spiritual things than you are of natural things.

At the moment I didn't know where I was. I wasn't aware that I was in Phoenix, Arizona. It seemed as though I knelt down in a white cloud. I prayed in tongues as hard and fast as I could pray and with groanings for about forty-five minutes.

I've prayed enough in the Spirit to know that I was interceding for someone who was lost. At the end of that time of praying, I had a note of victory.

I encourage people who are praying like this to continue to pray until they have a note of victory; that is, until they either laugh in the Spirit or sing in the Spirit.

When you pray until you have a note of victory, that means that whatever you were praying about, you have received the answer.

After I prayed this way, I had a vision. In the vision, I saw our church service on the following Sunday night, with between five and six hundred people present. When I had the vision it was Friday night and I was seeing three days ahead to my Sunday night service.

In the vision, I saw myself preaching and later giving the altar call. I saw myself with one elbow on the pulpit, and as I leaned over, I pointed to a man who was seated on the second row from the front in the center section.

I said to him, "My friend, the Lord shows me that you are past seventy years of age. You are not a Christian and you do not believe there is a hell. But God told me to tell you that you've got one foot in hell and the other one is slipping in."

In the vision I saw the man get up from his seat and kneel at the altar and be gloriously saved.

After the vision was over, the folks who were present knew that I had seen something and they asked me about it, so I told them. On Sunday night when we came to church, I looked immediately at that place where I had seen that man sitting in the vision. I had never seen him before in my life, but he was dressed just like I had described him to the people on Friday night.

I did just exactly what I'd seen myself doing in the vision. I preached my sermon and then I leaned over the pulpit and spoke those same words to him. He came forward, knelt at the altar and was gloriously saved.

Afterwards the man was telling the pastor everything I had said about him when I spoke to him in the Spirit. He said he was seventy-two and he actually had been taught that there wasn't a hell. He said he also knew what I meant when I told him that he had one foot in hell and the other one was slipping in. He had a serious heart condition and the doctors had told him that he might die at any minute.

He said that this was the first time he had ever been inside a church building in his entire lifetime. No one knew to pray for the man; not a person who was a member of that church knew him. He had come to that city five months prior to this time and had bought a motel. Some Christian folks traveling from the east had stayed at his motel and had witnessed to him. They had practically dragged him to church and he was saved that night.

The Holy Ghost knew he was coming and we already had him "prayed through" to victory before he ever got there. That's the joy and the benefit of praying in the Spirit.

After that vision had come to pass just as I saw it, the Lord Jesus Himself appeared to me. He began to talk to me about my ministry and about some things on a national scale concerning our own government, which came to pass the very next year. Then He talked to me about some financial matters concerning my own life that came to pass just like He said they would.

Then He said to me, "Be faithful and fulfill thy ministry, My son, for the time is short." You see, your time with God in eternity and your time with men on the earth are two different things.

I said to Him, "Dear Lord Jesus, before You go, may I ask You a question, please? I have two sermons that I preach from Mark chapter 5 concerning the woman with the issue of blood who touched Your clothes."

I had received both sermons by inspiration; one as I was driving my car down the highway, traveling to church and singing in tongues. I pulled over beside the road and wrote the sermon outline. I was preaching that sermon in the state of Alabama and I had just read the text and begun my sermon when it looked as though some of the words in the text were in print three times larger than the rest of the words in those verses. Those verses just seemed to leap off the page. I saw something that I had never seen before and that is how I received the second sermon.

I continued, "Lord, every time I preach those two sermons, I seem to be conscious in my spirit—I have the sense within me—that the Holy Spirit is trying to get another message over to me. I have the sense that this other sermon will complement these two sermons. Then in times of prayer when I have a greater anointing, it seems as if I'm going to receive the message and get that other sermon, but somehow or another, I fail to get it. I believe I'm right, and if I'm right, I wish You would tell me so. Then I wish You would give me that sermon."

The Lord said to me, "You are right. My Spirit, the Holy Spirit, has endeavored to get over to your spirit another sermon along that line, but you've failed to pick it up. While I'm here I'll do what you've asked. I'll give you that sermon outline. Now get your pencil and paper and write it down."

I reached for paper and a pencil in a hurry. I usually keep paper and pencil handy because God talks to me many times in times of prayer. If you don't write these things down you may let them get away from you.

Jesus said, "Write down, '1, 2, 3, 4.'" I did that. I had sensed in my spirit that there would be four points to this sermon. Then He said, "If anyone anywhere will take these four steps, or will put these four principles into operation, he will always receive whatever he wants from Me or from God the Father."

Four Steps to Receiving Your Answer From God

These are four steps that can be put into operation immediately concerning receiving anything God promises in His Word. For instance, you can take the four steps to salvation, to healing, to the baptism of the Holy Ghost, or to receive victory, finances, or any other answer you need from God.

However, there are some areas of faith that take time to develop. For instance, if you have a financial need, and you need a certain amount of money by the first of the year, then you may need to first develop your faith to the level of your need.

But even in the hardest areas, if you will put these four principles into practice over a period of time, they will produce results because they are Bible principles. Therefore, whether these principles are put into operation immediately or are practiced over a period of time, you can have whatever you say from God's Word. You can write your own ticket with God.

From what Jesus said, I wrote my own title to the sermon: "How To Write Your Own Ticket With God."

These four steps that Jesus shared with me and that I'm about to share with you are so simple that they almost seem foolish. But after all, Jesus in all of His preaching on the earth never did bring forth anything very complicated. He talked in terms that even the uneducated could understand. He talked about vineyards and orchards and sheepfolds and shepherds.

Jesus illustrated spiritual truths in such a simple way that the common people could understand. After all, the people Jesus preached to didn't have the advantages in education that we have today. God never did give anyone anything so complicated that it couldn't be understood. If it comes from the Father, it will be clear and concise.

Step Number One: *Say It*

MARK 5:25–34

25 And a certain woman, which had an issue of blood twelve years,

26 And had suffered many things of many physicians, and had spent all that she had, and was nothing bettered, but rather grew worse,

27 When she had heard of Jesus, came in the press behind, and touched his garment.

28 For she SAID, IF I MAY TOUCH BUT HIS CLOTHES, I SHALL BE WHOLE.

29 And straightway the fountain of her blood was dried up; and she felt in her body that she was healed of that plague.

30 And Jesus, immediately knowing in himself that virtue had gone out of him, turned him about in the press, and said, Who touched my clothes?

31 And his disciples said unto him, Thou seest the multitude thronging thee, and sayest thou, Who touched me?

32 And he looked round about to see her that had done this thing.

33 But the woman fearing and trembling, knowing what was done in her, came and fell down before him, and told him all the truth.

34 And he said unto her, Daughter, thy faith hath made thee whole; go in peace, and be whole of thy plague.

What is the first step that this woman took in order to receive from Jesus? Verse 28 says, *"For she SAID, If I may touch but his clothes, I shall be whole."*

The first step she took was, she *said* it. She said what she desired and it was in line with God's will.

There's a Godward side and a manward side to winning every battle, every victory, and to receiving anything from God. You have your part to play. There is something that *you* must do. God is not going to fail on His part. If there is any failure, it has to be on our part. If we see to it that we do our part, then we can be sure that there will be an answer and a victory for us every time.

Someone told this woman about Jesus. That is not something she did; that is something someone else did. So this woman knew about Jesus. She knew that He was healing people. She knew that He was the Healer. But the question was, what was she going to do about what she knew?

Jesus said to me in that visitation: "Step number one is to *say it*."

In the visitation, Jesus said, "Positive or negative, it is up to the individual. According to what the individual says, that shall he receive."

He said, "This woman could have made a negative confession instead of a positive one, and that would have been what she received."

Jesus continued, "She could have said, 'There's no use for me to go see Jesus. I've suffered so long. Twelve years I've been sick. All the best doctors have given up on my case. I've spent all of my living on physicians. I'm not better, but growing worse. I have nothing to live for. I might as well die.'"

Jesus said, "If that had been what she said, that would have been what she received. But she did not speak negatively. She spoke positively. For she said, 'If I may touch but his clothes, I shall be whole.'" And it came to pass!

You can have what you say. *You can write your own ticket with God.* And the first step in writing your own ticket with God is to *say it*.

Never Speak Defeat

As I discussed in a previous chapter, if you are defeated, you are defeated with your own lips. You have defeated yourself. The Bible says in Proverbs 6:2, *"Thou art snared with the words of thy mouth, thou art taken with the words of thy mouth."* Or we could say, "You are taken *captive* with the words of your mouth."

One writer put it this way: "You said that you could not, and the moment you said it, you were whipped. You said that you did not have faith, and doubt rose up like a giant and bound you. You talked failure, and failure held you in bondage."

Those words are well said. Believers should never talk defeat. We should never talk failure.

You talk about your trials, you talk about your lack of money, and your faith will shrivel and dry up. But on the other hand, if you talk about your lovely Heavenly Father and what He can do, your faith will grow by leaps and bounds.

If you confess sickness, you'll develop sickness in your system. If you talk about your doubts and fears, they'll become stronger. If you confess the lack of finances, your words will stop the money from coming in. I've proven this to be true in my own life.

Changing Lack of Finances to Provision by Faith

In 1951, I was scheduled to go to a certain church after Christmas and preach there. For three nights, I wasn't able to sleep, and the Lord kept talking to me about not going to that place. I kept arguing with Him and told Him that I had to go. Then the Lord got down to brass tacks with me. I told the Lord that it was a large church and they guaranteed so much money for holding the meeting. I told the Lord I needed that money.

But the Lord still didn't want me to go there. I finally told the Lord that I would call the pastor, and if he would let me off the hook, I wouldn't go. But I told Him that if the pastor wouldn't let me off the hook, I would have to go because I'd given my word. After all, one of the characteristics of a spiritual pilgrim is that he sweareth to his own hurt and changeth not (Ps. 15:4).

The next evening I started to call the pastor and the phone rang just as I started to make my call. It was a long distance telephone call from that pastor. I told him that I was just getting ready to call him.

He asked me if I was still coming and I told him that I planned to, but that the Lord had told me not to come at that time. He said that it really would be better if I came later because he had to go out of town to take care of some business. So it really worked out better for both of us.

When I hung up the phone, I asked the Lord where He wanted me to go to minister. God leads us one step at a time. If you want to get the whole picture before you make a move, you'll never make a move, and you'll miss the whole thing.

After I talked to that pastor on the phone, I told the Lord that I supposed He probably wanted me to call a pastor who had invited me to come and hold a meeting for him. This pastor was averaging three hundred in attendance in Sunday school and he just had a new auditorium built that would seat eight hundred people. He told me that if I would come and hold a meeting, he would guarantee me a full house every night.

But when I asked the Lord if He wanted me to go there, He said, "No." So I asked the Lord where He wanted me to go. He told me to go to a little church down in east Texas by the Louisiana border, out in the country.

This church ran seventy in Sunday school and that was tops for them. I asked the Lord if He knew what He was talking about! (You see, I talk to the Lord just like I do anyone else, because I'm closer to Him than I am to anyone else. He knows what you're thinking anyway, so you might as well be honest with Him!)

I told the Lord that I couldn't afford to go down there because that little church couldn't meet my budget. I had held a meeting for that pastor and I received $1.99 a week. This pastor would get up at the end of the week and receive my offering. He would say to the congregation that he had a few pennies and that surely they did too! So that's all I ever received—pennies! I would always give the offering back to them because if they were that short of money, they needed it more than I did!

So I told the Lord that this pastor didn't even know how to take up an offering. But the Lord told me that was where he wanted me to go. I said I would go, but I told the Lord that I expected Him to meet my budget just as He did when I was in the large churches. The Lord said it was for *me* to do the *going*, and *He* would do the *doing*. I went to that church the Sunday after Christmas. I drove all Sunday afternoon to get there. I was so far out in the country, it looked as if I had come to the jumping off place.

When I arrived at the parsonage, the pastor told me that he had almost called to tell me not to come because they'd had a crop failure. The town's main crops were tomatoes and cotton, and the hail got the tomatoes and the drought got the cotton. He said they couldn't promise me a dime. I said to him, "Well, I didn't ask you for a dime, did I?"

Then I told him not to get up and tell the people that he had told me they had had a crop failure. I told him that if he was going to say anything, he should get up and tell them what the Bible says. I told him to tell them that God says, *"for the world is mine, and the fulness thereof"* (Ps. 50:12).

I told him to tell the people that the silver and the gold and the cattle on a thousand hills are the Lord's (Hag. 2:8; Ps. 50:10), and what belongs to the Lord belongs to us. I told him to take the offering then, but not to make a pull for any money; just to give the people an opportunity to give.

I told the Lord that I was claiming a certain sum of money. The least I could get by on was $150 a week. I didn't tell the pastor that because I knew he would be alarmed. When it came time to take up the offering, he gave the people the scriptures I had told him to use. The Lord had told me to stay there only ten days, so I told the Lord that I would claim $200 for that ten-day period. That was the bare minimum I could get by on. When the ten nights were over, I had received $248.15 in offerings.

When I first went to that church, there was only one man attending the meeting. But during that week, we had thirty-two people come to receive the baptism of the Holy Ghost. Out of those thirty-two, twenty-nine received the Holy Spirit the minute I laid hands on them. Out of the twenty-nine, there were thirteen grown men and twelve of these were heads of families. So this pastor had received twelve new families in his church within ten days' time.

This was a little old country church with a one-room Sunday school. It was winter time, and they had a little country stove sitting out in the middle of the floor.

I told the pastor that he ought to build on some rooms so the children could have Sunday school separately from the adults. The pastor had intended to do that the previous fall. He had talked to a lumberman who was a good Baptist man who promised to furnish all the lumber they would need and all the foundation material, and everything except the windows and the doors. The lumberman had promised to give them all this for only $400. I asked the pastor why he didn't take the offer, and he said it was because of the crop failure; no one had any money.

After Sunday school on Sunday morning, before I began to preach, I told the people that I had sat in the back of the adult Sunday school class, but that I couldn't hear what was being taught because there were so many voices coming from all the age groups in this one room.

I told them that the pastor had found a good deal as far as purchasing the materials, but the crop failure and the lack of finances coming in had stopped him from going on with the building program. I told them I was interested enough in their building additional rooms that I would give the first $10 myself. Before I could get them stopped, we had more than $400!

Then in the Sunday night service, I told the folks that I had been staying over at the parsonage, and I had asked the pastor why he didn't buy a butane gas system for the church and parsonage. I told the congregation that we had been eating food cooked on a kerosene stove and that everything tasted like kerosene.

When I asked the pastor about it, he told me that a Baptist man had told him he would put in a butane system in the church and parsonage and put in a cooking stove and the heating stoves for a good price. The Baptist man also said he would furnish the gas after that for nothing. He also said he would give ten percent of the cost out of his own pocket toward the system.

I told the congregation that the pastor was going to do it, but had decided against it because of the crop failure and subsequent lack of finances.

I told the people that we should raise the money and buy the system anyway. And do you know that in a few minutes' time we had the money!

At the end of my ten-day meeting, I was talking with the pastor about all the finances that had come in. The pastor said that before he only had one man in the church and maybe a few visitors, and he would only average about $15 a week for his own salary, so he had to work another job on the side for a living. But on that particular Sunday morning, he had received $140 himself for his week's salary.

I had started preaching tithes to those new people who came in. The pastor said that the church had taken in a little more than $2,000 within those ten days, and that he would never talk failure again.

You see, if you talk about your lack of finances, it stops the money from coming in. And if you talk about your doubts and fears, you'll destroy your faith. But if you will speak words that line up with the Word of God, you will increase your faith, change your circumstances, and receive the answers to prayer you need from God.

Step Number Two: *Do It*

MARK 5:28

28 For she said, If I may TOUCH but his clothes, I shall be whole.

It wouldn't have done the woman with the issue of blood any good if she had said, "If I may touch but his clothes, I shall be whole," and then hadn't *acted* upon what she said.

Jesus told me that night in the vision, "Your actions defeat you or they put you over. According to your action, you receive or you are kept from receiving what you want from God."

The woman with the issue of blood *acted* upon what she said. She touched Jesus' clothes.

Step Number Three: *Receive It*

MARK 5:29

29 And straightway the fountain of her blood was dried up; and she FELT in her body that she was healed of that plague.

After the woman touched Jesus' clothes in faith, she felt in her body that she was healed of that plague (Mark 5:29). Jesus said, *"Who touched my clothes?"* (Mark 5:30). Jesus knew that virtue had gone out of Him. Or as the margin says, Jesus said that *power* had gone out of Him.

The disciples said to Jesus, *"Thou seest the multitude thronging thee, and sayest thou, Who touched me?"* (Mark 5:31). First, the woman said it. Then she *came* forward to receive her healing by touching Jesus. That was her faith in action. Then she received it and felt in her body that she was healed of the plague.

Saying and *Doing* Comes Before *Feeling* and *Healing*

Notice that the *feeling* and the *healing* followed the *saying* and the *doing*. Most people want the *feeling* and the *receiving* first and then they think they'll do the *saying* and the *doing*.

But you can't do that because it doesn't work that way. You have to have the *saying* and the *action* first. *Then* you'll have the feeling and the receiving. It was only after the woman with the issue of blood *said* and *did*, that Jesus said that the power had gone out of Him.

The whole world has become concerned about the nuclear bombs that have been exploded in the atmosphere because those bombs can release radioactive material into the atmosphere—power that cannot be seen or felt. And that power is deadly and dangerous.

Well, there is a power at work in this earth that is not deadly or dangerous, yet is far greater in strength than any bomb. There is a power that is good. That power is always present everywhere. If all the sick people knew about that power, they could be healed of every disease. Yes, there is power to deliver from anything that binds or hurts you. It is the power of God, the anointing which destroys every yoke (Isa. 10:27)!

If God's power is available, then why isn't everyone healed? We can find out by looking again at the woman with the issue of blood. We will see that it is *faith* that gives God's power action.

Step Number Four: *Tell It*

MARK 5:33

33 But the woman fearing and trembling, knowing what was done in her, came and fell down before him, and TOLD him all the truth.

This verse says the woman with the issue of blood *told Jesus* "all the truth" (v. 33). Jesus said to tell it so that others might receive it. The first step is to *say it*, but this fourth step is to *tell it*.

At first, we read that the woman *said* what she believed. Now she is *telling* what happened as a result of her saying, believing, and doing.

You have to *say* some things in faith before you ever receive them from God. Many times people say the wrong thing because they believe the wrong thing. I said before that wrong thinking produces wrong believing, and wrong believing produces wrong speaking. But when people start believing the right thing and saying the right thing, they'll have the right things in life. You'll have in life what you believe and say, either good or bad.

In this vision when the Lord was teaching me this, I told the Lord I could see that if anyone took these four steps, he could receive *healing* just like this woman did. But then I asked, "Lord, You said that if any believer anywhere would take these four steps, he would receive whatever it is he *wanted*. Does this mean that folks can receive the Holy Spirit this way too?" The Lord answered me that they could.

We Write Our Own Ticket of Victory

Then I asked Jesus, "Does this mean that any believer anywhere can write a ticket of victory over the flesh, the world, and the devil?"

Jesus answered, "Emphatically, yes." Then Jesus said that if the believer *doesn't* write his own ticket with God, nothing will be done about his situation.

Jesus continued, "If believers don't write their own ticket, it won't be done. It would be a waste of their time to pray for Me to give them the victory. *They* have to write their own ticket." Jesus was saying that believers must do something about their situations themselves and they can do that by following these four steps.

Old Testament Example of the Four Steps of Faith

I then asked the Lord to give me some more scriptures about these four principles. The Lord told me that David used these four principles in First Samuel 17:30–54.

David arrived at the Israelites' camp and found the Philistines camped on one side of a valley and Israelites on the other. The giant, Goliath, defied the armies of Israel and the people of God, and he challenged the Israelites. *"And David SAID"* (1 Sam. 17:32).

That's the first thing David did. He *said* that he would *fight* and prevail against the uncircumcised Philistine, Goliath.

1 SAMUEL 17:32–37

32 And David said to Saul, Let no man's heart fail because of him; thy servant will go and fight with this Philistine.

33 And Saul said to David, Thou art not able to go against this Philistine to fight with him: for thou art but a youth, and he a man of war from his youth.

34 And David said unto Saul, Thy servant kept his father's sheep, and there came a lion, and a bear, and took a lamb out of the flock:

35 And I went out after him, and smote him, and delivered it out of his mouth: and when he arose against me, I caught him by his beard, and smote him, and slew him.

36 Thy servant slew both the lion and the bear: and this uncircumcised Philistine shall be as one of them, seeing he hath defied the armies of the living God.

37 David said moreover, THE LORD THAT DELIVERED ME OUT OF THE PAW OF THE LION, AND OUT OF THE PAW OF THE BEAR, HE WILL DELIVER ME OUT OF THE HAND OF THIS PHILISTINE. And Saul said unto David, Go, and the Lord be with thee.

David didn't say that because he got a word from the Lord. But, you see, David knew he could have what he said. He knew he could write his own ticket with God. David knew that God would do anything David said that was in line with God's covenant with the Israelites.

And the reason God hasn't done any more for you is because you haven't said any more. All that you have today is the result of what you said yesterday. If you are at the bottom of the ladder, it is because that's all you've been believing for and saying for. If you'll talk right and believe right, you'll get to the top, instead of being under the barrel.

David went out with his shepherd's sling and crook, or staff, and the Bible says, *"when the Philistine looked about, and saw David, he disdained him: for he was but a youth, and ruddy, and of a fair countenance"* (1 Sam. 17:42).

1 SAMUEL 17:43–44

43 And the Philistine said unto David, Am I a dog, that thou comest to me with staves? And the Philistine cursed David by his gods.

44 And the Philistine said to David, Come to me, and I will give thy flesh unto the fowls of the air, and to the beasts of the field.

David let Goliath talk. You can't stop the devil from talking. But when he gets through, *you* have something to say.

Jesus didn't stop the devil from talking when Jesus was being tempted in the wilderness. But when the devil got through, Jesus had something to say. Jesus said, *"It is written"* (Matt. 4:4).

Well, David *said* to Goliath, *"Thou comest to me with a sword, and with a spear, and with a shield: but I come to thee in the name of the Lord of hosts, the God of the armies of Israel, whom thou hast defied"* (1 Sam. 17:45).

David also said, *"This day will the Lord deliver thee into mine hand; and I will smite thee, and take thine head from thee; and I will give the carcases of the host of the Philistines this day unto the fowls of the air, and to the wild beasts of the earth; that all the earth may know that there is a God in Israel"* (1 Sam. 17:46).

David was just a little country boy, and Goliath was a giant who may have been as tall as eleven and one-half feet. Goliath was so big, another man carried his shield.

Some people say, "How did David know what to do?" It's strange that when it comes to natural things, folks know exactly what to do. For example, if they are going to sell their automobile, they know exactly how much they're going to sell it for. If they're trying to get a job, they know exactly how to go about doing it. But when it comes to spiritual things, they don't know what to do. They don't know that they can write their own ticket!

You can write your own ticket with God. Whether you know it or not, that is what you've been doing. That's the reason people are where they are now. *God will do everything for you that you believe Him to do* (Mark 11:24). Many have read the scriptures concerning these things but those scriptures never mean a thing to them.

Living in the Protection of God by Faith

A number of years ago, we were going to Clovis, New Mexico, for a tent meeting. My children and wife were going with me. My mother had come over and she asked where I was going next. I told her about our planned trip to Clovis. She told me to be careful on the road because there were so many wrecks and people were getting injured all the time.

Then she said that when I was traveling, she stayed awake all night long and prayed for me. She said she just waited for the phone to ring. She was always afraid that a call would come saying I'd been in a wreck. So I told her that if she had been praying in faith, she would have gone to sleep. (I have to tell my own mother the truth just as I do you.)

She said, "Son, I know you have faith. I never had much myself." She was a member of a Full Gospel church too! But she was talking herself right out of God's blessings.

She said that when the family gets together for a family reunion, they all agree that I am a walking miracle. She said that she just knew I must pray every minute I'm on the road. I told her that I never did. I told her I never prayed that God would be with me.

She said, "What makes you talk that way? What's gotten into you?"

I told her, "Nothing but the Word." I told her that Jesus had already said, *"I will never leave thee, nor forsake thee"* (Heb. 13:5). She wanted me to pray all the time that God would be with me. But I told her

that I didn't have to go down the road bawling and squalling and begging Jesus to be with me. I always begin a trip saying, "Heavenly Father, I'm so thankful for Your Word. I'm so glad Jesus is with me."

Psalm 34:7 says, *"The angel of the Lord encampeth round about them that fear him, and delivereth them."* I told my mother that the angels are always with me. Also, the Holy Ghost is on the inside of me, so I can go singing and rejoicing. God has already told me that no evil will befall me (Ps. 91:10). One translation of this verse reads, "No accident shall overtake thee."

So my mother asked me where I was going next, and when I told her I was going to Clovis, New Mexico, she said, "Son, you're not going to take your wife and children there, are you?"

You see, this was before the Salk polio vaccine had been developed, and my mother had heard on the radio that there was a polio epidemic in that city. She said that if it got any worse, they were going to close down all the theatres; they had already closed down all the swimming pools.

But I told my mother that the meeting had already been slated and that we were going, and that neither of my children would ever have polio. I told her I had "vaccinated" my children with the Ninety-first Psalm when they were born. I thank God for the Salk vaccine, but it didn't always work. But I know something that works one hundred percent of the time. Psalm 91:10 says, *"There shall no evil befall thee, neither shall any plague come nigh thy dwelling."*

I told my mother that polio was a plague; therefore, my children would never have it. She said she knew a preacher who was a mighty good man and his boy had polio. I said I had to believe the Bible and I couldn't go by someone else's experience. Besides, maybe that preacher didn't know what the Bible taught and didn't know how to appropriate the promises of God. I told her that neither of my children would ever have polio.

Thank God, they never have. In fact, all my children ever cost me for medical expenses was $37.50. When Ken was born, the doctor charged me $25, and when Pat was born, he charged me $12.50. Girls are worth just half as much as boys! (I'm just joking. I had a different doctor with Pat and he didn't charge as much.)

Resisting the Devil With the Word

This doesn't mean that the blessings of God are going to fall on you like ripe cherries from a tree. You are not going to float through life on flowery beds of ease. The devil will try you and tempt you.

For example, in 1954 we had been in Oregon for meetings, and we were coming back to Texas in August for a tent meeting. We stopped on the way back in Utah and did some sightseeing. We saw the great Mormon Temple.

The guide was telling us about what is on the inside of the temple. I cannot accept the book of Mormon. I've read it, but it doesn't agree with the New Testament. The Apostle Paul said, *"But though we, or an angel from heaven, preach any other gospel unto you than that which we have preached unto you, let him be accursed"* (Gal. 1:8).

As we stood there on the lawn at the Mormon Temple, the guide told us about the likeness of the angel which stood on the spire of the Mormon Temple. He said that this figure was fourteen feet high and made out of beaten copper overlaid with gold. He said the angel has a trumpet in his hand, which he is pictured as about to blow.

About that time I heard someone behind me fall. The fall was so hard that I heard the head bounce up as it hit the ground twice. Some man said that a boy had fallen.

The guide said, "That happens very often when I'm telling this story." He thought it was a supernatural sign to corroborate what he was telling. He said to just drag the person into the shade and he would come to in a minute.

I hadn't looked back, but my wife did, and she said that it was our son, Ken, who had fallen. He was fifteen years old at the time. I looked back, and I saw Ken lying there. He had hit the ground so hard, the impact knocked his shoes off. His knees were drawn up to his chest. His hands were twisted and his mouth was working so that he was chewing his tongue in convulsions. His eyes were set and glazed.

Faster than machine gun bullets can fly, the devil shot his darts into my mind and said, "You said that nothing evil could happen to your child." He gave me mental visions of my child having epilepsy or some other disease and being in an institution while I was out preaching about God's healing power.

But, thank God, I knew how to write my own ticket with God! I grabbed Ken by the arms to lift him up and he was stiff. I said, "Come out of him."

I had sensed evil spirits when I had walked on the grounds. I said, "I command you to come out of him in the Name of the Lord Jesus Christ."

The man who had said that a boy had fallen had helped me lift him up. He heard me saying, "Come out of him," and he began to quickly walk backwards and then turned around and ran away. I tell you, when I said, "Come out of him," Ken straightened out and blinked his eyes. He called to me and asked where he was and asked what had happened to him. I told him that the devil had knocked him down, but that Jesus was bigger than the devil. We wrote our ticket of victory.

That guide had said that Ken's fall was a supernatural manifestation as a result of what he had been saying, but I got rid of his manifestation in the Name of Jesus!

Receiving Salvation by Faith

If you can *say* it and *do* it, you will *receive* it and *tell* it.

I then asked the Lord in the vision if the sinner could take these four steps and use them. He said that they could. He said that these were steps the sinner uses in receiving salvation.

I told Jesus that I had read the New Testament through many times and I had never found anything like this about these scriptures for salvation.

Jesus said, "Son, there's a lot in the New Testament you don't know yet." Jesus then referred me to Luke 15.

LUKE 15:11–24

11 And he said, A certain man had two sons:

12 And the younger of them said to his father, Father, give me the portion of goods that falleth to me. And he divided unto them his living.

13 And not many days after the younger son gathered all together, and took his journey into a far country, and there wasted his substance with riotous living.

14 And when he had spent all, there arose a mighty famine in that land; and he began to be in want.

15 And he went and joined himself to a citizen of that country; and he sent him into his fields to feed swine.

16 And he would fain have filled his belly with the husks that the swine did eat: and no man gave unto him.

17 And when he came to himself, he SAID, How many hired servants of my father's have bread enough and to spare, and I perish with hunger!

18 I will arise and go to my father, and will SAY unto him, Father, I have sinned against heaven, and before thee,

19 And am no more worthy to be called thy son: make me as one of thy hired servants.

20 And HE AROSE, AND CAME TO HIS FATHER. But when he was yet a great way off, his father saw him, and had compassion, and ran, and fell on his neck, and kissed him.

21 And the son said unto him, Father, I have sinned against heaven, and in thy sight, and am no more worthy to be called thy son.

22 But the father said to his servants, Bring forth the best robe, and put it on him; and put a ring on his hand, and shoes on his feet:

23 And bring hither the fatted calf, and kill it; and let us eat, and be merry:

24 For this my son was dead, and is alive again; he was lost, and is found. And they began to be merry.

Jesus said that the very first thing the prodigal son did was *to say*. *"And when he came to himself, he SAID"* (Luke 15:17).

Jesus said that the preaching of the Word convicts the sinner of his need for a Savior. He sees himself as lost.

First the son *said, "I will arise and go to my father, and will say unto him, Father, I have sinned against heaven, and before thee, And am no more worthy to be called thy son: make me as one of thy hired servants"* (Luke 15:18–19).

Second, *he did it.* He started down the road toward home.

Third, *he received it.* He was reunited with his father and received his rightful inheritance as a son. His father ran and met him and put a ring and shoes and a robe on him.

Then Jesus told me, "Those people who come to the altar and bawl and squall and pray for me to save them are not down there to get saved. *They're down there trying to talk themselves into the notion of believing something.* If they would come down there like the prodigal son did, God would meet them before they ever got to the altar."

Fourth, the father of the prodigal son *told it.*

The brother of the prodigal son wouldn't go see the prodigal and wouldn't go in to the party his father had prepared. The father went out and entreated the brother. This has to be a picture of the lost, because the father said, *"For this my son was dead, and is alive again; he was lost, and is found . . ."* (Luke 15:24).

Whatever it is you need from God—whether it is salvation, healing, receiving the Holy Spirit, protection, or deliverance—you will receive your answer if you will follow these four steps of faith that Jesus gave me. Remember, *say* it, *do* it, *receive* it, and then *tell* it—and write your own ticket with God!

Questions for Study

1. Give the four scriptural examples of being "in the Spirit" that are listed in this chapter.

   _____

   _____

2. Name the four steps to receiving your answer from God.

   _____

   _____

3. What will happen if anyone anywhere will take these four steps and put them into operation?

   _____

   _____

4. What are the two sides to winning every battle, every victory, and to receiving anything from God?

   _____

   _____

5. What will happen if you talk about your lack of finances?

   _____

   _____

6. What two things come before <u>feeling</u> and <u>healing</u>?

   _____

   _____

7. Give an Old Testament example of the four steps of faith.

   _____

   _____

8. All that you have _____ is the result of what you said _____.

9. What should you use to resist the devil?

   _____

   _____

10. Give a New Testament example of using the four steps of faith to receive salvation.

    _____

    _____

Chapter 22

Doubt, the Thief of God's Greater Blessings

The greatest enemy to faith is doubt. In the following scriptures we will see that doubt will always hinder the believer from receiving God's best. Jesus had much to say about doubt and unbelief and its ravages of one's faith.

MATTHEW 13:58

58 And he [Jesus] did not many mighty works there BECAUSE OF THEIR UNBELIEF.

MATTHEW 14:22–31

22 And straightway Jesus constrained his disciples to get into a ship, and to go before him unto the other side, while he sent the multitudes away.

23 And when he had sent the multitudes away, he went up into a mountain apart to pray: and when the evening was come, he was there alone.

24 But the ship was now in the midst of the sea, tossed with waves: for the wind was contrary.

25 And in the fourth watch of the night Jesus went unto them, walking on the sea.

26 And when the disciples saw him walking on the sea, they were troubled, saying, It is a spirit; and they cried out for fear.

27 But straightway Jesus spake unto them, saying, Be of good cheer; it is I; be not afraid.

28 And Peter answered him and said, Lord, if it be thou, bid me come unto thee on the water.

29 And he said, Come. And when Peter was come down out of the ship, he walked on the water, to go to Jesus.

30 But when he saw the wind boisterous, he was afraid; and beginning to sink, he cried, saying, Lord, save me.

31 And immediately Jesus stretched forth his hand, and caught him, and said unto him, O thou of little faith, WHEREFORE DIDST THOU DOUBT?

MATTHEW 17:14–20

14 And when they were come to the multitude, there came to him a certain man, kneeling down to him, and saying,

15 Lord, have mercy on my son: for he is lunatick, and sore vexed: for ofttimes he falleth into the fire, and oft into the water.

16 And I brought him to thy disciples, and they could not cure him.

17 Then Jesus answered and said, O faithless and perverse generation, how long shall I be with you? how long shall I suffer you? bring him hither to me.

18 And Jesus rebuked the devil; and he departed out of him: and the child was cured from that very hour.

19 Then came the disciples to Jesus apart, and said, Why could not we cast him out?

20 And Jesus said unto them, BECAUSE OF YOUR UNBELIEF: for verily I say unto you, If ye have faith as a grain of mustard seed, ye shall say unto this mountain, Remove hence to yonder place; and it shall remove; and nothing shall be impossible unto you.

MARK 4:35–40

35 And the same day, when the even was come, he saith unto them, Let us pass over unto the other side.

36 And when they had sent away the multitude, they took him even as he was in the ship. And there were also with him other little ships.

37 And there arose a great storm of wind, and the waves beat into the ship, so that it was now full.

38 And he was in the hinder part of the ship, asleep on a pillow: and they awake him, and say unto him, Master, carest thou not that we perish?

39 And he arose, and rebuked the wind, and said unto the sea, Peace, be still. And the wind ceased, and there was a great calm.

40 And he said unto them, Why are ye so fearful? HOW IS IT THAT YE HAVE NO FAITH?

MARK 11:23–24

23 For verily I say unto you, That whosoever shall say unto this mountain, Be thou removed, and be thou cast into the sea; and shall NOT DOUBT IN HIS HEART, but shall believe that those things which he saith shall come to pass; he shall have whatsoever he saith.

24 Therefore I say unto you, What things soever ye desire, when ye pray, believe that ye receive them, and ye shall have them.

Let's notice the expression in Mark 11:23, *"and shall not doubt in his heart."*

In these scriptural references we have read, you'll find in each instance, doubt caused people to receive something less than the best God had for them. And in each case, the Lord rebuked them for their doubt and unbelief.

God's Best: Receiving by Our Own Faith

The Lord intervened by His divine sovereignty, as in the case of Peter when he cried to the Lord to save him as he began to sink (Matt. 14:30). And Jesus moved sovereignly in Mark chapter 4 when His disciples awakened Him in the ship and said, *"Master, carest thou not that we perish?"* (Mark 4:38). Jesus said, *"Peace, be still"* (Mark 4:39). And the Bible says the wind ceased.

But, my friends, God's highest and His best was for His disciples to receive by their *own* faith. *That* was His best.

In this story in Matthew chapter 14, Jesus sent the disciples across the sea in a ship, while He went up to a mountain to pray. The Bible says that in the fourth watch of the night, *"Jesus went unto them, walking on the sea"* (Matt. 14:25). When the disciples saw Jesus walking on the water, they were afraid. They cried out for fear and said that it was a spirit, or in other words, a ghost.

Peter said, *"Lord, if it be thou, bid me come unto thee on the water"* (Matt. 14:28). Jesus said, "Come," and Peter began to walk on the water to go to Jesus (v. 29).

Don't Look at the Circumstances

Someone said it's okay to doubt once in a while because, after all, Peter himself began to doubt and then began to sink. I know it. But you can't use Peter as an excuse because God is enlightening you to show why Peter began to sink—so *you* won't have to! Peter began to sink because *"when he saw the wind boisterous, he was afraid"* (Matt. 14:30).

In other words, Peter got his eyes on the circumstances. He began to see the things that were going on around him. He quit looking at Jesus. He quit acting on what Jesus said.

Faith is acting upon the Word of God. When Peter quit acting in faith on what God had said, he began to sink. And that was doubt because Jesus said to him, *"O thou of LITTLE FAITH, wherefore didst thou DOUBT?"* (Matt. 14:31).

Peter did have some faith, but it only carried him for a little while. The miracle began, but it was not consummated. Many times miracles have begun but they have not been consummated because the person began to look at circumstances or symptoms. Jesus called that "little faith." He got his eyes off Jesus and off the Word of God. Then he began to sink and he didn't receive his miracle from Jesus.

Notice Jesus said to Peter, *"O thou of little faith, wherefore didst thou doubt?"* (Matt. 14:31).

Doubt robbed him of the best that God had for him.

Don't Criticize Others Until You've Walked on the Water Yourself

Jesus didn't intend for Peter to sink. Jesus meant for him to be able to walk back to the ship with Him. But don't criticize Peter until you've successfully walked on the water without sinking! Then we'll accept your criticism. Besides, when you criticize others, it hinders your own faith.

In the last church I pastored, we had to raise some money in order to pay the church insurance which came due every three years. Since we only had to pay every three years, it was a large sum to raise in one service in those days.

On Sunday night I explained to the congregation that we needed to raise money for the church insurance. Within about ten minutes all the money we needed was given or pledged.

The next day my wife and I were in town. A cafe there in town was owned by a man who wasn't saved, but his wife was. She was not a member of our church and neither was he, but they came to our church some on Sunday nights. He always wanted us to eat at his cafe free of charge, and we usually ate there every Monday at noon time.

One of the women in my church worked in that man's restaurant as a waitress and she came to wait on us. We were alone in the cafe, so she began talking to me and told me that she didn't like the way I had taken up the offering the night before. She really vented her feelings about it. I didn't say a word; I just let her talk. All the time she waited on us, she was fussing about that offering.

Finally, after we had prayed over the food, I asked her if she was through talking. I told her that we had some more things we were supposed to pay for that week and that on the next Sunday night we were going to raise money again to pay the lumber bill. I told her that she could take up the offering and that if she didn't get the money, she could pay it out of her own pocket. She said she wouldn't be there then; she'd just stay home.

So I told her that if she didn't come to church that Sunday night, I would announce to the congregation why she didn't come. And if she didn't come, the next time she did come to church, I would have her stand up and I would make another announcement to the congregation about it. She asked me if I really meant what I said and I said I did.

Then she said that if I would not make her do that, she would never criticize me again as long as she lived. I said I had made up my mind and I wouldn't change my mind unless the Lord changed my mind.

She came on Wednesday night and asked me if she would still have to take up the offering on Sunday night and I told her yes. I told her that she should never criticize anyone until she can beat what they can do. She repented and said she couldn't take up an offering better than I had. On Sunday morning she was there to teach her class and she said she was going to pray that the Lord would change my mind.

When it was time for the evening service, she was there. I hadn't really changed my mind, so I explained to the congregation about the offering and why we needed it. Just as I started to say that Sister So-and-so was going to receive the offering, she leapt to her feet and said that she would give the first portion of it.

Immediately people all over the building were pledging; and before I knew it, we already had the needed amount.

The next day my wife and I were in the cafe and this woman said that she would never criticize me again. She said that she would keep her mouth shut and she didn't care how I took up my offerings.

So don't criticize old Peter until you've walked on the water yourself! Don't use Peter's failure to believe as an excuse for you to be able to doubt God. When Peter saw the wind boisterous, the Bible says, he was afraid. Looking at the circumstances caused Peter to begin to sink.

Doubt and Fear Rob People of God's Blessings

Doubt and fear go hand in hand. But faith and love go hand in hand. The Bible says, *"perfect love casteth out fear"* (1 John 4:18). Faith gets the job done.

MATTHEW 13:58

58 And he [Jesus] **did not many mighty works there because of their UNBELIEF.**

Mark puts it another way.

MARK 6:5

5 And HE COULD THERE DO NO MIGHTY WORK, save that he laid his hands upon a few sick folk, and healed them.

In Jesus' hometown only a few folks were healed under His ministry. The *Amplified Bible, Classic Edition* brings out the fact that there were "a few sickly people" healed. A Bible dictionary says the Greek shows that there were a few folks with minor ailments who were healed.

What happened in Nazareth? Doubt robbed the people there of God's best. Mark 6:6 says, *"And he* [Jesus] *marvelled because of their unbelief."*

If words mean anything at all, then these scriptures are saying that doubt robbed that whole city of Nazareth of the blessings that God intended for them to have. When Jesus left that city, there were people who were left sick who should have been healed. They ought to have been healed, but doubt and unbelief robbed them of God's blessings.

If you doubt, it can rob you, but the unbelief of an entire congregation can keep God from working. Doubt, the thief of God's greater blessings, will do this.

Doubt and Unbelief Will Hinder Ministry to the Sick

I was preaching one time several years ago, in a Full Gospel church in Texas. It was in 1951 after the Lord had appeared to me in the first vision in 1950. This church was the hardest place in my ministry to get people healed I'd ever been to. I was so concerned that just a few were being healed until I went to the Lord in prayer and fasting about it.

The second day of my fasting and prayer, I stayed in the church to pray. I prayed much of the day. As I was praying, I began to see something from the Word. It is surprising to me how one can read over scriptures and really not even know they are there. Mark 6:5 had never really stood out to me until then.

The Lord spoke to my heart as I was kneeling around the altar and He said to me, "Don't feel too badly about it, because I only managed to get a few people healed in my own hometown." Then the Lord quoted the scripture that the servant is not above his master (Matt. 10:24). This shocked me, and I told the Lord that it just couldn't be true.

Then Jesus told me to turn to Mark 6:5. I read it. He said that I wasn't going to be able to do more than He had been able to do. I asked the Lord why only a few were healed in His own hometown. He said to read the next verse, which says, *"he marvelled because of their unbelief"* (Mark 6:6).

So I asked the Lord what I was going to do about ministering to the sick in that atmosphere of doubt and unbelief. He said in the service that night when I got ready to pray for the sick, I shouldn't minister to the sick out in the main auditorium. He told me to take all the sick back into some other room for ministry. He said I shouldn't even allow the pastor and his wife to come back there unless they were to be prayed for. I told the Lord that I didn't want to do it this way because if I did, the pastor and his wife might not understand why I was doing it that way.

Then the Lord reminded me about the scripture in Mark chapter 8 which tells how Jesus took the blind man out of the city to pray for him. And Jesus also reminded me of Mark chapter 7.

MARK 7:32–33

32 And they bring unto him one that was deaf, and had an impediment in his speech; and they beseech him to put his hand upon him.

33 And he TOOK HIM ASIDE from the multitude, and put his fingers into his ears, and he spit, and touched his tongue.

The Lord told me that He took the man aside because there was so much unbelief in the town. He often took the sick aside so He could get them healed. He said if the rest of the people fussed at me for doing this, I should show them the scripture where Jesus did the same thing in His earthly ministry. I did what Jesus said, and from the time I began praying for the sick in this way, more of them got healed.

There was a little girl in one of my services who was about eight or nine years old. Her knees were as big as her head and she was helpless, and she had to be carried everywhere. She had rheumatic fever and her joints were swollen. Her heart was in a very serious condition too. She had been to some of the best hospitals in the nation, and doctors had said she probably wouldn't live very long. They had said that she would never walk.

I had ministered to her before and nothing had happened because of the unbelief in the congregation. The Lord knew where the unbelief was coming from, and He had me take the child aside and minister to her. (It's hard to pray for the sick and do what the Lord says when the pastor sitting on the platform with you is breathing the hot breath of unbelief down your collar!)

I ministered to this child that night. I told the child's parents that I had cast out the spirit that had oppressed their daughter. I told them that she would

begin to get better and in a little while she would be walking. Before the meeting was over, her parents brought her to one of the services and she was walking!

The next year I was holding a meeting in a town close by, and these folks came over to visit. The mother had the child with her and that same pastor came also. He talked to me and wanted me to come back to minister in his church. He acknowledged that the little child really had been healed. The mother had taken the child back to the hospital and she had been checked by doctors. They said they had really seen a miracle. Her heart was perfect and she was walking.

The mother said that as a result of her child being healed, both the father and she had been born again. She told me then that they had been Roman Catholic. They had gone to another Protestant church because they thought all Protestant churches believed in divine healing.

They wanted to tell their testimony in this Protestant church about their daughter being healed, but when they tried to tell it, the people almost threw them out. So they returned to the Full Gospel church and had been going there ever since.

Doubt robbed the people of Nazareth of the greater blessings that God wanted them to have. And doubt can rob you, too, if you let it.

Not a Lack of Power—A Lack of *Faith*

MATTHEW 17:14–20

14 And when they were come to the multitude, there came to him a certain man, kneeling down to him, and saying,

15 Lord, have mercy on my son: for he is lunatick, and sore vexed: for ofttimes he falleth into the fire, and oft into the water.

16 And I brought him to thy disciples, and they could not cure him.

17 Then Jesus answered and said, O faithless and perverse generation, how long shall I be with you? How long shall I suffer you? bring him hither to me.

18 And Jesus rebuked the devil; and he departed out of him: and the child was cured from that very hour.

19 Then came the disciples to Jesus apart, and said, Why could not we cast him out?

20 And Jesus said unto them, BECAUSE OF YOUR UNBELIEF.

Matthew 10:1 says, *"And when he had called unto him his twelve disciples, he gave them power against unclean spirits, to cast them out, and to heal all manner of sickness and all manner of disease."*

If I say that the disciples didn't have *the power* to cast out that devil in Matthew 17, then I am making Jesus out to be a liar because the Bible says He gave them the power *"against unclean spirits, to cast them out"* (Matt. 10:1).

When the disciples asked Jesus why they couldn't cast out the devil, Jesus didn't say it was because they didn't have *the power* to do it. He said it was because of their *unbelief.*

For years I've heard many Full Gospel people say that they needed more power so they could cast out devils and do the works of Jesus.

But a lack of power is not what the trouble is at all. People who say that, miss the point because if you have the Holy Ghost, then you have the power. People think that if they had more power, the Word would automatically work, but the Word works by faith.

What's hindering people is a lack of faith—not a lack of power. Doubt is robbing them of the blessings of God. Jesus didn't say you couldn't cast out the devil because you don't have *the power.* He said if you can't cast out the devil, it is because of your *unbelief.*

It doesn't matter what you receive from God's Word, God's Word still only operates by faith. Salvation is the greatest gift you can receive from God. Being born again is the greatest blessing a person can receive. But you still have to receive salvation by faith. And after you're born again, to enjoy the blessings and the benefits of salvation, you must still have faith. The benefits of your inheritance in Christ just don't fall upon you like ripe cherries off a tree. Second Corinthians 5:7 says, *"For we walk by faith, not by sight."*

The baptism of the Holy Ghost is a mighty gift that God has for His children. But just because you are filled with the Holy Ghost, doesn't necessarily mean you are a successful Christian. All around us there are Spirit-filled Christians who are not successful Christians, and yet, their Spirit-filled experience is real.

But the power they have received in the baptism in the Holy Spirit with the evidence of speaking in tongues is still utilized through *faith.* And if there is a lack of faith in appropriating the promises of God, then they are simply ignoring the powerhouse that is in them. You don't need any more power. You need to learn how to put the power you already have to work for you.

Some people are so taken up with the natural realm; they are always trying to find a reason why something happened. They think the trouble is in the natural. But actually, the trouble is in the spirit realm.

Healing is a mighty gift that God has provided for us. Someone has said that it is not the will of God to heal everyone. But I would rather cuss than talk like that. To say something like that would be insulting my Lord Jesus. Matthew 8:17 says, *"Himself took our infirmities, and bare our sicknesses."* But healing is received *through faith*, and it also takes faith *to maintain* healing.

P.C. Nelson or "Dad" Nelson, founder of Southwestern Bible Institute, said that more people lose their healing over a counterattack than any other one reason. He was actually saying that the devil is going to come back against you with symptoms to make you think you didn't get your healing in the first place.

But if you'll stand your ground in faith on the Word of God and say that you are healed, then the devil will flee from you. The Bible says that we should resist the devil and then he will flee from us (James 4:7). Whatever you receive from God, you *receive* by faith and you hold on to by faith.

Stephen: A Man Full of the Holy Ghost, Faith, *and* Power

ACTS 6:1–5

1 And in those days, when the number of the disciples was multiplied, there arose a murmuring of the Grecians against the Hebrews, because their widows were neglected in the daily ministration.

2 Then the twelve called the multitude of the disciples unto them, and said, It is not reason that we should leave the word of God, and serve tables.

3 Wherefore, brethren, look ye out among you seven men of honest report, full of the Holy Ghost and wisdom, whom we may appoint over this business.

4 But we will give ourselves continually to prayer, and to the ministry of the Word.

5 And the saying pleased the whole multitude: and they chose Stephen, a man full of faith and of the Holy Ghost, and Philip, and Prochorus, and Nicanor, and Timon, and Parmenas, and Nicolas a proselyte of Antioch.

Let's look at Stephen for a moment. In this passage, we see that seven men were chosen, and all of them were full of the Holy Ghost. Stephen was not only full of the Holy Ghost, but he was also full of faith and power (Acts 6:8). You see, you can be full of the Holy Ghost and not do a thing in the world for God if you don't have faith. We have plenty of people like this.

Acts 6:8 says, *"And Stephen, full of faith and power, did great wonders and miracles among the people."* The Bible doesn't say that the rest of the men that were chosen had faith or not. In Acts chapter 8, we do read where Philip did great works also, but the other five men of the seven, we never hear about again. They were all full of the Holy Ghost, but evidently they didn't have the faith to put the power to work.

Utilize the Power of God Within You

Doubt is robbing many Spirit-filled believers of the best that God has for them. These believers have the power, but they are not using it; they are not putting the Powerhouse—the Holy Spirit on the inside—to work for them.

A number of years ago I read in *The Pentecostal Evangel* about a fellow down in Africa who was a convert of some of our missionaries; he was a native evangelist of Africa. He had been reading about what God had been doing here in America, and he'd read about the works that some evangelists were doing for God. He said he was going to fast and pray until God gave him that power also, so he decided to go on a twenty-one day fast so he could get the power of God.

About the tenth day of the fast, the Lord spoke to him and told him to get up and stop fasting because the power was already in him and all he had to do was start using it. So that's exactly what he did.

He began to utilize the power he already had and before he knew it, they were calling him the Billy Graham of Africa. His meetings drew crowds up to 80,000 people in attendance. He was going to fast until he got the power, but the Lord told him that he already had the power—the Person of the Holy Spirit dwelling in him.

Doubt robbed the people of Nazareth of the best that God had for them. Doubt robbed Jesus' disciples in Matthew 17. They failed to cast the demon out of the man. The Lord told them they failed because of their unbelief (Matt. 17:20).

Trying the Word Is *Doubting* the Word

On September 2, 1950, the Lord appeared unto me in a vision at about 10 o'clock at night. In that vision, Jesus laid the finger of His right hand upon the palms of my hands. When He did this, my hands began to burn as if I had a coal of fire in them.

Jesus told me that He had called me and anointed me to have a special ministry to the sick. I had been praying for the sick for years. He told me that when I was praying for a sick person, I should lay one hand upon one side of his body and the other hand upon the other side of the body. He said that if the fire within my hands jumped from hand to hand, that would mean there was an evil spirit within the body of the person. If it does not jump from hand to hand, then it is a case of healing only.

The Bible differentiates between the casting out of devils and healing of the sick. Jesus told me in this vision to lay hands upon the sick and pray for them. He said that if the fire does jump from hand to hand, then I should cast the devil out in Jesus' Name. He said that in His Name the devil or the demons would leave the person's body.

At my very next meeting, which was in Oklahoma, a fellow came over to the service from Arkansas. One night in the meeting, this fellow said that he had tuberculosis of the spine. Several different doctors had examined him. His spine was rigid, and his back was as stiff as a board.

I laid one hand on his chest and one hand on his back and I could feel that fire jumping from hand to hand, so I knew then that an evil spirit was oppressing his body. I commanded the evil spirit to come out of him in the Name of Jesus. (The evil spirit was in his body, not in his spirit. You see, your *body* is not redeemed yet.)

After I commanded the evil spirit to come out of the man's body, I missed it and got into unbelief. The Word of God operates by faith. How did I miss it? I asked the man if he could stoop over and he said he couldn't. I told him to *try* it again. But the Word won't work, by *trying*! It only works by faith.

I got into unbelief by saying this, so the evil spirit still didn't come out of the man's body. The man couldn't stoop over. I told him to try bending over a third time, and it still didn't work; the man couldn't bend over. So I sent him back to his seat. As he was walking down the aisle to return to his seat, Jesus appeared to me.

Jesus said to me, "I said in My Name demons will be cast out. Call them out in My Name." I spoke to Jesus and told Him that I knew He had said it but that the demon had not left the man's body. He told me the same thing again.

I said, "I know You said that, Jesus, but the evil spirit did not leave."

Jesus said, "I told you in My Name evil spirits will be cast out. Call them out in My Name."

So I said again, "Lord, I know you said that."

Then I realized what Jesus was trying to get over to me. I called the man back up to the front and I told the man that he was free, and I told him to reach over and touch his toes. (This time I didn't say "try.") He did and he was free.

Doubt had been robbing me of my faith. It isn't enough to sit there and agree and say amen. You've got to be a *doer* of the Word in order to make your faith work (James 1:22).

Are you going to quit doubting and start acting? Are you ready to quit *trying* the Word and start *doing* the Word? Don't let doubt rob *you* of God's best for your life.

Questions for Study

1. What is the greatest enemy to faith?

   _____

   _____

2. In each of the Scripture passages first listed in this chapter, what did doubt cause?

   _____

   _____

3. In Mark chapter 4, Jesus told the wind to be still and it obeyed Him. But what was God's highest and best in that situation?

   _____

   _____

4. In Matthew chapter 14, why did Peter begin to sink while walking on the water?

   _____

   _____

5. What is one reason many miracles have begun, but have not been consummated?

   _____

   _____

6. What two things rob people of God's blessings?

   _____

   _____

7. When the disciples asked Jesus why they couldn't cast out the devil, what did Jesus say was the reason?

   _____

   _____

8. According to P.C. Nelson, what is the number one reason people lose their healing?

   _____

   _____

9. According to Acts 6:8, what was Stephen full of besides the Holy Ghost?

   _____

   _____

10. _____ the Word is _____ the Word.

Chapter 23

You Can Have What You Say

What is in your heart will eventually come out of your mouth (Matt. 12:34). That's why the Bible says, *"Keep thy heart with all diligence; for out of it are the issues of life"* (Prov. 4:23). What you say locates you.

To show you what I mean, let's look again at the account of Mark 5 of the woman with the issue of blood.

MARK 5:25–34

25 And a certain woman, which had an issue of blood twelve years,

26 And had suffered many things of many physicians, and had spent all that she had, and was nothing bettered, but rather grew worse,

27 When she had heard of Jesus, came in the press behind, and touched his garment.

28 For she SAID, If I may touch but his clothes, I shall be whole.

29 And straightway the fountain of her blood was dried up; and she felt in her body that she was healed of that plague.

30 And Jesus, immediately knowing in himself that virtue had gone out of him, turned him about in the press, and said, Who touched my clothes?

31 And his disciples said unto him, Thou seest the multitude thronging thee, and sayest thou, Who touched me?

32 And he looked round about to see her that had done this thing.

33 But the woman fearing and trembling, knowing what was done in her, came and fell down before him, and told him all the truth.

34 And he said unto her, Daughter, THY FAITH HATH MADE THEE WHOLE; go in peace, and be whole of thy plague.

Let's focus our attention on verses 28: *"For she SAID, If I may touch but his clothes, I shall be whole"* (Mark 5:28).

What the woman with the issue of blood said, located her. And that is why she received her petition from Jesus. Because her faith had located her, Jesus said unto her, *". . . Daughter, thy faith hath made thee whole; go in peace, and be whole of thy plague"* (Mark 5:34).

Now let's look at another verse which illustrates the connection between saying and receiving from God.

You Can Have What You Say

MARK 11:23

23 For verily I say unto you, That whosoever shall say unto this mountain, Be thou removed, and be thou cast into the sea; and shall not doubt in his heart, but shall believe that those things which he saith shall come to pass; HE SHALL HAVE WHATSOEVER HE SAITH.

You can have what you say! The Bible says about the woman with the issue of blood, *"For she said . . ."* (Mark 5:28), and that woman received exactly what she said. What you say is your faith speaking. We know that is true because Jesus said to the woman, *"thy faith hath made thee whole"* (Mark 5:34). You can have what you say. The woman in Mark chapter 5 received exactly what she said.

An Evil Report vs. A Good Report

Another wonderful proof that you can have what you say is found in the Old Testament in Numbers chapter 13 where we read how Israel came to Kadesh-Barnea and Moses sent the twelve spies into Canaan to spy out the land. The Bible says that ten of them brought back an evil report, and that two of them brought back a good report (Num. 13:32; 14:6–9). Well, what is an *evil report* anyway? It is *a report of doubt.* What is a *good report?* A good report is *a report of faith.*

Ten of the spies said that there were giants in the land. When we analyze what they were saying, we see that they were simply saying that even though God had told them He was giving them the land, they couldn't take the land. They were affirming that they were not able to possess the land even though God had already said they could. All of Israel accepted the majority report.

Someone once said that the majority is always right, but that is not a Bible truth. If you follow the majority of people—and I'm even talking about Full Gospel Christians—you'll walk in unbelief. When Israel accepted the majority report, they were also saying that they couldn't take the land. Remember, *you can have what you say.* And they got exactly what they said. They believed that they couldn't take the land and they didn't.

After all, even when you doubt, you are believing something. But you're believing the wrong thing. You always receive and have in your life exactly what you believe for and what you say. If you don't believe what you're saying, then you don't have any business saying it. However, if you keep saying it long enough, your words will eventually register on your heart. And once those words register on your spirit, they will control your life.

These ten spies and all the rest of the Israelites got exactly what they *said*. They didn't enter the Promised Land. They wandered in the wilderness until they died. What they said came to pass. God told them they would have what they said (Num. 14:28–35).

But Caleb said, *"Let us go up at once, and possess it; for we are well able to overcome it"* (Num. 13:30). And in Numbers chapter 14 we read that Joshua had that same spirit of faith.

NUMBERS 14:8–9

8 If the Lord delight in us, then he will bring us into this land, and give it us; a land which floweth with milk and honey.

9 Only rebel not ye against the Lord, neither fear ye the people of the land; for they are bread for us: their defence is departed from them, and the Lord is with us: fear them not.

NUMBERS 14:27–33

27 How long shall I bear with this evil congregation, which murmur against me? I have heard the murmurings of the children of Israel, which they murmur against me.

28 Say unto them, As truly as I live, saith the Lord, AS YE HAVE SPOKEN IN MINE EARS, SO WILL I DO TO YOU:

29 Your carcases shall fall in this wilderness; and all that were numbered of you, according to your whole number, from twenty years old and upward, which have murmured against me,

30 Doubtless ye shall not come into the land, concerning which I sware to make you dwell therein, save Caleb the son of Jephunneh, and Joshua the son of Nun.

31 But your little ones, which ye said should be a prey, them will I bring in, and they shall know the land which ye have despised.

32 But as for you, your carcases, they shall fall in this wilderness.

33 And your children shall wander in the wilderness forty years, and bear your whoredoms, until your carcases be wasted in the wilderness.

The Israelites said that there were giants in the land and that all the Israelites were as grasshoppers in their own sight. But Caleb and Joshua said that God was well able to deliver the giants into their hands! Caleb and Joshua *said* that they were well able to possess the Promised Land. The other ten spies *said* they couldn't. And they all got what they said!

Locating People by What They Say

Many people come to me and ask me why they can't get healed. I always smile and tell them it's because they've already said they can't. Their words give them away. You can locate people by what they say.

Your confession locates you. Most of the time I try to get a confession from people before I pray for them. I ask them if they will be healed when I lay hands on them and pray. Many say that they *hope* they will be healed, and then I have to tell them that they won't because they are in *hope* and not in *faith*. Those who have a quick confession that is charged with faith receive almost instantly.

Some make a confession with a little bit of hesitancy. But that hesitancy will defeat them. It's the *little* foxes that spoil the vine (Song of Sol. 2:15). In other words, it's not always some big hindrance that can keep God's children from receiving from God or being healed.

Wrong Thinking, Believing, and Speaking— The Giants That Defeat You

For example, with the children of Israel, it wasn't the giants in the land of Canaan that kept Israel from possessing the land. It was the Israelites' doubt and unbelief and their confession of an evil report that kept them out of the Promised Land. And it really isn't the giants that defeat us either. It's our failure to cooperate with God and work with *God* in line with His Word that causes us to fail in life.

If it had just been the giants that hindered the Israelites from possessing their Promised Land, those giants would have defeated Joshua and Caleb, too, and no one would have ever possessed the land. No, it wasn't the giants who defeated the people. The people defeated themselves. It was their own thinking. It was their own unbelief. It was their own confession that defeated them.

It is *not* the giants in life that defeat you. It is *not* the storms of life that defeat you. It is *not* the devil who defeats you. If you are defeated in life, it's because you have defeated yourself.

You have defeated yourself by wrong thinking and wrong believing. Wrong talking has also defeated you.

Faith Confessions Bring Faith Victories

Caleb and Joshua *said* that they were well able to overcome the giants and eventually they did.

You can have what you say. The woman with the issue of blood in Mark 5 got exactly what she said. These Israelites who accepted the ten spies' report of doubt and unbelief got exactly what they said. They wandered in the wilderness until every single one of them died. Caleb and Joshua were the only ones of the older generation who went into the Promised Land, and Joshua became the leader.

Caleb said to Joshua, *"give me this mountain"* (Joshua 14:12). I like that fellow, Caleb. I like a man of faith. That fellow Caleb just has a special place in my heart because of his right believing, right thinking, and right talking. He went to Joshua and said, "Give me this mountain." Caleb was talking his faith!

Joshua probably looked back on that time and realized that their right thinking, believing, and speaking had won them victory. Joshua got a confession out of Caleb. It was a positive confession—a confession of faith and victory. Joshua told Caleb that there were giants in the mountain. But old Caleb told Joshua that he was well able to take the mountain anyway. Praise God! And bless God, he did.

Don't Prepare for Failure

Many unpleasant things happen in people's lives because they think they ought to happen that way. But, actually, some things happen because we believe wrong and talk wrong and then it comes to pass.

For example, in my own life sometime ago, I read about a scientist who said that when you get older your brain isn't as soft as it is when you are younger. The human brain keeps hardening a little bit over a period of time. Well, I got to the place where I couldn't remember things as well as I once did.

I went along this way for a short time until I realized that there wasn't any need for that. The mind is a part of the soul of man; it never grows old. But it does need to be renewed with the Word of God (Rom. 12:2). The very moment that I switched over and started believing right and talking right, I could quote all the scripture I'd ever known, and actually, my memory got better.

We fail sometimes because we get ready to fail. We prepare for failure. We think and believe in failure, and therefore we fail. As believers, however, we don't have any business talking failure or doubt. We should talk faith. I got that secret from Mark 11:23 and 24.

MARK 11:23-24

23 For verily I say unto you, That whosoever shall SAY unto this mountain, Be thou removed, and be thou cast into the sea; and SHALL NOT DOUBT IN HIS HEART, but shall believe that those things which he SAITH shall come to pass; he shall have whatsoever he SAITH.

24 Therefore I say unto you, What things soever ye desire, when ye pray, believe that ye receive them, and ye shall have them.

If you believe that you're going to receive something from God, then you will confess it. You will say what you believe.

Holding Fast to My Confession of Faith

About four months before I became sixteen, I became totally bedfast on the bed of sickness. Five different doctors were on the case. One of them had practiced at the Mayo Clinic. My grandfather was not a rich man. He did have quite a bit of property, but it was during the Depression Days and property wasn't worth much. But he was a man of some means, and if the Mayo Clinic had been able to help me, he would have sent me there.

My doctors said that the doctor who had practiced at the Mayo Clinic was one of the best doctors in America, and if he said nothing could be done, then I was simply wasting my money and time to go to the Mayo Clinic.

This particular doctor said that there wasn't any hope; I didn't have one chance in a million of living. He went on to say that as far as medical science knew, no one in my condition had lived past sixteen years of age. I had become totally bedfast by this time. But I had never really been able to run and play like normal children because I had been a semi-invalid all of my life.

My grandfather had several houses in town, which he rented out. He decided he wanted to move into one of his rental homes, so he gave one of the renters notice to vacate. He had given the people plenty of notice beforehand and the house had been redecorated. So on New Year's Day in 1934, we moved. The movers moved the furniture from other parts of the house first and left the furniture in my bedroom until the last load. When they came and moved the furniture in my room, the ambulance came and moved me.

As I was in the ambulance, one of the men remarked that he had heard I had been in bed about a year, but if I felt up to it, they would take me for a ride around the residential areas so I could see the scenery. I was able to move my head and look out the windows. So they drove slowly through town, and it was really good to be able to look out.

Then finally one of the men turned to me and said, "Son, if you feel up to it, we'll drive down across the townsquare." He said that since it was a holiday and there would be little traffic, it probably would be nice. I told him I would appreciate it. I lived in McKinney, Texas. At this particular time the population was between eight and nine thousand.

I remember that we came from the north and we were going down the west side of the square. At this time, there was a drugstore on the corner. Right next to it was J.C. Penney Company, and next to that was Mode O'Day dress shop. Next to that was Woolworth's; then a shoe store and on the corner was a women's ready-to-wear shop.

So we went down the west side of the square and then turned and went down the south side. I was looking at all the buildings. Just as we turned the corner and started down the south side of the square, I turned and looked at the old courthouse that sat in the middle of the square.

I shall never forget it as long as I live—now and even through eternity. As I looked at the courthouse, something said to me, "Well, you never thought you'd see these old buildings in the flesh again, and you wouldn't have if it hadn't been for the kindness of the man who is driving you around."

Immediately, something on the inside of me spoke up and said, "Mark 11:23 says 'he shall have whatsoever he saith.'"

I had read Mark 11:23 and 24 before which says to believe in your heart and say what you believe in your heart with your mouth. That's the principle of faith. You can have what you say.

I didn't understand all that I know now. I just had one little gleam of light—just like a little beam of light that might creep under a door or through a crack in a door. But this was the beginning point for me—that first day of January, 1933, at about 2 o'clock in the afternoon.

That "something" had said to me, "You'll never see these buildings again." But that day there in that ambulance, as the tears rolled down my face, I said, "Yes, I will see these buildings and this courthouse! And I will come in the flesh and stand in this courthouse square because Jesus said that what you believe in your heart and say with your mouth shall come to pass."

Once you've committed yourself with your confession then you've located what you believe in your heart.

January and February went by and I was still bedfast. March, April, May, June, and July went by. Someone might say that my faith wasn't working, and that's what the devil said to me over those months. But I was holding fast to my confession and I refused to give it up.

I kept telling Jesus, God, the Holy Ghost, and the angels, the devil, and evil spirits that I was going to hold fast to my confession of faith. I told God that if it didn't work for me, then it was because God's Word had failed—because I was standing on His Word and it had to work.

And the day came when I saw God's Word work! On the second Saturday of August in 1934, I did walk to that courthouse square! I had received what I had been believing and confessing.

The people always came to town on Saturday, and the crowd was so thick in that square that I had to elbow my way through people to get to the outside of the curb. But I stood there on that curb on the southeast corner, and the tears coursed down my face.

I stood there and I said, "Devil, I told you so! I don't know whether you can read or not, but in case you can't, this is what the Bible says." And then I read Mark 11:23 and 24 to him. I had my New Testament with me.

I don't know what people thought when they saw a young boy standing on the corner with tears in his eyes, reading a New Testament. But I couldn't have cared less. On the bed of sickness, I had gotten ahold of the scripture in First Thessalonians 5:21 which says, "Prove all things; hold fast that which is good." I proved that Mark 11:23 is true and I've been holding fast to it ever since.

Having What I Said in My Ministry

I began my ministry then as a young Baptist boy preacher. I was pastor of a community church which was eight miles from that courthouse square. I want to tell you something here. Don't ever say that people aren't *saved* if they don't have the baptism of the Holy Ghost and don't speak in tongues. In the first place, that's not scriptural; in the second place, when I first started preaching, I was saved, but I hadn't received the baptism in the Holy Spirit yet.

The first year I pastored, I wore out four pairs of shoes walking to preach the gospel. I walked down an old dusty road, and many times someone would stop and give me a ride. I had a hilarious time preaching the gospel.

I would walk down that old road and say, "I'll preach that Jesus saves, heals, and is coming again from the Red River to the Gulf of Mexico." Then after my faith grew a little, I would say, "I'll preach the gospel from the Louisiana border to the New Mexico state line." (I thought that this would be covering quite a bit of territory!) I said I'd do it because I knew I could have what I said. It had worked for me before and I knew it would work now.

Then I began associating with Full Gospel people who preached about divine healing because I believed in healing too. They also preached about being filled with the Holy Ghost and speaking with other tongues. One boy said, "It's like a slippery creek bank. If you keep fooling around it, you'll slip in." So I did!

I continued to associate with those Full Gospel people and I eventually "slipped in"—that is, I was baptized in the Holy Ghost, with the evidence of speaking in tongues. I continued to preach the same thing I was preaching and added a little bit to it as I got more revelation from the Word. The Holy Ghost will help you to enlarge your vision.

So then as I walked that dusty road, I would say, "I'll preach that Jesus saves; I'll preach that Jesus heals; I'll preach that He fills you with the Holy Ghost. I'll preach it from Los Angeles to New York. I'll preach it from the Gulf of Mexico to the Canadian border."

And bless God, I've done it. I've traveled more than a million miles by automobile throughout America and Canada. I've been going at a hop, a skip, and a jump in the ministry ever since I received my healing. And for many years throughout the land I've been telling that Jesus saves, heals, and is coming again!

You Can Have What You Say

My wife and I were married November 25, 1938. My wife was Methodist. I was Baptist. A few days after we were married, a cold wind blew in, and my wife's throat became sore. She said she supposed her throat would be that way all through the winter because that's what usually happened.

She had been ready to have her tonsils taken out several times before; but something always happened to prevent it, a little fever or something, and the doctor wouldn't take them out.

I remembered this scripture in Mark 11:23 so I said to her, "No, you won't. You'll be healed and won't ever have that problem anymore."

My faith could work for her because she was still a spiritual babe. Of course, God expected her to grow in the Word and begin to exercise her own faith, which she learned to do. But many years have come and gone and she has never had any more throat problems. God's Word works! You can have what you say.

In 1949 I went on the field ministering. We rented an apartment. My father-in-law died and I promised him on his deathbed that I would take care of his wife, my mother-in-law, and that she would always have a home with us. So my mother-in-law came to live with us in that apartment, but it was crowded, so I told my wife that we needed a house.

At first we rented a three-bedroom frame home, but later decided to buy it. We agreed in prayer about buying the house and later talked to the woman who owned the house. At that time, she and her husband didn't want to sell it.

However, in the process of time, the woman told my wife they wanted to sell the house. I told my wife that it was no news to me because I'd known it for months! Soon afterwards I came home from a meeting especially to see the owners about buying the house. But in the meantime someone had made them an offer of $500 more than I had. I told the woman and her husband that I sure would hate for them to miss God in selling their house. They said that the past several nights, they'd had the feeling that the house belonged to me. You can have what you say!

Having What I Said in My Finances

The first year I was on the field, the devil really tried to shut off my finances. When the year was over, I would have been $1,200 better off if I had stayed with the church I had been pastoring, where the parsonage was supplied and all my utilities were paid. On the field, I had to pay for a place for my family to stay and also for my traveling. At the end of the year, I had to sell my old car in order to pay the interest on the three notes I was keeping.

I said to the Lord, "Lord, something is wrong somewhere! I'm doing everything You told me to do. If there was any shadow of doubt about my being out in field ministry, I wouldn't even wait on the doubt; I would take advantage of the shadow and go back to pastoring!

"You said in Your Word that if we were willing and obedient we would eat the good of the land (Isa. 1:19). I know You want us to eat the good, and you want us to drive the good—the best. But I've had to sell my automobile."

The Lord told me, "You've been obedient but you haven't been willing." When He said that it did not take me long to get willing! I got willing in a hurry!

The Lord told me, "The trouble with you is you don't practice what you preach." I considered that sort of a low blow.

Then Jesus told me that I preached faith but didn't practice it. He said that when it came to healing, I did, but He told me that the principles of faith are just the same in the realm of finances as they are in the realm of healing.

I went home and told my wife that I was going to buy a car. She couldn't understand how we could do that when we weren't even meeting our budget as it was. But when you act because you've got a foundation of God's Word under you, you'll whip poverty, lack, and the devil in every combat. This car wasn't a brand-new one. It was a '49 Oldsmobile and it belonged to a pastor we knew. He had just a few miles on it and so we bought it from him.

We paid for it, and in the course of time, I said that I was going to buy a new car. I told every pastor in every church where I preached that when I got to Fort Worth, I was going to buy a new car while I was there. (Really, I didn't have enough money to buy one at all.)

I told the pastor in Fort Worth that I hoped it wouldn't hurt my offerings to say that. But he said his people were the kind who would be thrilled and would probably help me on it. Thank God for people like that. He knew a car dealer who always gave preachers a good deal. I wanted to buy an Oldsmobile 98. So we drove to the car lot and there was the exact car I'd had in mind, even to the very color.

I looked it over and decided to buy it. The pastor and I went into the office and he introduced me to the owner, who was sitting with his feet propped up on the desk, with a cigar in his mouth. When the pastor introduced me and told the man that I was interested in an automobile in his lot, the man plopped his feet down and said I could have it any way I wanted it. He knew I was a preacher. He told me he would take $1,200 off the list price of it and that he wouldn't make anything on it.

The car dealer asked me what I was driving, and I told him I was driving a 1949 Oldsmobile 88. It had 93,000 miles on it, the transmission was leaking oil, the tires were bare, and the valve lifters were rattling. But he told me that he would give me a good price for my car as a down payment—just as if it had been in good condition. He would still not get anything out of it because he would have to spend quite a bit fixing my old car up in order to be able to resell it.

This man said he believed every preacher should have a new car. He said he was an old sinner himself, but he still believed in God, in the work of God, and in preachers and the church. That beats what a lot of Christians believe in!

This car dealer named a preacher I knew who was going to buy a Chevrolet but had seen an Oldsmobile he really liked better. The car dealer asked the man why he didn't buy the Oldsmobile instead, if he liked it better. The man responded that he wouldn't be able to afford the payments on the Oldsmobile. So the car dealer said he would let him have the Oldsmobile and make payments he could afford. The car dealer told the preacher that he might be a sinner, but God would help him even if he lost money on the deal.

So when I told the car dealer what I wanted my payment to be, he wrote out the contract and said, "Sign here." He never did get out of his chair to look at my car or anything. But I drove off with the new car! You can have what you say! I know it works. I had learned that on the bed of sickness in 1934.

Having What We Say Works for All Believers

Someone might say, "Oh, well, you were in the ministry and you needed a car, and it worked for you." But I can tell you, lay members, that it works for you too.

It'll work for something little as well as for something big. In the last church we pastored, we had some good friends, and the husband was a medical doctor. When we were in their area, we would usually stop and visit them. He was a fine man and she was a splendid woman.

My wife was quite nervous and was having great difficulty in sleeping. We talked to him a little bit about it because he was a doctor, and he said he was going to put her on a diet. Then he asked my wife if she drank coffee. He did recommend that she quit drinking it, as it was a stimulant, and it was probably hindering her from sleeping. When she tried to quit, she couldn't. She told the doctor that she hadn't been able to quit, but the doctor said again that she needed to.

As we came back home, my wife told me she just knew she couldn't quit drinking coffee. I remembered the scripture that says you can have what you say. I told her that I was going to pray that the coffee would make her sick, and from then on, I wasn't going to pray about it anymore, I would just say it. Jesus said that you will have what you say.

So the next morning, she decided to cut down to one cup of coffee a day. She started to drink the coffee and it made her deathly sick. From that day to this, she has not been able to drink coffee. It works on little things. And it works on big things. *You can have what you say.*

I've also used this principle from God's Word a number of times with fellows who want to be delivered from tobacco. Nothing will help some hardheaded people who just don't want to quit, but I'm talking about people who are really sincere and honest and who want deliverance. I've just told them that the next cigarette they tried to smoke would make them sick.

One fellow who was a member of my church came to me and said that he had been smoking for forty years, but after we prayed, he hadn't been able to smoke another cigarette. One time after that, he had someone in his car who began to smoke, and he had to ask the person to put his cigarette out because it was making him so sick.

We can all use our faith to help those who really want help; of course, if a person doesn't want help, you won't be able to help him. You can't push something off on someone who doesn't want it.

Having What I Said in Buying a Home

In 1954 we moved to Port Arthur, Texas. Our pastor from Garland, Texas, had taken a Full Gospel church in Port Arthur. I decided to move my family to Port Arthur because this pastor had really seen after my family while I was out on the road, which was most of the time. Our wives were like sisters anyway.

We found a house we wanted to buy. When we went to see the man who was selling it, he said he had just put an ad in the paper to rent the house fully furnished. I told him that I already had my furniture, and he replied that he'd rather sell the house anyway.

He said he would sell it to me for $1,000 down and he would carry the note himself at a certain amount per month. The garage apartment on the house was being rented by some Full Gospel folks, and their rent was $45, which almost made the entire house payment every month because the house payment was $60 a month. That meant I only had to pay $15 a month for a three-bedroom, carpeted house.

I started to tell him that I didn't have even a dollar, but then I remembered Mark 11:23 and 24. I remembered that you can have what you say. So I said, "I'll have $1,000 for you in ten days." So the owner phoned the newspaper and cancelled the ad.

I really had myself on the spot now. The very next day in the parsonage the telephone rang and the pastor called me to the telephone. The person on the telephone was a woman who had received the Holy Ghost a year before in my Beaumont meeting. She asked me if I needed $1,000. I asked her why she was asking me this, because I knew just a few people knew about the house deal. She said that when she had been praying the night before, God had told her to give me $500 and loan me $500.

I answered, "I don't doubt it, Sister, bring it on over." She came over with an envelope that had ten $100 bills in it. She told me to forget about the loaned $500 till the end of the year.

You can't outdo God! If you'll believe His Word, you'll have what you say!

Having What I Say for My Family

My sister's home was broken by divorce, so my wife and I took in my niece, Ruth, who was fifteen years old. My sister had had to go to work to support her family, and when she worked, my niece had gotten in with the wrong crowd and had gotten into some trouble. We took her to live with us, and she was saved and filled with the Holy Spirit within about a month's time. She even began to teach Sunday school.

Ruth graduated from high school, and by the time she went to work, my sister had remarried and had moved to our town. So my niece went to live with her mother again and got out of church for a little while.

While Ruth was working, she met a fellow and married him. She wasn't in fellowship with God, but she told her husband that she did believe in God and in speaking in tongues. He was Baptist and pretended it was all right.

However, just as soon as they were married, he told her that he was the head of the house, and she couldn't fellowship with those tongue talkers anymore. He treated us very coolly. We were living in Port Arthur and they were living in Houston.

One morning about 5 the telephone rang. It was my sister, who was almost hysterical. She told me that Ruth's baby had been born, and that at first the doctors wouldn't let anyone see the baby because it was dead.

My sister said that later the doctor came out and said the baby was still alive, but it would probably die, and the doctors didn't want anyone to see it. He said that the baby's head and face were deformed and it didn't look like a human being, and that the baby couldn't possibly live. The doctors wanted to dispose of it because it would be better for no one to ever see it and have that memory of it.

Ruth's husband wanted me to pray. He had treated me coldly in the past, but he knew who to ask for prayer! My sister said he was standing right there by the phone and that he wanted me to pray.

I told her to turn to him the minute we hung up the phone and say, "Uncle Ken said the baby will live and not die and will be all right."

My sister said, "Oh, Ken, do you think so?"

I responded, "No, I don't think so; I *know* so because Jesus said, '*Whosoever shall say unto this mountain, Be thou removed, and be thou cast into the sea; and shall not doubt in his heart, but shall believe that those things which he saith shall come to pass; he shall have whatsoever he saith*'" (Mark 11:23).

Then I told my sister again what to say to Ruth's husband as soon as I hung up the phone. She said he still wanted me to pray. I told her there was no need to pray because Jesus said that you can have whatever you say.

Ruth wanted my wife, Oretha, to come because Oretha had been like a second mother to her. When my wife arrived at Ruth's, Ruth's husband threw his arms around Oretha and said, "I am a Pentecostal Baptist. Uncle Ken hadn't hung up the phone ten minutes when the nurse came out and announced that we could see the baby because his head just suddenly filled out like a balloon, and he was perfectly all right and would live!"

And you ought to see him today! Also, the father is filled with the Holy Ghost and speaks with other tongues. He later became a Sunday school teacher and youth director in a Full Gospel church.

You can't shut God out if you'll just believe Him. Jesus said you can have what you say.

Questions for Study

1. What will eventually happen to what is in your heart?

   _____

   _____

2. What locates you?

   _____

   _____

3. What is a wonderful Old Testament proof that you can have what you say?

   _____

   _____

4. What is an evil report?

   _____

   _____

5. What is a good report?

   _____

   _____

6. What are the three "giants" that defeat Christians?

   _____

   _____

7. What is one reason why we fail sometimes?

   _____

   _____

8. What will you do if you believe you're going to receive something from God?

   _____

   _____

9. What did God say in His Word that we must be in order to eat the good of the land?

   _____

   _____

10. Why won't your faith help someone who doesn't want help?

   _____

   _____

Chapter 24

How to Train the Human Spirit

Your spirit can be educated just as your mind can be educated. Your spirit can be built up in strength just as your body can be built up. There are four steps by which your spirit can be educated and built up.

1. By meditating in the Word.

2. By practicing the Word.

3. By giving the Word first place in your life.

4. By instantly obeying the voice of your spirit.

After a while you can know the will of God the Father even in all the minor details of life. It takes time to train the human spirit, but it is well worth the effort.

God communicates with the *spirit* of man, not with his *reasoning* faculties. As you train your spirit and as you instantly obey your spirit, you will find that you are obeying the Holy Spirit.

Remember that God said in His Word in Proverbs 20:27, *"The spirit of man is the candle of the Lord, searching all the inward parts of the belly."* This means that God is going to use your own spirit to guide you because the spirit of man is the candle of the Lord.

Now let's look in greater detail at the four steps to train and educate the human spirit.

Step Number One: Meditate on the Word

Notice that three of these four points—meditation in the Word, practicing the Word, giving the Word first place, and instantly obeying the voice of your spirit—have to do with *the Word*. We all know the importance of reading the Word, but we must also realize the value of quiet meditation in the Word.

The most deeply spiritual men and women I know are people who give time to meditation in the Word. You cannot develop spiritual wisdom without meditation. God taught Joshua that principle in the very beginning of his ministry after the death of Moses.

JOSHUA 1:8

8 This book of the law shall not depart out of thy mouth; but thou shalt meditate therein day and night, that thou mayest observe to do according to all that is written therein: for then thou shalt make thy way prosperous, and then thou shalt have good success.

The *Amplified Bible, Classic Edition* says, *"for then you shall make your way prosperous."*

You certainly wouldn't have good success if you couldn't deal wisely in the affairs of life, would you? God told Joshua to meditate in the Word. God told Joshua that *if* he would meditate in the Word, then Joshua would make his way prosperous and he would have good success.

I was teaching one time at a district convention along this same line. Afterwards, a minister asked me to come to his church and hold a meeting, and I did. He told me he had been trying to make a success of his church by visiting every successful pastor he knew.

For example, he would go and visit a pastor and watch what he did and see what kind of programs he was using and then try to implement them in his own church. But he said when he tried to put another man's program into action in his own church, it never worked. This minister traveled all around the country doing this.

I think that many of us are like this pastor. After my meeting, that pastor told me he decided that instead of trying to implement other pastors' programs, he would meditate on the Word the way I taught and take a little time out each morning to do so.

After thirty days of doing this and not making such a pull on the people, but just by meditating on the Word, they just had a landslide service one Sunday. More people were saved in one day than they had the entire two or three years before!

You see, once this pastor began to meditate on the Word, his people were revived, and he began to have good success.

That was this pastor's life and calling, so of course, that was where he needed to have good success. But your life's calling is something else. It is certainly true, however, that your way can be prosperous, too, and you can have good success in your own life and calling by meditating on the Word.

Take time to meditate in the Word. Shut yourself in alone with your own spirit where the world is shut out. If you are ambitious to do something worthwhile for God, I would suggest that you just begin by taking ten or fifteen minutes daily for meditation in God's Word. That isn't much. Begin the development of your own spirit. And this is the way to do that.

Step Number Two: Practice the Word

Practicing the Word means being a doer of the Word. James said, *"be ye doers of the word, and not hearers only, DECEIVING your own selves"* (James 1:22). The margin reads, "He *deludes* himself." We have many self-deluded people. The sad part is, they have deluded *themselves.*

Begin to practice being a doer of the Word; under all circumstances do what the Word tells you to do. Some people think that being a doer of the Word is to keep the Ten Commandments. No, that is not what the Bible is talking about here. After all, we under the new covenant, have one commandment, and that is the commandment of love (John 13:34).

If you love someone, you won't steal from him. You won't lie about him either. Paul said love is the fulfilling of the Law (Rom. 13:10). If you walk in love, you won't break any law that was given to curb sin.

So being a doer of the Word means to walk in love, all right, and if you're walking in love, you will already be keeping the Ten Commandments. But being a doer of the Word also means to do primarily what is written in the Epistles because those are the letters that are written to the Church. The Epistles belong to us.

Practice the Word by Not Fretting

Philippians is just one of the New Testament Epistles written to the Church.

PHILIPPIANS 4:6–7

6   BE CAREFUL FOR NOTHING; but in every thing by prayer and supplication with thanksgiving let your requests be made known unto God.

7   And the peace of God, which passeth all understanding, shall keep your hearts and minds through Christ Jesus.

The AMPC translation of this verse brings out the meaning a little clearer that we are not to fret.

PHILIPPIANS 4:6–7 (AMPC)

6   DO NOT FRET OR HAVE ANY ANXIETY ABOUT ANYTHING, but in every circumstance and in everything by prayer and petition [definite requests] with thanksgiving continue to make your wants known to God.

7   And GOD'S PEACE [be yours, that tranquil state of a soul assured of its salvation through Christ, and so fearing nothing from God and content with its earthly lot of whatever sort that is, that peace]

WHICH TRANSCENDS ALL UNDERSTANDING, shall garrison and mount guard over your hearts and minds in Christ Jesus.

We usually practice only part of this verse. For example, we don't mind practicing the part that says to pray, but if you just practice that part and not the entire verse, you're not practicing the Word. You are not being a doer of the Word.

First, God says not to fret. If you're going to fret and have anxieties, then it isn't going to do any good to make requests. We teach prayer, but why don't we just go ahead and teach the whole story on prayer? Why teach just part of it? That kind of praying doesn't work. The kind of over-anxious praying that is full of fretfulness doesn't work.

I read a little saying years ago in a newspaper which said, "A scared prayer ain't no account." The man who wrote it said that down in the state of Georgia years ago there was a man, his wife, and his son who had an experience while they were out in the field chopping cotton.

This boy was a grown man, nearly thirty years old but still lived at home. He was a little mentally retarded. As they were all out picking cotton, a storm came up and it began to thunder. The boy and his mother wanted to go into the house, but the old man wanted them to hoe out the row first, so he told them to finish the rows they were on.

But before they could finish, the lightning grew worse and they all just threw down their hoes and began to run toward the house. When they saw that they couldn't make it in time, the man and his wife got down on their hands and knees and began to pray. Then the boy, who hadn't knelt to pray, turned around to them and said, "Come on Ma and Pa. A scared prayer ain't no account."

There is much truth to this statement. That is what the Spirit of God is saying through Paul here. Paul is telling believers, "Be careful for nothing—don't have any anxiety."

A minister came to me some time ago. I felt so sorry for him but sometimes sympathy doesn't help anyone at all. Just to sympathize with a man doesn't give him the answer. In this minister's case, several tests and trials had come against him, and he just couldn't sleep. His stomach was upset, and he wasn't able to keep anything down that he ate. His nerves were just shot because of worry and fretfulness. He came to see if I could help him and, thank God, I could.

At first, he sort of rebelled against my help, though really it was *God's* help because I gave him the Word. I began to tell him what the Word says and how to pray about his situation. I had him read this scripture in Philippians 4:6.

He would read it and then say, "Oh, yes, Brother Hagin, but everyone doesn't have the faith you have."

I answered, "Maybe they don't, but they do have the same Bible I have. And anyone can develop their faith." I told him that it wasn't a matter of having a lot of faith. It is a matter of acting on the Word and exercising the faith you do have.

This minister told me that it seemed that I didn't have a care in the world. I told him I didn't and that it was because I was practicing the Word; I was a doer of the Word. I kept telling him that even though some people hadn't developed their faith to the extent that they could, they still had the same Bible I did and that it was a matter of practicing the Word.

I also told him that as long as he was going to worry and fret, he wasn't going to sleep or eat. I told him that when I get alone and read this verse out loud, I tell the Lord that His Word is true and I believe it. I explained to this minister that he would be tempted to say he couldn't help worrying and fretting, but that God hasn't asked us to do something we can't do.

When God said not to fret, that means we can keep from fretting. God is a just God, and He won't ask us to do something that we couldn't do. At one time, I believed I could make my requests known unto God, but it was hard for me to believe that I couldn't fret. But God said that we don't have to fret. So I would agree with what the Bible said and refuse to fret or have any anxiety about anything. I told all of this to this minister.

I would also tell the Lord that I was bringing my requests unto Him, and then I would thank Him. This quieted my spirit and helped me resist the troubled spirit the devil wanted me to have. I would get up from praying and go on about my business, and before I knew it, the devil was trying to trouble or harass me again with anxious thoughts. But I would just simply go right back and read this verse again and keep claiming it.

After I explained to this minister about resisting the devil with the Word, he told me later that when he started doing this, too, the problem worked out and did not get as big as he was expecting. He was going to be sued over a certain situation but the lawsuit didn't amount to anything; God helped him out of it all.

You can become so fretful over something that you don't eat or sleep. But all you have to do is practice the Word and you can overcome all anxiety and fear.

PHILIPPIANS 4:6–8

6 BE CAREFUL FOR NOTHING [do not fret or have anxiety about anything]; **but in every thing by prayer and supplication with thanksgiving let your requests be made known unto God.**

7 And the PEACE OF GOD, which passeth all understanding, shall keep your hearts and minds through Christ Jesus.

8 Finally, brethren, whatsoever things are true, whatsoever things are honest, whatsoever things are just, whatsoever things are pure, whatsoever things are lovely, whatsoever things are of good report; if there be any virtue, and if there be any praise, THINK ON THESE THINGS.

Many people want what verse 7 promises—the peace of God—but they don't want to do what verse 6 says in order to get it. They don't want to practice not fretting or having any anxiety about anything. They don't want to practice casting their cares upon the Lord.

But in order to get what verse 7 promises—the peace of God—you have to practice verse 6—Be not fretful. If you will practice verse 6, then as the AMPC says, *God's peace will garrison and mount guard over your heart and mind. God's peace will keep guard over your heart and spirit.*

The education of our spirits comes by practicing the Word. Can you reap the results and have peace and not be a doer of the Word? No, you can't. It is impossible.

Some people who worry and fret continually think on the wrong things in life. They continually think and talk doubt and unbelief. You won't be able to educate and train your spirit by continually thinking and talking doubt and unbelief.

Don't Talk the Problem

The more you talk about some problems, the bigger those problems seem to get. But if something isn't true, honest, just, pure, and lovely, or of a good report, then you shouldn't be thinking about it. It may be true but it might not be lovely. So don't talk about it.

The AMPC translation of First Corinthians 13:7 says that God's love in us is "... *ever ready to believe the best of every person.*"

I've found out through the years that most of the bad stories I've heard about people aren't true anyway. It seems as if you can hear everything in the world in Christian circles about other people. Some things you hear might be true, but they might not be pure and lovely, so therefore you should not be thinking about them.

We give place to the devil by thinking and talking about these things. The devil's greatest weapon against us is the power of suggestion.

The devil is ever seeking and endeavoring to enter into your thought life. That's why the Apostle Paul is instructing believers and saying this. He says in Philippians 4:8, *"think on these things."* Meditate and feed on the letters that were written to the Church, the New Testament Epistles. Here is God, the Holy Spirit, speaking to the Church. Be a doer of the Word. If you do, you'll grow spiritually.

Step Number 3:
Give the Word First Place In Your Life

The scriptures tell us exactly how to give the Word first place in our lives.

PROVERBS 4:20–22

20 My son, ATTEND TO MY WORDS; incline thine ear unto MY SAYINGS.

21 LET THEM not depart from thine eyes; KEEP THEM in the midst of thine heart.

22 For THEY ARE LIFE unto those that find them, and HEALTH to all their flesh.

JOHN 6:63

63 It is the spirit that quickeneth; the flesh profiteth nothing: the words that I speak unto you, they are spirit, and they are life.

There is healing in the Word. Jesus said, *"the words that I speak unto you, they are spirit, and they are life"* (John 6:63). Always put the Word of God first in your life. It is a strange thing to me that some people just won't do this.

I pastored nearly twelve years, and I had members who would get sick and go to the hospital and *afterwards* ask for prayer. I am not saying that it is wrong to go to a doctor. But why not just put God's Word first, instead of using it as a *last* resort. It is regrettable that many Christians only turn to the Word as a last resort.

A Baptist minister down in Texas who didn't even particularly believe in divine healing said that he'd had problems with his throat and tonsils. The doctor kept telling him that he would need to have his tonsils taken out, so the date was finally set to have them removed.

Every morning the minister and his family would read the Bible and pray. One morning when they were reading (it was the day he was supposed to go into the hospital), he read the scripture about King Asa who got a disease in his feet and instead of seeking the Lord, he sought physicians and he died (2 Chron. 16:12–13).

The minister said that this stood out to him, and he realized that he hadn't even prayed about healing for his tonsils! So he told the children and his wife that they should all pray about his tonsils. When they prayed, the Lord told him not to have them removed. To his astonishment, the Lord healed him, and he has not had any trouble with his tonsils since.

There is a lesson to be learned here. This verse in Second Chronicles doesn't say that the king died because he put the physicians first, but it certainly implies that he ought to have put the Lord first.

We should train ourselves and ask ourselves what God's Word says about every situation and circumstance in life. Sometimes in ignorance, family and friends can try to rush us into things, but we need to think about what the Word of God says and put that first. Many difficulties in life will be spared us if we will only put God's Word *first*.

Step Number 4:
Instantly Obey the Voice of Your Spirit

The human spirit has a voice. We call that voice the *conscience*. Sometimes we call it *intuition*. Sometimes we also refer to it as an *inner voice* or an *inward guidance* from the Lord.

The world calls it "a hunch." But really it is the voice of man's spirit talking to him.

Every man's spirit has a voice whether he is saved or unsaved. But the new birth is a rebirth of the human spirit. As you give your born-again, recreated spirit the privilege of meditating upon the Word, your spirit gets correct information and it will then become an accurate guide. Then you must learn to *obey* your spirit.

Your spirit has the life and nature of God in it, for the Holy Spirit dwells within you. The devil can't be guiding you in your spirit because he is not in you. As the god of this world (2 Cor. 4:4), he is on the *outside* of you. But God communicates with you on the *inside* of you in your spirit because that's where He is. God isn't in your head; He is in your spirit. Your spirit gets its information from God through the Holy Spirit. Learn to obey your spirit.

Some people say that the conscience isn't a safe guide. But that statement isn't always true. That statement needs to be qualified, because the conscience is a safe guide for the believer, as long as he is walking in fellowship with God and His Word.

Your conscience, the voice of your recreated spirit, becomes the voice of God to you when it is trained in line with the Word of God. God is speaking to you. The spirit of man is the candle of the Lord (Prov. 20:27). God will use your spirit to guide you. He will use it to enlighten you.

As your spirit has the privilege of meditating and feeding upon the Word, it becomes more and more a safe guide. As you feed and meditate upon the Word, you are training your spirit in the Word of God.

Paul said that he always obeyed his conscience (Acts 23:1). The Holy Spirit does speak to some of us who stand in certain ministries a little differently; however, in the lives of believers, the inward voice is the voice of one's spirit speaking, and not just the Holy Spirit.

I hear what the Holy Spirit says often but I usually never hear Him for my own benefit. For my own personal guidance and direction in life, I have to follow my inward voice, the voice of my spirit. The Holy Spirit will speak to me about others.

The reason I say this is that a prophet's ministry isn't given for *his* benefit. The ministry of a prophet is given for the benefit of others. I have to know through my own inward voice or spirit about my own personal life, just as any believer does.

Don't Put Out a Fleece—Look to Your Spirit

We miss it by not always looking to our spirits. Many times we put a fleece out and tell God, "You do this if You want me to do that." But when you do this, what you really want God to do is come over in the sense realm and give you direction, and that is dangerous because that is the realm where Satan operates (2 Cor. 4:4).

Gideon put out a fleece (Judges 6:37–40). But he didn't have the Spirit of God in the sense that he was not born again. Therefore, he couldn't be led by his spirit—it wasn't recreated. Gideon was just a natural man, walking by his natural senses.

You see, in the Old Testament, the Holy Spirit only came *upon* the prophet, priest, and king. Those in the Old Testament we would call lay members didn't have the Holy Ghost. Because of this, God had to deal with the Old Testament saints through their senses. That's why God had to deal with Gideon through the senses because Gideon didn't have the Holy Spirit.

God might do that today, but if He has to deal with us through circumstances and the sense realm, it is because we are so spiritually dull. Believers are supposed to walk by their spirits (Prov. 20:27). And under the New Testament, Jesus said another Comforter would come who would lead and guide us into all truth (John 14:16–17; John 16:13). Therefore, believers have a safe Guide. But Gideon didn't know the Holy Spirit.

You as a believer know the Holy Spirit because He lives inside of you in your spirit (Rom. 8:14; John 14:16–17,23). God deals with man through his own spirit by the Holy Spirit. He sent the Holy Spirit to dwell in us, and Jesus said that He would guide us into all truth (John 16:13). Satan, not God, operates through the sense realm (2 Cor. 4:4).

Learn to Obey Your Spirit Even in the Affairs of Life

One Christian businessman told me that he lost $10,000 because he got involved in a business deal, and a fleece made it look as though he should do it. All the time, the inward voice of his spirit was telling him not to do it. He followed the fleece and lost the entire $10,000.

He said that for many years after he had done this, he wondered where he had missed God. He had been confused until he saw the truth of walking by his spirit as it is trained and developed by the Word of God. He had remembered an inward voice telling him not to do it.

When I was in the Baptist church, I had never heard about fleeces, but when I came to the Pentecostal church, people kept talking about fleeces. And years ago when I was pastoring a church, I began to think about changing churches, so I put out a fleece. It was the only fleece I ever put out in my life.

I told the Lord that if it was His will for me to take a certain church, then He should let such and such a thing happen. The answer to my fleece indicated that I should take the church, so I did, and God let me get fleeced! I missed it. It wasn't God's will for me. But I learned my lesson. I never missed God again. I've never fooled with fleeces again.

God has a better way than a hit-and-miss system in the sense realm. You know that. Learn to obey the voice of your *spirit*. You won't get there quickly, but eventually as you train and develop your spirit by feeding and meditating in God's Word, you will come to the place where you'll know in your spirit what you should do in every area of life. You'll get a yes or a no and you'll be able to deal wisely in all the affairs of life.

As you diligently follow these four steps outlined in this lesson, you will build up your spirit and train and educate your spirit man to dominate over your flesh and your mind. If you will put God's Word first in every area of your life, you will find that this walk of faith we have been discussing in all these lessons will become like second nature to you. The spirit realm will become more and more real and distinct to you as you learn to appropriate God's blessings in your own life by faith in His Word.

God has called us to a life of faith, a life of victory over circumstances, the flesh, and the devil. And by choosing to think, believe, and speak according to His Word in all areas of our lives, we will walk in the victory that God has provided for us through Jesus Christ.

Questions for Study

1. Name the four steps by which your spirit can be educated and built up.

   _____

   _____

2. What do the first three of the four steps have to do with?

   _____

   _____

3. What part of man does God communicate with?

   _____

   _____

4. What does practicing God's Word mean?

   _____

   _____

5. In order to get what Philippians 4:7 promises—the peace of God—What must you not be?

   _____

6. According to John 6:63, what are Jesus' words?

   _____

   _____

7. What are four other ways you can refer to the voice of the human spirit?

   _____

   _____

8. When you tell God, "You do this if You want me to do that," what are you really wanting God to do?

   _____

   _____

9. Why was it okay for Gideon in the Old Testament to put out a fleece?

   _____

   _____

10. When will the spirit realm become more and more real to you?

    _____

    _____